THE QUALITY OF

GROWTH

A Note about the Cover

Future: Bright or Dark? by Maja Sasek, age 12, Skopje, FYR Macedonia.

The future is a chance you should take. It is a creation and everyone has his or her own vision. It will look the way we make it look.

—Maja Sasek

Over 5,000 children and students from Albania, Bosnia-Herzegovina, Bulgaria, FYR Macedonia, and Romania took part in art and essay contests on their vision of the future for themselves, their cities, and their countries and regions. A selection of their paintings was displayed in an exhibit entitled "Children Look to the Horizon," which was shown at the World Bank, Washington, D.C., April 1999; in Vienna, Austria, September 1999; and in Florence, Italy, October 1999.

THE QUALITY OF

GROWTH

Vinod Thomas
Mansoor Dailami
Ashok Dhareshwar
Daniel Kaufmann
Nalin Kishor
Ramón López
Yan Wang

Published for the World Bank
Oxford University Press

Oxford University Press

OXFORD   NEW YORK   ATHENS   AUCKLAND   BANGKOK   BOGOTA   BUENOS AIRES
CALCUTTA   CAPE TOWN   CHENNAI   DAR ES SALAAM   DELHI   FLORENCE   HONG
KONG   ISTANBUL   KARACHI   KUALA LUMPUR   MADRID   MELBOURNE   MEXICO CITY
MUMBAI   NAIROBI   PARIS   SÃO PAULO   SINGAPORE   TAIPEI   TOKYO   TORONTO
WARSAW

and associated companies in

BERLIN   IBADAN

© 2000 The International Bank for Reconstruction
and Development/The World Bank
1818 H Street, N.W., Washington, D.C. 20433, USA

Published by Oxford University Press, Inc.
198 Madison Avenue, New York, N.Y. 10016

Oxford is a registered trademark of Oxford University Press.

Manufactured in the United States of America
First printing September 2000

Library of Congress Cataloging-in-Publication Data
The quality of growth/Vinod Thomas ... [et al].
        p. cm.
    Includes bibliographical references.
    ISBN 0-19-521593-1
        1. Economic development. 2. Sustainable development. I. Thomas, Vinod,
1949–

HD75.Q35 2000
338.9–dc21   00-028324

CONTENTS

Boxes

Tables

FOREWORD

We have much to celebrate as we begin the new millennium. A child born today in the developing world can expect to live 25 years longer and be healthier, better-educated, and more productive than a child born 50 years ago. The spread of democracy has brought new freedoms and unprecedented opportunities for many people throughout the world. And the communications revolution holds the promise of universal access to knowledge.

But, if we take a closer look, we see something else—something alarming. In the developing countries, excluding China, at least 100 million more people are living in poverty today than a decade ago. And the gap between rich and poor yawns wider. In many countries the scourge of AIDS has cruelly cut life expectancy—in some African countries by more than 10 years. More than 1 billion people still lack access to safe water, and each year 2.4 million children die of waterborne diseases. As many as a billion people have entered the 21st century unable to read or write. Some 1.8 million people die every year of indoor air pollution in rural areas alone. Forests are being destroyed at the rate of an acre a second, with unimaginable loss of biodiversity.

Those are some measures of our shortcomings: that despite prosperity for some, the quality of life has remained bleak for many. In the face of almost two decades of rapid economic growth in some countries, others have not benefited from such progress. In many settings policies have favored vested interests of the elite, and thus not promoted adequate investments in human capital and natural capital, which are essential for broad-based growth. The quality of the factors contributing to growth requires fundamental attention if poverty is to be reduced and a better quality of life attained by all. This is the central theme of this book.

A better quality of life for the poor calls for higher incomes. This requires sound economic policies and institutions conducive to sustained growth. Achieving higher incomes and a better quality of life also calls for much more—improved and more equitable opportunities for education and jobs, better health and nutrition, a cleaner and more sustainable natural environment, an impartial judicial and legal system, greater civil and political liberties, trustworthy and transparent institutions, and freedom of access to a rich and diverse cultural life. The World Bank's recent book *Voices of the Poor: Can Anyone Hear Us?* reinforces this message. Poor women and men from around the world noted emphatically the importance of dignity, respect, security, gender issues, a clean environment, health, and inclusion in addition to material well-being.

As incomes per capita rise, several aspects of quality of life improve as well, but not all, not at the same rate, and not inevitably. In different countries the same pace of economic growth has been associated with very different degrees of improvements over time in education, health, civil liberties, citizens' participation in the decisions affecting their lives, freedom from corruption, and environmental quality and sustainability. This book demonstrates that how growth is generated and whether it is sustainable matter crucially for the quality of life of everyone.

The World Bank's strategy is to design and evaluate its activities through the lens of poverty reduction, the vision that informs the Comprehensive Development Framework we have embraced in the countries we work with. This framework encourages countries to pursue a balanced approach to development, simultaneously trying to augment the human, social, natural, and physical dimensions. Only then are the fruits of development widely shared and sustained.

In aligning these complementary dimensions, this integrated framework also attempts to bring together the key development actors. It puts institutions, governance, corporate responsibility, and issues of inclusion, voice, liberties, and participation on par with conventional economic concerns and policymaking. In addressing these related issues simultaneously, the framework emphasizes the need for the country's leadership, as well as for partnership among government, the private sector, civil society, and the international community, in driving the development agenda. We are committed to assisting this framework not only with financing, but increasingly also with state-of-the-art learning and knowledge programs using new data, toolkits, and methodologies, and supported by the latest information and communication technologies.

Indeed, travelling throughout all continents I am constantly reminded by the people—in rural villages and overcrowded urban centers alike—that the quality of life for them transcends the contribution of just financing. That quality is about access for girls and boys to education, and to jobs when they graduate. It is about access for the rural poor to basic medicine when they go to their village clinic. It is about the cleanliness of the air and water and about protecting the precious biodiversity. It is about the dignity the poor might enjoy and the security of their lives. It is about the participation of people along with reformers in the government in implementing an anticorruption program. It is about fighting the vested interests of an economic elite that unduly influences, or even purchases, the policies, regulations, and laws of the state.

This volume makes a compelling case for focusing on these policy and institutional dimensions, and for doing so with country ownership and partnership among participants in the development process. Investing in people, sustaining natural resources, managing risks, and improving governance, it shows, are dimensions that make up quality growth. It is more of such growth that can best promote poverty reduction, environmentally and socially sustainable development, and an improved quality of life shared by all.

James D. Wolfensohn
President
The World Bank Group

PREFACE

The 1990s—at the end of a century and a millennium—were a period of stocktaking about development. Studies reexamined and assessed some of the central tenets of development. Sustained economic growth emerged unscathed as fundamental for reducing poverty. And the development record confirmed the efficacy of certain reforms for sustaining growth in both developing and industrial countries: investing more—and more efficiently—in education and health, reducing barriers to trade and investment, dismantling domestic price controls in agriculture and industry, and reducing fiscal deficits. Neither the economic ups nor the downs of the 1990s called these relationships into question.

The assessments also uncovered some crucial gaps. Missing from country policymaking as well as the advice, conditions, and financing of external entities has been adequate attention to the quality and sustainability of growth. Without that, the real potential of reforms cannot be realized.

And the assessments highlighted some profound changes in development thinking over the past 50 years as our understanding of development processes has matured, shaped by experience. Not that interpretations have been entirely uniform. For example, some have understood the "Washington consensus" solely as a policy prescription for liberalizing markets. Others have accepted the extended interpretation of the *World Development Report 1991's* market-friendly approach as a market-plus view, involving both liberalization and a strong, positive role for the state and other stakeholders.

Differing interpretations aside, the assessments show an emerging consensus on some key lessons about complementarity and balance among policies and institutions. Functioning markets and liberalization are crucial. But so is acknowledging the limits of the market and an essential role for governments and other stakeholders in the reform process.

Sometimes expectations based on experience have been borne out, sometimes not. Early discussions predicted the success of such natural resource-rich countries as Myanmar, the Philippines, and some in Africa and the failure of such natural resource-poor economies as the Republic of Korea or Singapore. Expectations of rapid development through market liberalization in the transition economies failed to materialize. And in the 1980s, the slowdown of productivity growth in North American and European industrial economies contrasted with the marked success of Japan, prompting calls for changes in the growth paradigm.

Sometimes reality fell short of expectations because changes in global and local circumstances blunted the impact of actions and forced governments to revise priorities. "Heavy industries first" seemed the best way forward at the turn of the 19th century; information technology seems to be the key to success at the turn of the 20th. And as markets were liberalized in recent decades, sometimes disappointing outcomes exposed the importance of institution building to make markets work.

We present this book in this spirit of continuous inquiry and feedback in framing development thinking. It is addressed to policymakers, practitioners, and others in developing as well as industrial countries. It reaffirms the crucial contribution of market-friendly policies. It also highlights key missing ingredients and fresh evidence. Not a complete review of development, the book examines vital issues that are often overlooked as a basis for action: the distribution of opportunities, especially education; environmental sustainability; management of risks; and governance and anticorruption. It does not address such important factors as the political economy of change, the influence of social instability, the consequences of communicable diseases such as HIV/AIDS, or the impact of cross-border and global issues—population pressures, labor migration, global warming, information technology, and the global financial and business architecture. It concludes that growth is crucial, and so is the quality of growth.

The work for this book was carried out by a team at the World Bank Institute. The work was supported by a research grant from the World Bank as a contribution to the learning material for a course on development as well as background for the *World Development Report 1999/2000: Entering the 21st Century* and the *World Development Report 2000/2001: Attacking Poverty*. It was inspired by a keynote paper and discussion by Stanley

Fischer at the 1998 Annual World Bank Conference on Development Economics. The team benefited from comments from many people outside and inside the World Bank. Special thanks are due to those who provided suggestions for the development of the book. These include Nancy Birdsall, Paul Collier, Eduardo Doryan, Ravi Kanbur, Mats Karlsson, Gautam Kaji, Rung Kaewdang, Vijay Kelkar, Mohsin Khan, Aart Kray, Nora Lustig, Rakesh Mohan, Mohamed Muhsin, Robert Picciotto, Jan Piercy, Jo Ritzen, Lyn Squire, T. N. Srinivasan, Nicholas Stern, Thomas Sterner, Joseph Stiglitz, Anand Swamy, Shahid Yusuf, Shengman Zhang, and the *World Development Report 2000/2001* team.

The team thanks the following for their inputs to the volume: Montek Ahluwahlia, Jane Armitage, Kaushik Basu, Surjit Bhalla, Jan Bojo, Deepak Bhattasali, Gerard Caprio, Shaohua Chen, Kevin Cleaver, Maureen Cropper, Monica Dasgupta, Shanta Devarajan, Ishac Diwan, David Dollar, William Easterly, Gershon Feder, Andrew Feltenstein, Deon Filmer, Pablo Guerrero, Cielito Habito, Kirk Hamilton, Jeffrey Hammer, Joseph Ingram, Farrukh Iqbal, Ramachandra Jammi, Emmanuel Jimenez, Mary Judd, Philip E. Keefer, Homi Kharas, Elizabeth M. King, Kathie Krumm, Ashok Lahiri, Kyung Tae Lee, Andres Liebenthal, Magda Lovei, Muthukumara Mani, Michele de Nevers, David Nepomuceno, Jostein Nygard, Michael Pomerleano, Tanaporn Poshyananda, Lant Pritchett, Martin Ravallion, David Reed, Neil Roger, William Shaw, Mary Shirley, Ammar Siamwalla, Hadi Soesastro, T. G. Srinivasan, Tara Vishwanath, Christina Wood, Michael Woolcock, Roberto Zagha, and discussants and participants in seminars at the International Monetary Fund/World Bank Annual Meetings, the National Council of Applied Economic Research (India), Asian Development Forum (Singapore), Thailand Development Research Institute, as well as a presentation at an International Monetary Fund conference on reforms. Several units of the World Bank reviewed the manuscript.

THE REPORT TEAM

This work was carried out by a team at the World Bank Institute led by Vinod Thomas and comprising Mansoor Dailami (chapter 5), Ashok Dhareshwar (chapter 1), Daniel Kaufmann (chapter 6), Nalin Kishor (chapter 4), Ramón E. López (chapter 2), and Yan Wang (chapter 3 and task manager). The team was assisted in its research by Cary Anne Cadman, Xibo Fan, and John Van Dyck. Taji Anderson, Alice Faria, and Jae Shin Yang provided support.

Bruce Ross-Larson and Meta de Coquereaumont of Communications Development Incorporated and International Communications, Inc. (ICI) of Sterling, Virginia, edited the manuscript at different stages. ICI also provided typesetting and proofreading. Product development, design, editing, production, and dissemination were directed and managed by the World Bank's Office of the Publisher.

OVERVIEW

The last decade of the 20th century saw great progress in parts of the world. But it also saw stagnation and setbacks, even in countries that had previously achieved the fastest rates of economic growth. These gaping differences and sharp reversals teach us much about what contributes to development. At the center is economic growth, not just its pace but—as important—also its quality. Both the sources and the patterns of growth shape development outcomes.

Have those patterns been adequate for rapidly reducing poverty or improving the quality of people's lives? Why have so few countries sustained robust growth rates for prolonged periods? Why have some crucial dimensions—income equality, environmental protection—deteriorated in so many economies, both fast- and slow-growing? How does governance underpin the growth process? As answers, we offer three principles of development and a set of actions for enhancing the quality of growth processes.

Development Outcomes and Growth Processes

Development is about improving the quality of people's lives, expanding their ability to shape their own futures. This generally calls for higher per capita income, but it involves much more. It involves more equitable education and job opportunities. Greater gender equality. Better health and nutrition. A cleaner, more sustainable natural environment. A more impartial judicial and legal system. Broader civil and political freedoms. A richer cultural life. As per capita incomes rise, several of these aspects improve in varying degrees—but others do not. How can growth processes be influenced so that the qualitative dimensions of development outcomes also improve? This book explores these issues of faster and better growth.

A recent study, *Voices of the Poor: Can Anyone Hear Us?* (Narayan and others 2000), indicates that raising incomes is one part of poverty reduction. Greater security in life and a more sustainable environment are others. The experience of the past decades and the voices of the poor offer compelling reasons to emphasize these qualitative factors.

Indeed, from Bolivia, Egypt, and Uganda to Romania, Sri Lanka, and Thailand, the development community is broadening the traditional definition of poverty and welfare. Beyond an individual's or household's measured income, welfare includes opportunity, as assessed by the functioning of markets and investments and improvements in health and education. It includes security, as reflected by reduced vulnerability to economic and physical shocks. It includes empowerment, as evaluated by social inclusion and the voice of individuals. And it includes sustainability, as represented by the protection of the environment, natural resources, and biodiversity.

Economic growth has been associated positively with poverty reduction. Early assessments projected a growth rate for the developing world for the 1990s of a little over 5 percent, or about 3.2 percent per capita. They projected a reduction in the number of poor people of some 300 million, or an annual rate of decline of nearly 4 percent. But actual growth during 1991–98 was about half that, at 1.6 percent per capita. If the countries of Eastern Europe and Central Asia are excluded from these estimates (as in the above-mentioned projections), actual per capita growth is closer to projected growth, at 3.5 percent—with the number of poor people unchanged and the incidence of poverty down 2 percent a year (World Bank 2000a).

The poverty reduction associated with growth has varied widely, as have social progress and welfare improvements, whether in education, health, voice, or participation (chapter 1). Where growth has stagnated or declined, social and welfare dimensions have deteriorated. The widely differing measure in which growth contributes to welfare improvements means that there must be a direct concern for sustainable advances in welfare. It also means that the way growth is generated is very important. The quality of the growth process, not just its pace, affects development outcomes—much as the quality of people's diets, not just the quantity of food, influences their health and life expectancy. That is why it is essential to explore the complex interactions of the factors shaping growth.

The pace of growth has been more sustainable in developing and industrial countries that pay attention to the qualitative attributes of the growth process. Indeed, there is a two-way relationship between economic growth and improvements in social and environmental dimensions. Attention to the sustainability of the environment, for example, helps to deliver more sustained growth, especially where growth rates are highly variable and the negative impacts are particularly pronounced for the poor. This suggests a premium for steady growth rates over stop-and-go growth, even if the go includes short periods of fast growth. As countries exhaust the possibilities for increasing growth through market reforms, the qualitative factors supporting long-term growth become much more important.

These dimensions of the growth process often interact positively in a virtuous cycle. But there can also be some difficult tradeoffs between quantity and quality. Fast, temporary growth relying on such distorted policies as subsidies to capital, neglect of environmental externalities, and biased public expenditure allocations can actually diminish prospects for more sustained growth. Even more difficult to correct are situations in which growth conflicts with environmental and social sustainability, which both contribute directly to development. Managing these qualitative aspects becomes essential for achieving sustainable improvements in welfare.

What then is the quality of growth? Complementing the pace of growth, it refers to key aspects shaping the growth process. Country experiences bring out the importance of several such aspects: the distribution of opportunities, the sustainability of the environment, the management of global risks, and governance. These aspects not only contribute directly to development outcomes. They also add to the impact that growth has on these outcomes, and they address the conflicts that growth might pose to environmental or social sustainability. It is the mix of these policies and institutions shaping the growth process that is the main focus of this study.

Principles of Development

Viewing the quantitative and qualitative sides of the growth process together puts the spotlight on three key principles for developing and industrial countries:

- Focus on all assets: physical, human, and natural capital
- Attend to the distributive aspects over time
- Emphasize the institutional framework for good governance.

The Major Assets

Broadly speaking, the assets that matter for development are physical capital, human capital, and natural capital. Technological progress affecting the use of these assets matters as well. For accelerating growth rates, much attention has traditionally gone to the accumulation of physical capital. But other key assets also deserve attention—human (and social) capital as well as natural (and environmental) capital (box 1). These assets are also crucial for the poor, and their accumulation, technological progress, and productivity, along with that of physical capital, determine the long-term impact on poverty.

By focusing predominantly on physical capital, industrial and developing countries can be tempted to implement policies that subsidize it at a cost (chapter 2). This can create a situation that benefits vested interests and is hard to reverse. Meanwhile, from the social viewpoint there is

---

Box 1. Asset Accumulation, Growth, and Welfare

Figure 1 lays out a simple schema of how human (H), natural (R), and physical (K) capital contribute to economic growth and welfare. Physical capital contributes to welfare through economic growth. Human (and social) capital and natural (and environmental) capital also do that; they are also direct components of welfare.

Human and natural capital also contribute to the accumulation of physical capital by increasing its returns. Physical capital increases the returns to human capital and natural capital and, if markets reflect this, their accumulation. Adding to all this, investments in physical, human, and natural capital, together with many policy reforms, contribute to technological progress and the growth of total factor productivity, thereby boosting growth (chapter 2).

But policy distortions, corruption, misgovernance, market failures, and externalities can put countries on a path of distorted or unbalanced asset accumulation. This situation can hold income growth and welfare improvements below their potential. More specifically, it can lead to lower total factor productivity and underinvestments in

- Productive physical capital, by reducing the profitability of investment through bribes and red tape or by distorting the allocation of physical investments—say, toward certain lucrative contracts
- Human capital, by promoting such favored areas as the military and large infrastructure and

by regressively reallocating public expenditures
- Natural capital, by undermining taxes, royalties, and regulations that could sustain natural resources.

Distortions, market failures, implicit government guarantees, and inadequate regulation can cause

- Overinvestment or wasteful investment in physical capital by increasing the profitability of certain physical assets through guarantees—which influence risk-taking behavior by banks, corporations, and investors—and by lowering the value of certain natural resources
- Underinvestment in human and natural resources by underpricing these assets and by reducing resources devoted to them.

The effects of these policy distortions on the accumulation of human and natural capital relative to physical capital can reduce growth and welfare. Conversely, if corruption is controlled and governance is adequate, undistorted policies could boost asset accumulation, contributing to faster growth (chapter 6). So, by removing policy distortions, fostering good governance, and addressing market failures and externalities, countries can achieve less distorted, more balanced asset investments. And that can lead to more stable and sustained growth and to broadly based increases in welfare.

(box continues on following page)

Box 1 continued

Figure 1.   A Framework

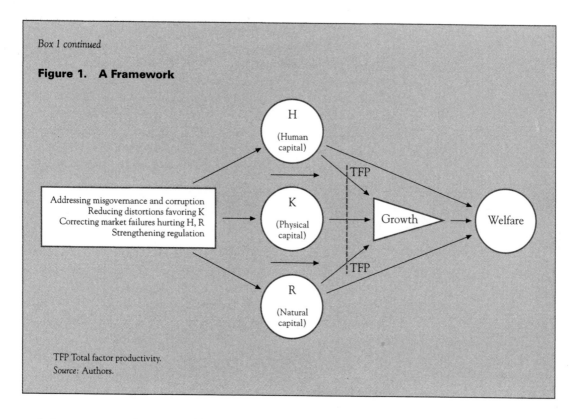

TFP Total factor productivity.
Source: Authors.

underinvestment in education and health (chapter 3) and overexploitation of natural capital, often because of its underpricing or weak property rights (chapter 4). At an aggregate level, (gross) subsidies to agriculture, energy, road transport, and water amounted to an estimated US$700 billion to US$900 billion in the early 1990s, about two-thirds of it in the industrial countries and one-third in the developing ones (de Moor and Calamai 1997).

Sustaining a relative dependence on physical capital accumulation could require continuing distortions. For example, as physical capital deepens, sustaining its rate of return could require larger public subsidies, for example, to attract foreign capital. Furthermore, accelerating growth through policies that lead to the overexploitation of forests and other natural assets runs down natural capital and hurts environmental sustainability. In 1997, gross domestic savings were about 25 percent of gross domestic product (GDP) in the developing world. Corrected for the depletion of environmental capital, however, genuine domestic savings were only an estimated 14 percent of GDP. This includes the case of Nigeria, with gross domestic savings of 22 percent but genuine savings of negative 12 percent, and the Russian Federation, with rates of 25 percent and negative 1.6 percent (World Bank 1999d).

A less distorted (more neutral or balanced) approach to the accumulation of the three types of assets is preferable. Policies can contribute to the accumulation of these assets. Investments in education at all levels, while helping to generate growth, also contribute to the accumulation of human capital and welfare. Investing in natural capital is essential to human health and, for the many poor people who depend on natural resources for their livelihoods, to economic security (chapter 4). As important as the accumulation of these assets is their efficient use. For that—and for greater total factor productivity of these assets—good governance, mitigating the undue influence of elite interests, and anticorruption actions are vital.

Distributional Aspects

This focus on quality brings to light the importance of distributional aspects to the growth process. A more equitable distribution of human capital, land, and other productive assets implies a more equitable distribution of earning opportunities, enhancing people's capacity to take advantage of technologies and to generate incomes. That is why a given growth rate is likely to be associated with better poverty outcomes in settings where educational opportunities are distributed more equitably (chapter 3).

Stability in growth outcomes over time is also likely to be important. The incomes of the poor can be very sensitive to cycles and crises, especially because the poor lack assets—land, skills, and financial savings—to smooth their consumption in bad times. Living barely above the poverty line, millions of near-poor have been thrown back into poverty by external shocks. So for growth to reduce poverty, it usually needs to be relatively stable, and its benefits need to be widely spread.

What, then, of the income gains expected from globalization in the 1990s? These have begun to materialize, but not everywhere. One reason is the inadequacy of regulatory and supervisory frameworks both at the global and country levels, and the overall lack of preparedness for participating in the global economy. Another is the volatility sometimes related to moral hazard and the responses of external players. A third is that, by some estimates, incomes in the last decade or so have become more unequal. Aims of development policy thus include reducing not only the inequality of opportunities, but also the inequality and volatility of growth outcomes. In this it is important to enhance financial risk management and reduce the sensitivity of poor people to changing economic fortunes (chapter 5).

The Governance Framework

The institutional structures of good governance underpin everything done to boost growth. The effective functioning of bureaucracies, regulatory frameworks, civil liberties, and transparent and accountable institutions for ensuring the rule of law and participation matters for growth and development. The effects of poor governance, bureaucratic harassment, and corruption are regressive and harmful to sustained growth. The capture of state policies, laws, and resources by elite interests often biases incentives and public expenditure toward less socially productive assets and, by eroding the benefits that would go to society, reduces the impact on welfare. Estimates of the "development dividend" in the form of higher incomes or better social outcomes are dramatic, in going from low levels of rule of law or high levels of corruption to even middling levels. (A difference in corruption levels of even one standard deviation can be associated with enormous differences in the development impact.) Thus investing in the capacity for better governance is a top priority for better economic performance (chapter 6).

A vibrant civil society—empowered by Internet computing tools, diagnostic survey techniques, and the latest information on governance—is indispensable in the fight against corruption and other forms of misgovernance. Civil liberties are not only linked positively to improved governance, reduced corruption, and increased productivity of public investments, but they also contribute to welfare directly. Indeed, attention ought to go beyond getting the government side of the equation right. It also needs to go to enhancing civil rights and giving greater voice to diverse groups, promoting competitive enterprises, and complementing top-down government policy reforms with bottom-up formulation and implementation of development strategies.

Neglected Actions in the Growth Process

While we now see the development process more broadly, there is often inadequate attention, especially in a crisis, to two of the three assets that the poor rely on: human and natural capital. This neglect in turn seems to have led to the neglect of some key actions:

- Improving the distribution of opportunities
- Sustaining natural capital
- Dealing with global financial risks
- Improving governance and controlling corruption.

Addressing them contributes not only to asset accumulation, but also to technological progress and greater total factor productivity.

Improving the Distribution of Opportunities

The main asset of poor people is their human capital. Of 85 economies examined, Poland and the United States (estimated to have the highest average years of schooling) have the most equitable distribution of educational attainment among people in the labor force. And the Republic of Korea recorded one of the largest improvements in educational equality over the past three decades. But inequality in education remains staggering, as in Algeria, India, Mali, Pakistan, and Tunisia.

The relation of any given growth rate to poverty reduction depends on the investments in people. The more equitable the investments, the greater the impact of growth in lowering the incidence of poverty, as seen in a comparison of the effects of growth on poverty across Indian states (Ravallion and Datt 1999). If people's abilities are normally distributed across the population, the skewed distribution of education and health outcomes would seem to represent especially large welfare losses to society as a significant proportion of people are deprived of opportunities to use new technologies and to lift themselves out of poverty.

A review of education spending for 35 countries finds it to be weakly related to educational attainment after controlling for incomes. In health, the United States, with the highest per capita health expenditure, ranks 37th among 191 countries in a measure of overall health system performance. France, with less than 60 percent of the U.S. per capita health expenditure, ranks first. Colombia, which is much further down in per capita health expenditure, ranks first in the category of fairness of financial contribution (WHO 2000). So spending on education and health services is not enough. Also demanding attention are the breadth and depth of human capital—its quality and equity, as measured by girls' education, access for the poor, and school attainment.

Governments need to reallocate public expenditure for basic education to ensure its quality and equitable distribution. Private-public partnerships need to be encouraged through market-based policies to increase efforts in education at all levels, including higher education. Also needed are supportive labor market policies and social protection policies. In addition, the human capital of the poor can be better applied by addressing the distribution of land and pursuing labor-intensive strategies in an open global environment (chapter 3).

Sustaining Natural Capital

Environmental degradation has worsened sharply. Contributing factors include population growth; domestic and global pressures on scarce resources; economic policies, for example, subsidies that ignore environmental consequences; and the neglect of local and global commons. The costs of environmental pollution and resource overexploitation are enormous; the losses in many cases are irreversible. Indonesia's forest fires—the result of human, policy, and natural factors—produced some US$4 billion in direct losses in 1997 and again in 1998, with extensive damage in neighboring nations. And it is poor people, because of their reliance on such natural capital as land, forests, minerals, and biodiversity, who suffer disproportionately from environmental degradation.

Few countries have adequately confronted the underlying causes of environmental and resource degradation—the policy distortions, market failures, and lack of knowledge about the full benefits of environmental protection and resource conservation. Growth and higher incomes can create conditions for environmental improvement by increasing demand for better environmental quality and by making resources available to meet that demand. However, only a strong combination of domestic and global market-based incentives, investments, and institutions can make environmentally sustainable growth a reality—as in examples from China, Costa Rica, Indonesia and many European countries (chapter 4).

Dealing with Global Financial Risks

Global financial integration has large benefits, but it also makes countries more vulnerable to hidden risks and sudden swings in investor sentiment. Volatile private capital flows seem to be associated with volatile growth rates, which hurt especially the poor, who lack the assets to weather an economic storm. To deal better with such risks, countries need to maintain sound macroeconomic policies. They also need to deepen domestic financial markets, strengthen domestic regulation and financial supervision, introduce corporate governance mechanisms, and provide social safety nets.

For all this they need sound institutions and strong capabilities, which take time to cultivate. Developing them, while opening a country's capital markets, can help deal with the risks for the financial system and the economy. In the meantime, as governments open their capital accounts, they can consider a spectrum of actions as in Argentina, Chile, Mexico, and elsewhere. One is to shun special incentives for short-term flows. Another is to set up reserve requirements and taxes for risky short-term flows. Yet another is to strengthen prudential regulation and supervision. International policy coordination and lender-of-last-resort activity can provide liquidity and emergency financial assistance (chapter 5).

Improving Governance and Controlling Corruption

Governance needs to move to center stage in institution-building strategies. That requires better analysis and measurement of the dimensions of governance and a clearer understanding of the vested interests of powerful groups. Where the legal and judicial frameworks are weak and vested interests have taken over the state policymaking and resource allocation apparatus, the social cost can be enormous. In that case the institution building needed for effective development interventions may be extensive, warranting an active approach.

Participation and voice would be vital for increasing transparency, providing the necessary checks and balances, and countering state capture by the elite. The engagement of civil society in participatory and transparent processes with reformists in the executive, legislative, judiciary, and private sectors can make the difference between a well-governed and a misgoverned state, between a stagnant and a thriving society. A rigorous understanding of governance would need to be supported by new technologies (as in Albania, Bolivia, Georgia, Latvia, and several African countries).

Creating a climate for successful development thus requires an integrated approach linking economic, institutional, legal, and participatory elements: building transparent and effective institutions for budgeting and public investment programs (as in Australia, New Zealand, and the United Kingdom), as complements to macroeconomic policies; establishing merit-based public administration (as in Malaysia, Singapore, and Thailand) and efficient and honest customs and procurement agencies; and promoting civil liberties and popular participation (chapter 6).

Shifting Priorities

Why focus on quality when the pace of growth is slow in many parts of the world? Growth has been modest in many countries—about 1.6 percent per capita for low- and middle-income countries since the 1980s and lower still when China and India are excluded. Some countries are also facing or coming out of financial crises. In these circumstances, the issue is not one of quality *or* quantity. Both are essential, and both are involved in a two-way relationship.

A relative shift in priorities could boost the pace of long-term growth. Investments in human capital—education, health care, and population policies—can directly improve the quality of life. They can also improve investment incentives through the effect of a healthier, more educated work force on the productivity of capital. So shifting the emphasis more toward human capital could promote faster growth in the long run. The key point? A focus on the quality of outcomes could help to sustain more rapid growth.

Addressing the quality dimensions that contribute to the pace of growth can in turn enhance welfare directly. For example, less air and water pollution or less degradation of natural resources, in addition to contributing to growth, enhances welfare directly by improving health or providing greater opportunities for income and consumption.

This book shows that some processes and policies in developing or industrial countries generate economic growth with greater equality of human development, sustainability of the environment, and transparency of governance structures. Others do not. Furthermore, sequencing actions is unlikely to be effective—whether liberalizing first and regulating later, privatizing first and ensuring competition later, growing first and cleaning up later, or growing first and providing civil liberties later. To do the most for long-term growth, liberalization, for example, needs to go together with regulatory actions, environmental management, and anticorruption measures.

Defining the Shift

The actions focusing on the quality of growth need to be a core part of the policy package, not add-ons to an already crowded agenda. That means that stakeholders will have to augment actions by governments, shifting the emphasis to

- *Asset accumulation and use*, by reducing policy distortions, for example, those favoring or subsidizing physical capital, while complementing markets in valuing natural resources and investing adequately in human resources. The implication is to ensure broadly based, sustainable growth, not to slow growth.
- *Regulatory frameworks*, by building regulatory frameworks for competition and efficiency to accompany liberalization and privatization and giving legal and judicial reforms greater attention, while ensuring macroeconomic stability. The implication is to take supportive regulatory actions along with liberalization, not to slow liberalization.
- *Good governance*, by nurturing civil liberties, participatory processes, and accountability in public institutions; promoting anticorruption efforts; and actively involving the private sector to reduce the influence

of vested interests, while building capacity for policy changes. The implication is to increase the attention to coalition building in civil society, not to detract from government policy and capacity building.

Making the Shift—Now

How can more and better investment in people and natural capital be financed? In several ways. First, improving governance, reducing rent-seeking and corruption, and encouraging greater corporate responsibility can increase national savings. Second, increasing the charges for the use of natural resources and taxing such externalities as pollution can make more resources available for development. Third, reducing distortions that favor physical capital can be beneficial—as with much of the experiences in removing such distortations. It can allow a reallocation of national savings in favor of human development. And fourth, reducing subsidies within sectors for services that are regressive or damaging to the environment can reallocate public resources to benefit the poor or to promote sustainable development.

In sum, this book supports broadening the focus of actions to encompass a comprehensive development framework, a qualitative and fuller agenda involving structural, human, social, and environmental aspects of the growth process. This broader focus complements liberalization with a build-up in the assets and capabilities of the poor. It shifts attention from an exclusive reliance on government as the agent of change to the engagement of all parts of society. And it requires much more effective capacity building across the board.

With all development partners complementing one another, a more integrated framework can be implemented more effectively. First, the large inequalities in opportunities—especially in education—if addressed now, present the greatest promise for welfare gains to society. Second, the environmental damage and biodiversity losses from current growth patterns are frightening, but if they are addressed now, growth can achieve a better natural environment and reduce the number of poor. Third, globalization presents risks to the poor, but if those risks are addressed now, globalization could make possible the technological wherewithal for reducing poverty. Fourth, corruption, misgovernance, and a lack of civil liberties and voice threaten the gains from any action, but if those threats are addressed now, better governance presents great promise of improved welfare.

The opportunities afforded by increased openness, knowledge, and technologies have never been more plentiful. Equally, the challenges of poverty, population growth, environmental degradation, financial distress, and misgovernance have never been greater. Needed is more growth with a focus on quality. This is not a luxury. It is crucial for countries to seize the opportunities for a better life for their present and future generations.

A MIXED DEVELOPMENT RECORD

Economics is not only concerned with generating income, but also making good use of that income to enhance our living and our freedoms.

—Amartya Sen, *A Conversation with Sen*

I n the 1990s, a group of economies in East Asia posted some of the fastest growth rates and sharpest declines, as well as recoveries, giving market liberalization policies both strong support and serious qualification. In many ways the 1990s concentrated the development experiences of the previous decades, offering approaches and cautions to guide action in the 21st century.

Looking at the previous decades of development, various studies from around the world in the 1990s spotlighted the successes in East Asia, the setbacks in Sub-Saharan Africa, and the modest gains elsewhere. The *World Development Report 1991* (World Bank 1991) articulated an emerging consensus under the rubric of a market-friendly approach, calling for a reappraisal of the roles of state and market. This and other reviews signaled the crucial roles of the state and markets in poverty reduction (World Bank 1990), in environmental protection (World Bank 1992), in infrastructure provision (World Bank 1994), and in the legal and governance frameworks and the financial system (World Bank 1997j).

Here we examine how the lessons of development have played out over the past decade. We update earlier assessments of how countries are performing with regard to poverty reduction, sustainable development, and economic growth. And we examine the global factors and policy and institutional changes underlying the countries' performance.

Evidence from the 1990s expands the development story, especially concerning institutional requirements for success, and provides a rich set of hypotheses to consider with regard to policy. First, investments in people need to be concerned with the quality and distribution of those investments. Second, rapid growth, while it supports social development when broad based, can hurt environmental sustainability in the absence of appropriate actions. Third, while market openness and competition continue to provide benefits, the financial risks must be managed with attention to country-specific factors. Fourth, good governance and institutional factors should be given priority and not postponed for later stages of reform.

Assessing Development

Development is about people and their well-being, which involves their ability to shape their lives. Accordingly, development must be inclusive of future generations and the earth they will inherit. It must engage people, for without their participation, no strategy can succeed for long. This notion of development as well-being means that measures of development must include not just rates of growth, but the dispersion, composition, and sustainability of that growth.

Development practitioners have often used growth in gross domestic product (GDP) per capita as a proxy for development, partly because social progress is associated with GDP growth and partly because of expediency. However, reliance on GDP as the sole measure of development is seriously limiting. GDP growth can be of high quality or of poor quality. Some processes and policies generate GDP growth along with the growth of human and natural assets that directly affect people's welfare beyond their productive roles. Others generate poor quality growth that is not associated with improvements of human and natural assets. To integrate the quality of growth in assessments of development, multidimensional indexes of welfare are needed.

Economic theory distinguishes the concept of growth from the broader idea of development. How carefully this distinction has been made has varied over time.[1] The rapid growth of the 1950s and 1960s motivated an increased concern for broader development goals. Over the following decades, as stagnation set in, the emphasis shifted to economic growth. In the 1990s, the broader outlook reemerged, as exemplified in the United Nations Development Programme (UNDP) *Human Development Report* (produced annually since 1990) and the World Bank's *A Proposal for a Comprehensive Development Framework* (Wolfensohn 1999).

In an ideal assessment of development, progress would be measured by human and environmental advances before considering intermediate indicators, such as GDP. However, we lack good quality data to construct robust indicators of human and environmental progress and consequently rely heavily on GDP. We supplement the analysis with indexes of human development and environmental sustainability, keeping in mind serious data limitations on some variables. Lack of consistent data on the incidence of poverty, comparable internationally and over time, forced us to exclude a poverty reduction component in our human development index. However, we document, where possible, progress in poverty alleviation and the impact of growth and development policies on poverty (see also Dollar and Kraay 2000; Ravallion and Chen 1997; World Bank 2000i). Future work should improve the scope and empirical basis of these indexes and expand the discussion to other dimensions, including cultural well-being.

Table 1.1 shows correlations among the components of the three indicators of progress since 1981: human development, income growth, and environmental sustainability. It shows that GDP growth is correlated

A step toward better and broader measures of development
Table 1.1. Correlations of Measures of Development, 1981–98

Measure of development	Human development					Income growth	Environmental sustainability		
	Decrease in poverty	Increase in literacy	Decrease in infant mortality	Increase in life expectancy	Decrease in income inequality	Growth of GDP	Decrease in carbon dioxide emission	Increase in forest cover	Decrease in water pollution
Human development									
Decrease in poverty	1.00	−0.40	0.18	0.14	0.44	0.52	−0.45	−0.23	0.28
		27	28	28	20	27	27	26	22
Increase in literacy		1.00	0.15	−0.19	−0.23	0.03	−0.14	0.15	−0.21
			115	115	41	89	102	94	72
Decrease in infant mortality			1.00	0.54	0.28	0.20	−0.20	−0.12	−0.13
				146	43	104	121	107	81
Increase in life expectancy				1.00	0.54	0.17	−0.16	−0.15	−0.05
					43	104	121	107	81
Decrease in income inequality					1.00	0.34	−0.33	−0.20	0.32
						39	41	41	37
Income growth									
Growth of GDP						1.00	−0.53	−0.06	0.33
							100	81	65
Environmental sustainability									
Decrease in carbon dioxide emission							1.00	0.27	−0.38
								87	70
Increase in forest cover								1.00	−0.14
									70
Decrease in water pollution									1.00

Note: The two values in each cell are the correlation coefficient and number of countries. Entries in bold italics are significant at the 10 percent level or better.

Sources: World Bank (2000c); authors' computations.

- Positively with reduction in poverty, income inequality, infant mortality, and increase in life expectancy, with considerable differences in strength
- Negatively with decline in carbon dioxide emissions and positively with decline in water pollution.

Other associations between GDP growth and changes in the components of human development and environmental sustainability are not statistically significant. These preliminary correlations suggest that GDP growth is a crucial, yet partial, indicator of development, as when it is imperfectly associated with certain aspects of human development, and at times when it is associated with an increase in environmental damage.

Easterly (1999a) applied several techniques to a large set of quality of life indicators, including tests of causal relationships. He found that fewer than 10 percent of the 81 examined indicators improved with growth. A similar fraction deteriorated with growth, and many showed no significant association with growth (figure 1.1). These findings strengthen the case for broadening the measures of development.

It is very important to note that the relationships discussed above are between *growth* of income and *changes* in human development and environmental sustainability. Relationships in most cases are much stronger with *levels* of income and indicators, particularly for human development indicators (Dasgupta 1993; Fedderke and Klitgaard 1998; Kakwani 1993; Sen 1994;

Figure 1.1. GDP Growth and Changes in Quality of Life, 1960s and 1990s

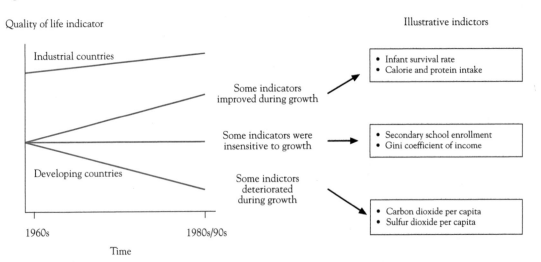

Quality of life indicator

Illustrative indictors

Industrial countries

Some indicators improved during growth

- Infant survival rate
- Calorie and protein intake

Some indicators were insensitive to growth

- Secondary school enrollment
- Gini coefficient of income

Developing countries

Some indictors deteriorated during growth

- Carbon dioxide per capita
- Sulfur dioxide per capita

1960s   1980s/90s

Time

Note: The schematic trends are applicable for countries with positive GDP growth.
Source: Easterly (1999a).

World Bank 2000i). Easterly's study also looks at this discrepancy, hypothesizing that cross-country analysis of income levels may capture long-term trends that are not discernible in analysis of shorter periods, and that growth may lead to improvements in human development with long and varying lags. Alternatively, country-specific factors, such as endowments, location, and social infrastructure, could be dominant determinants of levels of both income and human development indicators. In that case the cross-country correlations between income and quality of life indicators would need to be qualified.

The Development Record

Progress in some areas of human development, especially in extending people's lives and increasing literacy, has been considerable over the 1960s through the 1990s, a period over which some data are available. However, many other qualitative aspects of life, including steady and sustained increase in incomes, poverty reduction, equality gains, and environmental quality, have lagged.

Human Development

Robust economic growth is accompanied by improvements in measures of human development, such as higher literacy and life expectancy. The broad association is seen in figure 1.2.

Overall, the gains in human development over the past four decades have been enormous in some areas—partly reflecting technological improvements—and modest in others. Infant mortality and adult illiteracy rates fell dramatically almost everywhere.

Progress in raising incomes and reducing poverty has been mixed, based on the data and estimates available (figure 1.3). In the developing world, the poverty headcount index, defined as the proportion of people with an income of less than US$1 a day based on 1993 purchasing power parity (PPP) prices, decreased from 28.3 percent in 1987 to 24 percent in 1998. The East Asia and Pacific region showed the largest improvement, particularly China in the mid-1990s. Improvements were modest in the Middle East and North Africa and the South Asia regions. Poverty rates remained stubbornly high in Sub-Saharan Africa and Latin America and the Caribbean and increased sharply in Europe and Central Asia. Overall the decrease in the poverty rate could not keep pace with population growth, and the number of poor in the developing world outside China increased by about 106 million between 1987 and 1998 (World Bank 1999c).

At the end of the 20th century, the incidence of poverty increased in many parts of the world. In particular, the East Asian countries directly

Figure 1.2. Change in Human Development and Growth of Income, 1981–98

Change in human development (index)

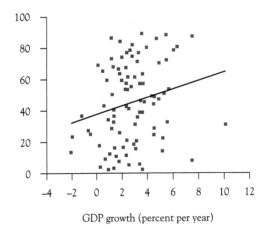

GDP growth (percent per year)

Note: $r = 0.22$, $p < 0.05$, $n = 89$. The data are for 89 developing countries. Controlling for per capita income in 1981 gives a stronger pattern with a correlation coefficient of 0.33.
    Source: World Bank (2000c); authors' computations.

affected by the 1997 financial crises and the consequent slowing of growth experienced reversals in poverty reduction achieved during their period of rapid growth (World Bank 2000f). Even greater is the poverty increase in the transition economies of Europe and Central Asia, where as recently as 1987 poverty and income inequality were both extremely low. Survey data show an enormous increase in the number of poor as a result of sustained declines in economic output and worsening income distributions (Milanovic 1997) (figure 1.4).

Environmental Degradation

The impact of economic growth on environmental conditions has been mixed and is a serious concern. In many instances GDP growth and higher incomes are associated with better sanitation and water quality, as well as investments in cleaner technologies. But growth is also related to increases in particulates and carbon dioxide emissions.[2] With equal weights for the changes in indicators of water quality, air quality, and deforestation, between 1981 and 1998 income growth was associated with environmental deterioration and depletion of natural resources as in figure 1.5.

Between 1990 and 1995, the *rate* of forest clearing slowed in most developing regions, but forest cover was still disappearing rapidly. Forest cover

Figure 1.3.   Poverty Rates and Number of Poor, Selected Years

Poverty Headcount Index

Percentage (of population living on less than US$1 per day)

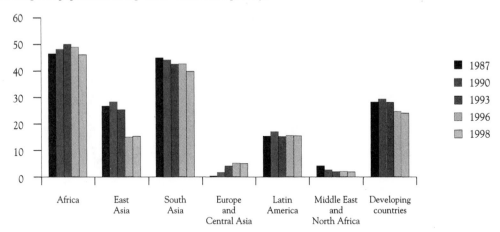

Number of Poor

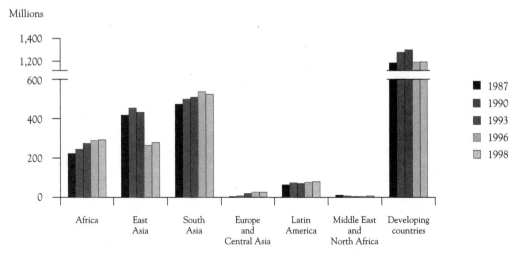

Note: Based on 1993 purchasing parity rates. The 1998 values are estimates. Poverty is defined as income of less than US$1 a day.
Source: World Bank (1999d).

increased only in high-income countries and in developing Europe and
Central Asia. It is unclear how much of the improvement in the latter is
the result of concerted environmental action.

Between 1980 and 1995, carbon dioxide emissions, total as well as per
capita, increased across income groups and regions. Only Sub-Saharan

Figure 1.4. Poverty Incidence in Selected Transition Economies, 1987–88 and 1993–95

Percent (population living on less than US$4 a day)

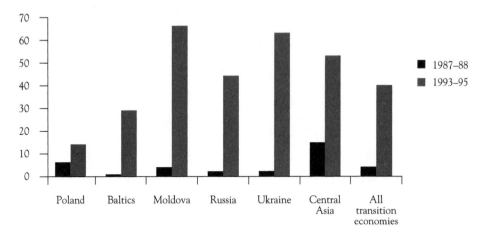

Note: The poverty line of US$4 a day is considerably higher than that used elsewhere.
Source: Milanovic (1997).

Figure 1.5. Environmental Changes Versus Growth of Income, 1981–98

Change in environmental quality (index)

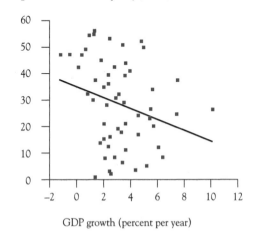

GDP growth (percent per year)

Note: $r = -0.27$, $p < 0.05$, $n = 56$. The data are for 56 developing countries. Controlling for per capita income in 1981 gives a similar pattern and the same value for the correlation coefficient (–0.27).
Source: World Bank (2000c); authors' computations.

Africa, probably because of general economic stagnation, did not experience increased carbon dioxide output. East Asia had the fastest deforestation and highest carbon dioxide emissions per capita, suggesting a conflict
between growth and sustainable development (World Bank 2000c).

In much of the developing world, the environmental quality is far worse
than indicators portray. Air quality worsened as incomes rose.[3] Exposure to
high levels of air pollution, that is, total suspended particulates, sulfur dioxide, and nitrogen dioxide, poses a major threat to human health. In Delhi,
one of the world's most polluted cities, total suspended particulates were
more than four times the level identified as safe by the World Health Organization (WHO) (World Bank 1999d). For particulate levels in selected
cities, see figure 1.6.

The human cost of environmental deterioration is staggering. Poor water
supply, inadequate sanitation, indoor air pollution, urban air pollution, malaria,
and agro-industrial chemicals and waste account for an estimated one-fifth of
the total burden of disease and premature death in the developing world, based
on a standardized measure of health outcomes—disability adjusted life years, or
DALYs. For Africa, poor water supply, inadequate sanitation, and indoor air
pollution account for 29.5 percent of the disease burden, a share larger than
that attributed to malnutrition, 26 percent (Lvovsky and others 1999).

Air pollution is alarmingly high in many cities in developing countries

Figure 1.6. Total Suspended Particulates, Selected Cities, Early 1990s

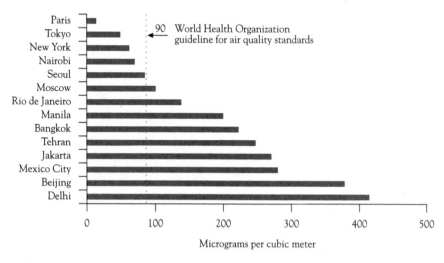

Microgams per cubic meter

Note: Most data are for 1995. The figure for New York is for 1990.
Source: World Bank (1997i, 2000c).

Income Growth, Inequality, and Volatility

Long-term progress in income growth in the world has been very uneven. Figure 1.7 show the trends in per capita incomes in the developing regions and the industrial countries since 1975. East Asia has improved living standards significantly, while Sub-Saharan Africa has seen the opposite trend. The large variation in growth rates at the level of individual economies may be seen in figure 1.8. Of the 15 fastest growing economies, 8 are in East Asia. Many of those at the other end of the spectrum are countries affected by civil strife and other dislocations.

Judging by customary growth rates, weighted by incomes of countries, the 1980s were a lost decade for the developing world. The picture looks better when growth rates are weighted by population, because the decreases among middle-income countries, especially in Latin America, weigh less and the increases in the larger low-income countries, China and India, weigh more. In the 1990s, the difference between income-weighted and population-weighted aggregate growth rates for developing countries narrowed as growth improved in the middle-income countries in Latin America.

Figure 1.7. Purchasing Power Parity–Adjusted GDP Per Capita, 1975–98

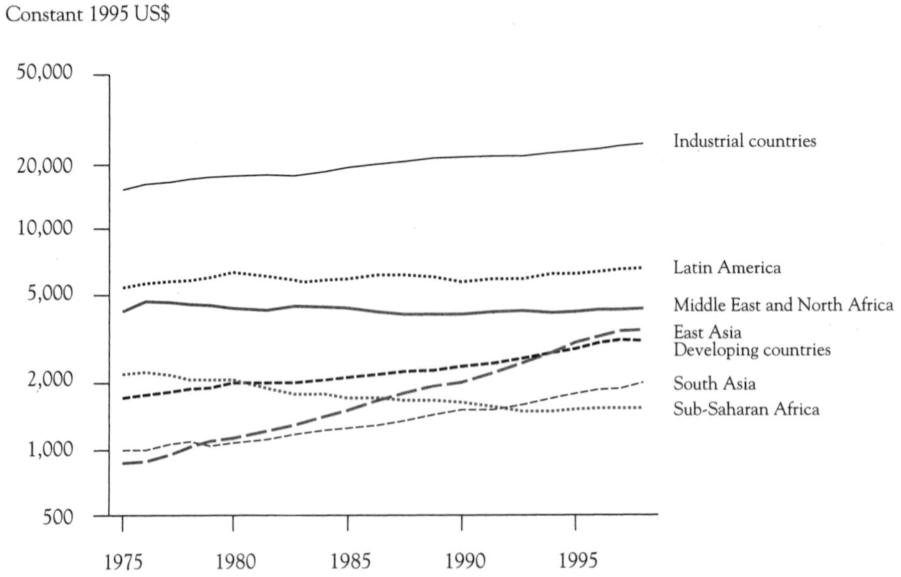

Constant 1995 US$

Note: Europe and Central Asia is excluded for reasons of data availability.
Source: World Bank data.

Figure 1.8. Growth in GDP Per Capita, Selected Economies, 1975–98

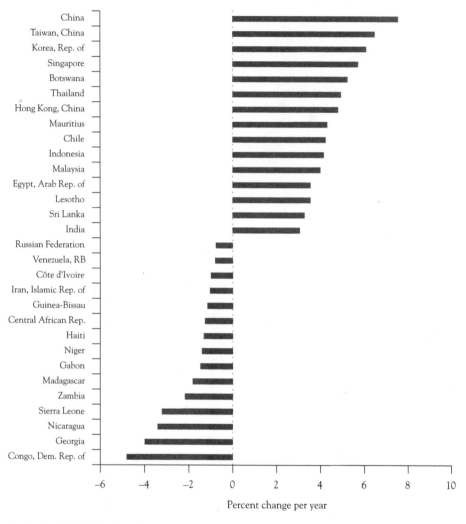

Source: World Bank (2000c); authors' computations.

Income Inequality. Within this picture of overall income growth, it is also important to consider how the income was being shared by looking at changes in income inequality. Several dimensions of income inequality are relevant here: between countries, across households within countries, and within households. As noted in World Bank (2000i), the gap between the average income of the richest 20 countries and the average for the poorest 20 has doubled in the past 40 years—to more than 30 times.

The data requirements for estimating the distribution of personal incomes in the world are onerous, and the available data have severe weaknesses. That said, Dikhanov and Ward (2000) estimated such distributions for 1988 and 1993 and found that the overall inequality of personal incomes in the world increased from a Gini coefficient of 0.63 to 0.67 (see also Cornia 1999).

Schultz (1998) looked at the trends in between-country inequality of income. The results differ considerably based on whether China is included in the analysis. Income inequality between countries increased from 1960 through 1968, stayed high through 1976, and gradually declined after that, ending up slightly higher in 1989 than in 1960. If China is excluded, the decline in inequality among countries from 1976 disappears. Extension of the analysis through 1994 for a slightly smaller set of countries confirmed these trends.

Using comparable data on income Gini coefficients for 45 countries from the early 1960s to the early 1990s, Deininger and Squire (1996) found no general trend in within-country inequality, which stayed approximately the same in 29 countries, rose in 8, and fell in 8. For a different comparison, between the early 1980s and early 1990s inequality increased in 19 countries and decreased in 24 (figure 1.9). Among the countries in which inequality increased are those with large populations: Brazil, China, and India. Population-weighted, average inequality for the 43 sample countries increased by 0.52 percent a year in the 1980s and the early 1990s.[4]

Growth Volatility. Economic fluctuations seem to affect the poor disproportionately, but the impact is likely to be particularly severe in countries where social safety nets are typically less well developed (Furman and Stiglitz 1998). Declines in economic growth were directly associated with sharp increases in poverty in Eastern Europe, and more recently in East Asia. Economic downturns appear to have enduring adverse effects on the economy. Studies suggest that bigger fluctuations in growth rates are associated with slower average growth.[5] The volatility of growth would seem to matter.

On average, volatility of growth by some measures is estimated to have declined in the 1980s for most country groups (except middle-income countries, mainly because of the debt crisis in Latin America), compared with the 1970s when the oil shocks occured. The picture is more mixed in the 1990s. Volatility is estimated to have declined for Latin America, the Middle East and North Africa, and South Asia, but increased slightly for industrial countries and for East Asia (figure 1.10).

No general trend in within-country inequality

Figure 1.9. Income Inequality within Countries: 1980s and 1990s

Reduction in Gini coefficient (percent per year)

FSU Former Soviet Union.
Note: The quantity plotted is reduction in income Gini coefficients, in the early 1990s over the early 1980s, in percentage declines per year. Negative values indicate an increase in inequality.
Source: Deininger and Squire (1996).

Figure 1.10. Volatility of GDP Growth Rates by Decade

Percent (standard deviation of growth rates)

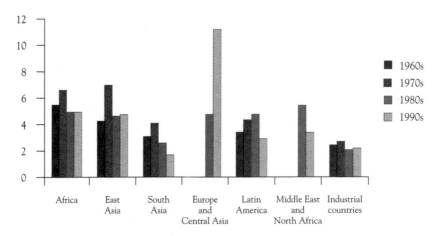

Note: Volatility in a decade was computed by taking the standard deviation of growth rates in the decade for each country and the unweighted average across the countries in the group.

Sources: World Bank (2000c); authors' computations.

Developing Europe and Central Asia had especially more volatile growth than other regions in the 1990s compared with the 1980s.

Developing countries seem to have experienced higher volatility than industrial countries. Easterly, Islam, and Stiglitz (1999) explore the determinants of the increased volatility of countries, finding that

- Openness to trade and the volatility of capital flows are associated with increased volatility of growth
- Improvement in indicators of financial development are associated with lower volatility
- Constraints on policy from institutional limitations and financial sector underdevelopment contribute to the variability of outcomes
- Wage flexibility does not seem to be an important factor.

Growth and Welfare

Table 1.2 places developing countries in three groups, based on their per capita GDP growth rates: high-growth countries, those with moderate or improving growth rates, and low-growth countries.[6] By the definition used here, 13 had rapid growth, 53 had moderate growth, and 39 had low

Table 1.2. Development Outcomes by Growth Class, 1980s and 1990s
(unweighted means)

Change in indicator: comparing 1980s and 1990s	Unit	Period	High growth	Moderate or improved growth	Low growth
Poverty	Percentage with less than US$1 a day	1990s	24.1	31.4	36.9
		1980s	31.0	32.1	30.2
Infant mortality	Per thousand	1990s	29.2	54.3	60.7
		1980s	41.0	66.6	71.0
Illiteracy	Percent	1990s	17.2	31.2	31.4
		1980s	22.9	37.6	38.8
Life expectancy	Years	1990s	70.0	62.9	59.8
		1980s	66.8	60.6	58.4
Carbon dioxide emission	Tons per capita	1990s	2.4	2.3	1.7
		1980s	1.5	2.3	1.8
Deforestation	Percent per year	1990–95	0.83	1.05	1.11
		1980–90	1.08	0.65	1.15
Water pollution	Kilograms per day per worker	1990s	0.16	0.21	0.21
		1980s	0.18	0.21	0.21
GDP growth	Percent per year	1990s	5.3	4.2	0.3
		1980s	6.5	2.3	2.1
Number of countries			13	53	39

Note: See text for details regarding country classification. Some variables are missing for some of the countries. In particular, poverty data are available for only a small number of countries.
Sources: World Bank (2000c); authors' computations.

growth. Also by this definition, the moderate-growth countries had the strongest improvement in growth. Several of the human development indicators generally improved for all three groups, with the high-growth countries showing the strongest improvements. The high-growth countries had higher and increasing carbon dioxide emissions per capita.

External Factors Matter

In the 1990s, externally- and domestically-driven political and social upheaval and wars continued to derail progress in numerous countries (Collier 1999; Collier and Hoeffler 1998) (table 1.3). Global and cross-border issues related to financial crises, population pressures, labor migration, and environmental distress continued to affect domestic outcomes. Despite

Table 1.3. External Factors Matter for Domestic Outcomes, Examples from 1997–99

	Financial crises	Natural disasters	Conflicts	Human-caused disasters
Region or country in crisis	East Asia Russia Brazil	Bangladesh Central America	Albania Bosnia Congo, Dem. Rep. of Yugoslavia Rwanda Sierra Leone	Indonesia (forest fire)
Impact	Short-term increase in poverty	Loss of human lives and physical and natural capital	Destruction of human and social capital	Long-term increase in poverty

Source: Authors' compilation.

progress in slowing population growth, population increases in many countries could undermine efforts to achieve sustainable development. Global warming, environmental degradation, and the loss of biodiversity continue to worsen as an ever more crowded planet puts more pressure on limited global resources (World Bank 2000b and various editions of the World Bank's *Global Economic Prospects* and *Global Development Finance*).

The quarter century or so after World War II marked a period of rapid and steady growth for both industrial and developing countries, and the economic environment was relatively free of major shocks. The international economic environment changed dramatically in 1973 with the oil price shock and the end of the Bretton Woods system of fixed exchange rates among major industrial countries. Subsequent decades saw sharp declines in the productivity growth of industrial countries, high inflation and interest rates, and cycles of large amplitude in commodity prices and exchange rates of major currencies.

It has been argued that the low growth record of most developing countries (with some exceptions, mostly in East Asia) after 1973 and into the 1990s was due primarily to the growth slowdown in industrial countries (Easterly 1999b). While that was a significant factor, the record of the developing countries that prospered during this period, such as those in East Asia, suggests that domestic policy, governance, and institutions also influence outcomes. The damage caused by shocks and conflicts depends on the institutions in place and their effectiveness in strengthening governance, civil rights, the rule of law, social programs, and safety nets (Collier 1999; Collier and Hoeffler 1998; Easterly, Islam, and Stiglitz 1999; Rodrik 1998, 1999).

The global economic environment experienced another significant change in the 1990s, becoming more conducive to development in some respects, less so in others (see various editions of the World Bank's *Global Economic Prospects*). Import demand by Organisation for Economic Co-operation and Development (OECD) nations was less volatile in the 1990s than in earlier decades, partly because the cycles of North America, Europe, and Japan were no longer synchronized, and partly because of the increased weight of developing countries, especially East Asia, in world trade. Thanks to monetary restraint and progress in fiscal consolidation, real interest and inflation rates in the major OECD countries dropped in the 1990s, and volatility in the exchange rates of major currencies was considerably smaller relative to the pronounced dollar cycle of the 1980s.

Particularly important was the relative steadying in developing country terms of trade with industrial countries, especially in prices of the nonenergy primary commodities. Non-oil exporters saw a serious deterioration in their terms of trade from the mid-1970s to the early 1990s. However, for much of the 1990s, non-oil commodity prices held firm, and the decline since 1997 has been less steep than in earlier price cycles. Although export prices are far more volatile for commodities than for manufactured products, commodity prices were less volatile in the 1990s than in the 1980s for 22 of 30 key commodities (World Bank 2000a; various issues of *Commodities Quarterly*).

The robust growth in world trade sharply surpassed growth in world output through 1998. The international trading environment remained liberal on the whole, with increased multilateralism, notwithstanding the rise of such questionable practices as antidumping. And there was a phenomenal increase in private capital flows to developing countries, albeit only to a few.

The East Asian financial crisis revealed that while opportunities have grown enormously, so have the demands on institutions and the costs of mistakes. Success in a highly globalized setting requires adequate mechanisms for managing risks, and successful policies for openness and competition need effective regulatory and legal frameworks.

Domestic Policies Make a Crucial Difference

Underlying the varied development outcomes has been the effectiveness of policy, notably in the following four areas: the quality and distribution of education and health services, the stewardship of the environment, the management of opportunities and the risks of globalization, and the effectiveness of governance. These links are analyzed in the subsequent chapters.

Investing in People

No country has achieved sustained development without investing substantially and efficiently in the education and health of its people. Developing countries have generally been spending more public resources on education, and many regions have expanded that spending in the 1990s (figure 1.11). Public spending in education has declined in East Asia and the Middle East and North Africa. There is evidence that in East Asia, the share of private expenditure is on the rise. Cross-country data on health expenditures are available only for the 1990s, so long-term trends are not known.

What happens to the share of social expenditures in countries undergoing adjustment and fiscal austerity? Analyses have been divided on the question. The World Bank (1992) concluded that the shares remain unchanged, while Corbo, Fischer, and Webb (1992) found that education shares declined. A recent International Monetary Fund (IMF 1998) study of low-income countries undergoing adjustment found that the shares of education and health expenditures have generally been protected. Private spending is also important in social services funding, especially in East Asia, where its share rose with economic growth. But public spending does not always produce good outcomes. Those depend on the distribution and quality of the public spending and on the incentives for more private spending. These issues are explored in chapter 3.

Figure 1.11.   Public Expenditures on Education by Region, Selected Years

Percentage of GNP (medians)

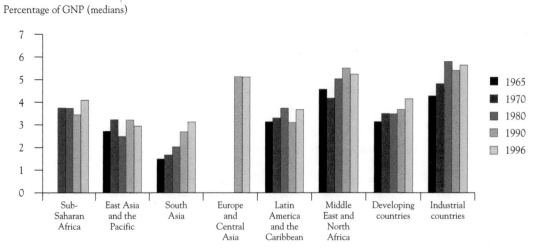

Source: World Bank (2000c).

Managing the Environment

We know that government policies have neglected the environment, but we have no standard measures for evaluating a country's environmental policies. One recently developed indicator, *genuine saving*, measures the rate of saving after accounting for investments in human capital, depreciation of produced assets, and depletion and degradation of the environment (World Bank 1999f, pp. 175–77). Such measures are still experimental and reflect both policies and outcomes.

We have looked at progress in agreements reached on environmental issues. From this, however, we get only a sense of the commitment of governments from having completed a country environmental profile, formulating conservation and biodiversity strategies, and participating in global treaties. These measures appear to be only weakly related to environmental outcomes. We need better ways to capture country policies for environmentally sustainable development.

Creating Market-Friendly Policies

Openness and Liberalization. Openness increased in developing countries in the 1990s. The ratio of trade to GDP rose in all developing regions. Levels of trade protection have declined in most regions, aided by successive rounds of multilateral trade negotiations. Average tariffs came down in the 1990s, sharply in many cases (figure 1.12). Nontariff barriers have also been reduced significantly in most regions, with the exception of Sub-Saharan Africa (Rodrik 1999; UNCTAD 1994).

Openness to capital also increased dramatically in some regions. An index of financial controls shows a sharp decline in the 1990s, following a sharp increase in the previous decade (chapter 5). Liberalization has also taken hold in domestic markets, as governments have become more willing to rely on markets and to increase incentives for private initiative by privatizing industries and have lifted other restraints on marketing and distribution. Many primary commodity exporting countries in Africa are liberalizing control boards, allowing for more pass-throughs of international commodity prices to producers (Akiyama 1995).

Macroeconomic Stability. Two often used reflectors of economic management are parallel-market exchange rate premiums and government deficits. Figure 1.13 shows that parallel-market premiums declined sharply in the 1990s in most countries. After sharp increases in the 1980s, government deficits declined in most regions, except Europe and Central Asia. Partly as a result, inflation was down in most developing countries.

Trade barriers decline in most regions

Figure 1.12.   Trade Barriers, Selected Regions, 1984–93

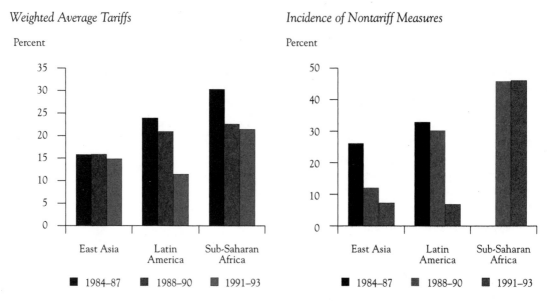

Weighted Average Tariffs

Incidence of Nontariff Measures

Source: Rodrik (1999).

Growth Outcomes and Policy Performances. Table 1.4 shows policy profiles for three growth classes and for the 1980s and 1990s. They do not claim to establish the direction of the link between policies and outcomes, but the patterns and trends are noteworthy. A great deal of previous work has shown the impact of policies on growth (a literature survey summary is available on request.) Although some market-friendly policies remain contentious, many developing countries made significant efforts to adopt them in the 1990s. Average budget deficits were lower for all groups in the 1990s—sharply so for the high- and moderate-growth groups. All three groups had significantly lower tariffs and a higher trade-to-GDP ratio in the 1990s than in the 1980s. All three groups were more open for capital account transactions in the 1990s—the high-growth group more cautiously so. Domestic financial systems were also generally less repressed in the 1990s, relative to the 1970s—again the high-growth group more cautiously so, relative to the moderate-growth group. The fast growers had greater financial depth, measured by the M2-to-GDP ratio, and more prudent macroeconomic policies, partly evident in increased reserves. And they had higher ratings on governance measures. There is an immense empirical literature on some of these policy-outcome links.

Figure 1.13. Parallel-Market Premium, 1970s–1990s

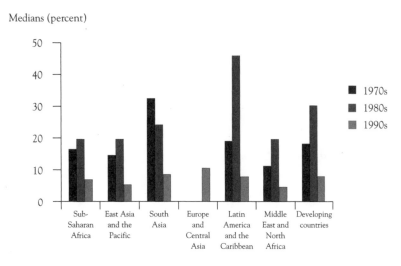

Note: The values plotted are (parallel market rate/official rate – 1) as a percentage, for a unit of foreign currency in terms of local currency units..

Sources: Easterly and Yu (2000); World Bank (2000c).

Crucial Issues for Action

The developing world continued to move forward in the 1990s. Progress on policy was substantial: reducing fiscal deficits, investing more in education, lowering trade and investment barriers, and dismantling domestic price controls in agriculture and industry. The record was more mixed on development outcomes. But both the 1990s and the longer-term record confirm that these actions go with improved economic growth. They also corroborate the link between economic growth and poverty reduction. Thus, on the whole, the developing world recovered from the setbacks of the 1980s, but both the depth and the breadth of the recovery left much to be desired.

The record also suggests that actions, by government and others, to affect the quality and sustainability of growth have lagged. Events in East Asia, Europe, Central Asia, and elsewhere underscore the fragility of advances in reducing poverty and achieving sustainable development. The numbers of poor people continue to increase, and today an estimated 1.2 billion live in absolute poverty, on less than US$1 a day. The incidence of poverty is highly sensitive to changes in income distribution and to population growth. So, policies affecting broad and equitable growth and population growth deserve considerable attention.

Table 1.4. Policy Performance, by Growth Class, 1980s and 1990s
(unweighted means)

Change in indicator: comparing 1980s and 1990s	Unit	Period	High growth	Moderate or improved growth	Low growth
Budget surplus	Percentage of GDP	1990s	−1.8	−1.4	−3.4
		1980s	−4.2	−2.9	−4.7
Effective tariff rate	Percent	1990s	22.7	25.4	18.3
		1980s	29.1	31.9	22.7
Trade/GDP	Percent	1990s	92.1	77.0	70.2
		1980s	82.0	71.0	59.9
Capital account openness	Index	1996	2.4	3.0	3.1
		1988	1.7	1.9	1.7
Financial repression	Index	1996	3.6	3.2	4.0
		1973	5.9	6.8	4.5
M2/GDP	Percent	1990s	55.4	36.9	28.6
		1980s	42.8	34.6	28.4
International reserves	Months of imports	1990s	4.2	3.9	2.9
		1980s	3.1	2.8	2.4
Rule of law	Index	1997–98	0.2	−0.2	−0.7
Control of corruption	Index	1997–98	−0.1	−0.2	−0.6
Education spending	Percentage of GNP	1990s	3.7	4.4	4.3
		1980s	3.6	4.2	4.4
Environmental action	0-1 Index	International	0.89	0.95	0.88
	0-1 Index	Domestic	0.89	0.86	0.65
Number of countries			13	53	39

Note: See text for details regarding country classification. Some variables are missing for some of the countries. In particular, the following variables are available for only a small number of countries: effective tariff rate and financial repression. Variables are described in annex 1.

Sources: World Bank (2000c); authors' computations.

The relationships between development goals and policy instruments have been investigated in considerable detail in the development literature. The annex to chapter 1 includes a set of correlation coefficients for goals and policies in the spirit of providing the basic data. As correlations, they say nothing about the direction of the causality or the mechanisms. Nevertheless, the combinations shown to be significant are worthy of further investigation as hypotheses. Equally important are the plausible combinations that are not significant with the expected sign. Many of the hypothesized relations are taken up in chapters 3 through 6, and in chapter 2, which elaborates a basic framework.

Here, we frame the relationships in the form of questions that motivate this study:

- Are the observed improvements in human capital sufficient to sustain growth in countries that experienced accelerated growth in the 1990s?
- Is the increased human capital in the slow-growth countries sufficient to propel faster and better growth in the near future?
- Will the deterioration of natural capital reduce the potential for future growth, especially among poor countries?
- Is the degradation of natural capital becoming a serious obstacle to improving the welfare of the population?
- Can the risks of financial globalization be managed in a way that diminishes the volatility of growth and improves its sustainability?
- How serious is the manner of governing for growth processes and outcomes, and how can progress be made in controlling corruption?

The chapters ahead provide insights into these questions, if not answers.

The rest of this publication is organized as follows. Chapter 2 provides an analytical framework for interpreting the development experience outlined in this chapter and derives lessons on the importance of undistorted growth of human, natural, and physical assets and the welfare significance of alternative growth patterns (see also the box in the Overview). Chapter 3 explores how investments in people—in quantity, quality, and distribution—can augment welfare directly and also make growth processes more sustainable. Chapter 4 does the same for environmental and natural resources, where the conflict between growth and welfare is apparent and the tradeoff that much tougher. Chapter 5 revisits the issue of growth volatility and financial risks and considers the quality aspects of reforms that would render growth processes more sustainable in today's globalized setting. All three—human, natural, and financial sides—hinge on the quality of overall governance, which is fundamental to the quality and sustainability of the growth processes. Formal and informal institutions of governance are discussed in chapter 6, with a special focus on fighting corruption. Chapter 7 considers an agenda for action.

Why is there a failure to take up policies that have shown themselves sound? Policymakers' lack of understanding of these policies is unlikely to be the main reason. More likely is the political difficulty of implementing sound policies. Interest groups limit the range of feasible reforms and open a gulf between policy design and implementation. How best to counteract these forces through enhanced participation and stronger government ownership is an important topic not fully explored in the report (except for a brief discussion of selected aspects in chapter 6).

Another crucial topic is the special circumstances facing the formerly centrally planned economies as they strive to make the transition to market economies. These economies are included in the analyses when data permit, and illustrations and cases drawing on their experience are used in some of the chapters, especially the one on governance and anticorruption (chapter 6). However, a full discussion of the issues for transition economies is beyond the scope of this volume.[7]

Notes

1. Many studies have addressed the multidimensional view of development objectives (Dasgupta 1993; Hicks and Streeten 1979; Lewis 1955; Nordhaus and Tobin 1972; Sengupta and Fox 1969; Tinbergen and Theil in Hughes-Hallet 1989). Some studies used multivariate analysis of a large number of economic, social, and political variables (Adelman and Taft-Morris 1967; Baster 1972; Morris 1979; UNRISD 1970). Some constructed indexes of quality of life or human development (Dasgupta 1990a; Diewert 1986; Drewnowski and Scott 1966; Griliches 1971; McGranahan 1972; Ram 1982a,b; Slottje 1991). The frameworks in some of these works are touched upon in chapter 2.

2. Carbon dioxide emissions do not have much local health impact directly, but are important in the context of greenhouse emissions and the associated problem of global climate change. Also, carbon dioxide emissions are usually associated with emission of other air pollutants that do have a local health impact, but about which data are less widely available.

3. Measures of air quality for many cities became available only in the mid-1990s. An inverted U-shaped relationship between pollution and per capita income, the environmental Kuznets curve, has been estimated for several types of pollutants (Grossman and Krueger 1995). This does not, however, invalidate the need for environmental intervention, because the per capita income turning points for improved environmental indicators are generally quite high. This issue is discussed in chapter 4.

4. Data on income distribution are scanty for the more recent years. A World Bank study of 29 countries estimated that 5 countries experienced a decline in inequality, while about 5 times as many countries (24) saw an increase (Buckley 1999).

5. For example, a regression of average rates of GDP growth for 112 countries against the volatility of GDP growth rates, measured by the standard deviation of growth rates, yielded a significant negative coefficient (see also Ramey and Ramey 1995).

6. High-growth countries as defined here are those with per capita income growth of more than 2.3 percent per year in the 1980s and the 1990s, a rate that doubles incomes in 30 years. The second group—moderate or improved growth—includes countries that maintained a positive growth of per capita income in both decades, or improved growth in the 1990s by at least 2 percentage points. The rest are classified as low-growth countries.

7. See World Bank (1996b) for a full treatment of transition issues. See also recent papers by Åslund (1999); Commander, Dutz, and Stern (1999); Kornai (2000); Qian (1999); Stiglitz (1999); and Wyplosz (1999).

ASSETS, GROWTH, AND WELFARE

The difficulty lies, not in the new ideas, but in escaping from the old ones which ramify…into every corner of our minds.

> —John Maynard Keynes, *The General Theory of Employment, Interest, and Money*

Rapid economic growth has usually been considered the prime indicator of development. Yet, there has been dissatisfaction with using growth measured by national accounts as the yardstick (see, for example, Adelman 1975; Dasgupta 1993; Dréze and Sen 1995; Lewis 1955; Sen 1988). More meaningful is welfare, comprising consumption, human development, and environmental sustainability, and their quality, distribution, and stability. Often per capita income growth and welfare improvements go hand in hand. But sometimes they do not.

Large divergences between growth and welfare improvements may arise when growth is volatile and unsustained. Can such divergences between growth and welfare change still arise when economic growth is sustained? That is, can countries maintain rapid growth for prolonged periods without commensurate increases in welfare? If not, the focus should be on policies that assure sustained growth—because those policies would also generally improve welfare. But if yes, the focus on growth has to be complemented with an examination of alternative patterns of (sustained) growth.

The analysis here focuses on investment patterns in three key assets: physical and the closely associated financial capital,[1] human and the closely associated social capital, and natural and the closely associated environmental capital. Technology affecting the use of these assets matters a great deal too. The central hypothesis, which is assessed empirically subsequently, is that promoting adequate investment in all forms of capital is a way to induce more and better growth and improvements in welfare. But policies often introduce distortions that encourage either over- or underinvestments in different forms of capital. Examples of these distortions are artificially low interest rates, underpricing of natural resources, or underemphasizing basic education in public policy. Focusing mostly on physical capital accumulation to the relative neglect of human and natural capital is no guarantee to sustain growth. Some recent evidence shows little correlation between investment rates and growth rates in the short term (Easterly 1999c). Special efforts to encourage physical capital accumulation per se are likely to impose large costs.

Some policy changes in the 1980s and the early 1990s would seem to have especially raised the rate of return to physical capital, reflected by investment booms in many countries. But these reforms by themselves have not automatically assured sustained growth, to the extent that there have not been complementary investments in human and natural assets. Moreover, some countries have not generated growth—partly because of wrong regulation (for example, licensing that reduces investment incentives), and insufficient regulation (for example, for financial markets and to deal with monopolies).

Alternatively, growth induced by relatively undistorted or a balanced expansion of human, physical, and natural capital can be sustained for prolonged periods.[2] Balanced does not signify an equal expansion in the assets. Rather, it refers to assest accumulation in response to an undistorted policy framework. Such a pattern is more likely to reduce poverty and improve income distribution. That, in turn, creates the conditions for faster growth that improves welfare more rapidly. So, preventing underinvestment in human and natural capital is one way of promoting rapid and sustained growth.

We begin with a framework that allows us to explore these hypotheses and their implications: patterns of asset accumulation, factor productivity, and social welfare. In particular, we look at the implications of distorted asset growth for the poor. The next section provides empirical evidence from a variety of sources. In addition to a historical review of 60 countries, we provide econometric evidence from two groups of countries on the determinants of growth. Finally, we turn to the empirical evidence on a variety of (gross) subsidies, followed by an evaluation of the impacts of capital subsidies.

A Framework

Improving the quality of national accounts by including human and natural capital at shadow prices (notwithstanding the complexities in computing them) is one way of reconciling the divergence between growth and welfare improvements. But even the limited progress in valuing these assets has not yet been incorporated into national accounts, and there still are serious conceptual problems with incorporating (and weighting) them. For these reasons, a more practical (and more modest) approach is to identify measurable growth patterns and policy instruments likely to promote greater welfare.

Three Patterns of Growth

Consider these alternatives:

- *Pattern 1*. Unsustained growth, where the economy grows with some phases of fast growth, but at a declining rate, eventually leading to stagnation or near stagnation.
- *Pattern 2*. Distorted growth bought at the expense of deteriorating natural resources, for example, from their underpricing; lagging investments in human capital, for example, inadequate safeguards regarding child labor; and subsidies to physical capital, such as tax exemptions, allowing tax arrears, giving financial grants to reward certain investments, and providing investment credit subsidies.
- *Pattern 3*. Sustained growth through undistorted or balanced asset accumulation, with public support to developing primary and secondary education, improving public health, and protecting natural capital. This prevents a decline in returns to private assets (especially physical capital) and provides the minimum and increasing levels of human capital needed to facilitate technological innovation and the growth of total factor productivity (TFP).

Pattern 1 usually is associated with slow and highly unstable or volatile growth. Slow and unstable growth prevents poverty reduction and leads to inadequate resources for investing in human capital and natural capital. That is, pattern 1 causes economic stagnation and welfare losses. Pattern 1 usually occurs in a context of poor governance and corruption that brings about low investment and inefficient allocation of public expenditures.

Compared to pattern 1, the stop-and-go growth of pattern 2 is better for welfare improvement and poverty reduction. But pattern 2 growth might depend on public support to physical capital, which is difficult to sustain. Pattern 3 is better for improving welfare and for reducing poverty. To sustain a reasonable rate of economic growth, therefore, the principal assets of the economy—physical and financial, human and social, natural and environmental—need to grow at undistorted or fairly balanced rates. The distribution of assets among the population, especially of human capital, is also important. Stable, sustained growth is highly beneficial for the poor, who usually suffer the most in the reversals of stop-and-go growth.

Externalities and Asset Accumulation

All forms of capital may involve externalities. Components of human capital and natural capital often have a social value that goes beyond that accruing to the individuals using it. As (partly) public goods, they have positive spillovers that are not necessarily fully accounted for by the actions of individuals or firms. That is why public policy and other mechanisms must prevent underinvesting in them. There has been some emphasis on the positive production and technological externalities associated with physical capital accumulation (Barro and Sala-I-Martin 1995; Romer 1986). But the externalities associated with human and natural capital are much harder to account for, and are probably larger.[3] Human and natural capital are important not only as factors of production, but as direct determinants of societal welfare.

Governments can use market instruments to deal with these external effects. But the issue also involves the allocation of public expenditures. Government spending typically accounts for 25–30 percent of GDP, exerting a powerful direct effect (as opposed to the effect of policies and regulations) on resource allocation and income distribution. Few countries have used market instruments successfully to account for the true social value of natural and human capital. Governments responsible for the Amazon region, for example, have exacerbated the negative environmental externalities. Public subsidies and tax incentives to large cattle producers and loggers were responsible for more than 50 percent of the deforestation in the Amazon region in the 1970s and the 1980s (Binswanger 1991). Moreover, public investments in infrastructure into the frontier areas have magnified the externalities associated with the lack of well-defined property rights in such areas.

Doing little to prevent underinvestment in human and natural assets is likely to lead to unbalanced asset accumulation, at least in the short term, by focusing on physical capital accumulation. Relying mostly on physical capital accumulation instead of balanced asset growth may increase the growth of GDP (using conventional national account methods). But welfare might not improve as fast—and it could even decline, if, for example, natural capital were to decline dramatically, or if the quality of public education and health care fell. The distributional consequences of distorted or unbalanced asset growth could also be severe, especially if the imbalance makes growth unstable, hurting the poor disproportionately.

Fast GDP growth without some degree of balanced asset augmentation may also be difficult to sustain. Unless there are very high technological spillovers or scale economies, rapid physical capital accumulation with slow growth in human capital and a depletion of natural assets would lead to declining marginal productivity of capital—as capital stocks increase relative to other productive assets (see annex 2).

Growth in Total Factor Productivity and Asset Accumulation

So far most of the emphasis in this chapter has been on asset accumulation and asset structure as a source of growth. An important set of analyses argues that the main source of growth is not asset accumulation—it is the growth of TFP (Easterly and Levine 2000; King and Rebelo 1993; Klenow and Rodríguez-Clare 1997a; Romer 1986, 1993). This conclusion, elaborated from theoretical models based on endogenous growth, is supported by earlier empirical studies showing that growth over time, especially in the United States and some other industrial countries, is indeed heavily explained by TFP.

Analyses of East Asian countries, however, suggest that TFP growth may not be as important a source of growth for developing countries as it has been for the United States and some other industrial countries. East Asian countries are practically the only developing countries that have experienced persistent, fast growth over long periods. Collins and Bosworth (1996), Kim and Lau (1994), Krugman (1996), and Young (1991, 1994, 1995) show that East Asia's rapid growth (before 1997) was based on strong asset accumulation. Two recent papers, however, point to factors that qualify these analyses. Klenow and Rodríguez-Clare (1997b) and Nelson and Pack (1998) emphasize improvement in asset measurement and methodological refinements that could significantly alter the conclusions reached by the above authors.

TFP in developing countries is potentially important for growth. It is also closely linked to asset accumulation for two reasons. First, a main vehicle of new technology is embodied in imported capital and new intermediate goods. Second, to benefit from technological progress, the level of education needs to be continually increasing both in depth and breadth. Expanding general education is more crucial in the developing countries than in the industrial countries, where it is already broad-based. But in most developing countries, general education is still insufficient to facilitate technological diffusion. So, TFP growth can be fast only if human capital rapidly broadens and deepens. That is why it is closely linked to asset accumulation and why it may be difficult to disentangle TFP and asset growth as sources of growth.

Investments in Physical Capital

Market reforms—trade and capital market liberalization, privatization, elimination of price controls, liberalization of labor and other markets—have been vital instruments in increasing the rewards to all forms of capital. Given the greater responsiveness of private investments in physical relative to human and natural capital, they have helped some countries (especially those countries not severely affected by corruption) to enjoy an investment boom, accelerating growth. Several of these reforms, for example, trade liberalization or removing anti-agricultural biases, also raise the rewards to human capital. However, in the absence of complementary investments in these assets (especially human capital), the expansion of physical capital could bring about a declining return and eventually a deceleration of growth (see annex 2). For some countries this tendency has been countered by deepening the reform process. Others have used increasing public resources to sustain distortions (thereby generating pattern 2 growth).

Moreover, as developing countries participate more in global markets, national (and subnational) governments can engage in competition to attract capital by artificially creating favorable conditions, as seen in recent evidence on subsidies to attract foreign investments in industrial and developing countries. (For a review of countries such as Argentina, Brazil, Canada, China, India, Malaysia, Singapore, and the United States, as well as Western Europe, see Oman 2000; also the next section.) There is a variety of evidence of incentives and subsidies relating to investments in industries such as the automobile industry from various regions or in the overexploitation through the underpricing of natural resources as in mining or forestry. A mechanism to increase the attractiveness of domestic and foreign investments is to "give away" human and natural resources at low costs, for example, by allowing child labor; not enforcing health and sanitation regulations in the workplace; not regulating banks and other financial institutions; not enforcing environmental regulations; and giving away mining, water, and logging rights.[4]

In some countries these capital subsidies and tax exemptions may offset the firms' costs associated with misgovernance and corruption that reduce their incentives to invest in productive activities (see chapter 6). This suggests that by reducing corruption and misgovernance, it may be possible for countries to save resources. In addition to governance, another ingredient that can play a positive role in enhancing quality growth is the strength of informal institutions in a country, often referred to as social capital (box 2.1).

Box 2.1. Social Capital

The notion of social capital has received a lot of attention from scholars and development professionals of late. The phenomena grouped under the rubric of social capital have included trust, cooperative norms, voting, participation in referenda, and horizontal associational activities in diverse groups.

How does social capital affect economic performance?

- Fewer resources have to be spent to protect against fraud in economic transactions, which would almost be a corollary of high-trust environments.
- There is less need for entrepreneurs to monitor suppliers and workers, freeing more resources for innovative activity.
- Interpersonal trust can substitute for formal property rights.
- The greater confidence in government policy is good for investment.
- A higher degree of trust seems important for human capital accumulation. Galor and Zeira (1993) suggest that higher trust is associated with higher enrollment in secondary education.
- Trust and civic participation are also associated with better performance of government institutions, including those for public education.
- Community or cooperative action by local groups can alleviate "the tragedy of the commons," overexploitation, and undermaintenance (Ostrom 1990).
- Greater links among individuals facilitate better information flows and faster diffusion of innovation (Besley and Case 1994; Foster and Rosenzweig 1995; Rogers 1983).
- Social capital may act as informal insurance, much the same as the diversification of a portfolio. Risk sharing by many households can act as a social safety net and enable them to undertake higher-risk and higher-return activities (Narayan and Pritchett 1999).

But can social capital be measured, and what is its effectiveness in contributing to growth? And are there policy interventions that can contribute to its

formation? Evidence involving both aggregate cross-country and within-county microdata is accumulating to suggest the potential of social capital. Knack and Keefer (1997) use data from the World Values Survey for 29 market economies over 1980–94 to probe the importance of trust and civic involvement. After controlling for initial per capita income, human capital, and capital goods prices, they found that both social capital indexes show significant links to economic growth. They also found that trust is even more important for poorer countries with weak legal systems and financial sectors. A policy implication: establishing formal legal and credit institutions is especially important in low-trust societies.

The concept of social capital has generated discussions and debates. Its proponents claim it to be as important as—or encompassing—physical, human, and natural capital. Others see this focus as excessive and inappropriate. Some of the work in the area is also criticized for leaving out important social dimensions. Temple and Johnson (1998) suggest a general perspective: simply that society matters. They analyze the data on socioeconomic variables compiled by Adelman and Taft-Morris (1967) and show that several social variables have significant explanatory power for predicting long-term economic growth. These variables go beyond the "trust variables" typically studied by researchers in social capital. Among these variables, the ones important in capturing differences in social arrangements include the extent of mass communication (newspapers and radios), the character of basic social organization, the modernization of outlook, the extent of social mobility, and the importance of the indigenous middle class.

Some key readings are Dasgupta and Serageldin (1999), Narayan and Pritchett (1999), and Woolcock (1998). See also two sets of articles that appeared in special sections of *World Development* (Evans 1996) and the *Journal of International Development* (Harriss 1997). Included in the latter is an article critical of the World Bank's use of the notion of social capital (Fox 1997).

Investments in Human and Natural Capital

The other side of the coin of special incentives to physical and financial capital is the insufficient attention paid to human capital and the rapid destruction of various forms of natural capital through overexploitation. Efforts to raise artificially the incentives to investment in physical and financial capital could be linked to insufficient investment in human and natural capital.

The private sector contributes to human capital accumulation—through training, private schools, and private health care. But private schooling and private health care go mostly to the better-off, who can afford to pay for their human capital up-front. Most people, particularly low- and middle-income people, depend on public support to accumulate human capital. Imperfections in capital markets prevent them from borrowing against future earnings, making this dependence even more marked.

Growth in physical capital may spill over into human capital through private investment in research and development and training in higher technologies—that is, in knowledge-driven growth. But to sustain this growth, a large (and growing) part of the work force must have enough general schooling to acquire skills and technology and participate in the expansion of research and development activities. So, publicly provided general schooling and privately generated knowledge are complementary. If the quality and coverage of general schooling do not increase fast enough, knowledge-driven growth may be stifled, particularly in poorer countries where most of the labor force does not have primary school education (chapter 3).

Growth without complementary environmental policies may damage the environment as the accumulation of physical capital accelerates. This is especially likely in countries with comparative advantages in natural resource-intensive industries that also require a lot of physical capital for their exploitation, such as mining, forestry, and fisheries. Preventing excessive environmental and natural resource degradation also depends on public policies and investments. Many environmental resources have social values—as inputs in production and as consumption—that are generally well above those that the private sector considers in its resource allocations. When natural resources are plentiful, degrading natural capital is not likely to have much effect on the productivity of physical capital. But after natural resources fall below certain thresholds, further degradation could reduce the productivity of physical capital (chapter 4).

While degrading natural capital is likely to reduce welfare, its impact on economic growth is subject to debate (see the exchange between Daly,

Solow, and Stiglitz in Daly 1997). That impact hinges on the substitution of other assets for natural capital (see annex 2). Some recent evidence implies that human capital, but not physical capital, can substitute for natural capital. So, economies that expand human capital can reduce the dependence of output growth on natural capital. The high levels of human capital permit the economy to diversify into activities progressively less intensive in natural capital. For example, a country with a high level of human capital can specialize in knowledge-intensive activities, making the exploitation of natural capital less essential for sustaining income growth.

But degrading natural capital is likely to be devastating for the poor, who generally have little human capital and continue to depend on natural capital (soils, natural water sources, fisheries) for their incomes, even in middle-income economies. Because the poor have few possibilities for substituting other assets for natural resources, the degradation of those resources could lead to irreversible vicious circles of poverty and environmental destruction (see López 1997 for an analysis of the dynamic features of natural resource degradation and institutional change for the rural poor).[5]

Distorted Asset Growth and the Poor

The poor, due to their lack of assets, would have more difficulties than the rich in smoothing their consumption in bad times. Close to the limits of subsistence, they usually work in activities hit most by economic cycles (agriculture, construction). So, unstable growth can have harsh effects for them, and an economic crisis can so degrade their human and natural assets that they may not be able to benefit from subsequent booms (see annex 2).

The economy of the poor is often separate in many ways from the modern economy, but the demand for their products depends at least in part on the modern economy (exchange rates, for example, affect the prices of their export products). Instability in the modern economy thus affects the incentives for the poor, and a deterioration of these incentives hurts the poor. Even if incentives return to original levels, the poor may not be able to take advantage of them. This implies two possible alternative equilibria: a sustained growth equilibrium and a stagnant subsistence equilibrium. During bust times, the poor lose the assets needed to maintain consumption at subsistence levels and to respond to stronger incentives in the next boom.

Some developing countries, for example, in Latin America, have a relatively high income inequality especially because of the skewed distribution of physical capital, education, and land. Expanding education could change that. Making education less concentrated through, say, reallocating public spending toward basic and secondary schooling, is probably the least controversial asset redistribution, and likely the most feasible.

Asset inequality affects social welfare through two mechanisms. One is a direct effect: large segments of the population have few assets and consume little, while a minority has large amounts of assets and consumes a lot (see annex 2). The other is indirect: asset inequality has been shown to reduce the potential for economic growth and poverty reduction through a variety of channels (see, for example, Alesina and Rodrik 1994; Deininger and Squire 1998; Persson and Tabellini 1994; Ravallion and Sen 1994 on asset inequality and growth and chapter 3 and annex table A3.5 for a literature review).

Even small changes in income distribution can have large effects on the extent and depth of poverty in developing countries (Lundberg and Squire 1999). Several studies have tried to establish a relationship between income distribution and growth. However, as Lundberg and Squire argue, growth and inequality should be analyzed as joint endogenous variables. How asset inequality affects both growth and income distribution is closely related to the way that the level and composition of public spending on education and health affect the inequality of human capital.

Skewed distributions of education are unlikely to produce the best growth outcomes.[6] If human capital is relatively concentrated, any further concentration would slow growth, while efforts to improve its distribution would benefit growth (chapter 3). An economy with a small number of highly educated people and a large number that is illiterate may find it difficult to sustain high rates of return to physical capital, because the potential technological spillovers associated with capital accumulation may not materialize. Greater access to secondary and higher education would allow for more technological spillovers.

Empirical Evidence

In this section we provide four types of evidence as follows:

- *Experience in 60 developing countries.* Growth experience has often followed patterns 1 and 2, relying mostly on a rise in investment in physical capital, while investment in human capital has lagged and investment in natural capital has been mostly negative (see box 2.2).
- *Econometric evidence.* Growth based mostly on physical capital expansion is unlikely to be sustainable. The possible positive spillovers of physical capital investment do not seem to be sufficient to maintain a stable rate of growth in the absence of significant expansion in human capital and a sustainable use of natural capital.

Box 2.2. Alternative Approaches to Sustain Growth: Brazil, Chile, and the Republic of Korea

Two approaches to pursue sustained growth might be noted:

- *Approach 1.* Increasingly large policy and expenditure distortions (incentives and subsidies) in favor of capital (pattern 2 growth).
- *Approach 2.* High levels of support to the growth of other assets as well, particularly human capital (pattern 3 growth).

Approach 1 implies that maintaining a high growth rate requires that the pro-capital bias has to be increasing over time. Apart from being less effective than approach 2 in sustaining long-run growth, this approach means unstable growth in the short run and increasing concentrations of income and wealth. The second approach is more likely to sustain a reasonable growth rate in the long run, reducing short-run instability and promoting equity.

Favoring Physical Capital

Most countries use a combination of these two approaches with different emphases. Brazil, like several others, at times seems to have used approach 1. Reviews of several countries show examples of public allocations to support the profitability of capital through direct financial subsidies to domestic and foreign investors; efforts to build infrastructure and services with public monies oriented to expand particular industries and develop environmentally sensitive areas; as well as credit, tax, and price policies in favor of capital. In many countries, the allocation of public resources to education has emphasized subsidies to tertiary education and underinvested in primary and secondary schools.

Over the past two decades, the standard deviation of annual growth rates has been more than the average growth rate (table 2.1). Such instability could be due in part to the varying capacity of the public sector to generate resources needed to continue to support physical capital in relative

terms. Also, the relatively small support to the social sectors would seem to have contributed to social inequity.

Attention to Human Capital

Korea also seems to have subsidized investors starting before the 1990s. Its subsidies were selective, focusing mostly on a few industries at a time—aiming at developing a few industries into exporters within a reasonable time. Some favored industries have become leaders in causing growth spillovers to others. While this approach was problematic in many ways, it implied relatively less of an explicit financial burden on the public sector. In addition, the allocation of public resources to education has prioritized basic education. This has allowed the public sector to support a fast buildup of human capital, along with a rapid decline of the education Gini coefficient (chapter 3). This has also balanced the incentives for the growth of physical and human assets, has permitted income inequality to remain at acceptable levels, and has helped poverty to decline.

There was sustained economic growth during the 1980s and the 1990s through 1997. Growth was relatively stable—possibly in part because the public sector maintained its support to both human and physical capital over the years.

Relative Neutrality

Since the early 1980s, Chile's public sector has generally abstained from directly favoring physical capital. Nor have the social sectors, particularly education and health, received special support, except for the period 1997–2000. The public sector has not taken on any significant role in especially orienting growth strategy in these areas. However, Chile has low taxation on using its natural resources, providing strong incentives for foreign investors to exploit mining, forestry, and fisheries.

(box continues on following page)

Box 2.2 continued

There was a boom in 1987–95, which benefit-
ted from a large acceleration of investment in
physical capital, with human capital lagging be-

hind. The lack of dependence of capital on direct
public subsidies may have led to stable growth
rates in an eight-year expansion.

Table 2.1. Selected Variables for Brazil, Chile, and Korea

Variable	Brazil	Chile	Korea
GDP growth (percent per year)			
Average level	2.8	5.9	7.6
Coefficient of variation[a]	1.4	0.9	0.4
Public expenditures on education and health (percentage of GDP)			
Average level	2.9	5.6	3.4
Trend over time	0.1	–0.1	0.0
Gross domestic investment (percentage of GDP)			
Average level	20.5	19.7	32.6
Trend over time	–0.1	0.6	0.4
Memo items (latest available year)			
Poverty (percentage below US$1 a day)	23.6	15.0	—
Gini coefficient of income	0.60	0.59	0.32
Gini coefficient of education	0.39	0.31	0.22
Illiteracy (percent)	16.7	4.8	2.0
Infant mortality (per 1,000)	34.0	11.0	9.0

— Not available.
Note: The values are for 1978–97, except for expenditures on education and health, which are for 1980–97 (1980–
94 for Brazil), and specific years for some variables.
a. Standard deviation of the growth rate divided by the growth rate.
Source: Various issues of the World Bank's World Development Indicators and the International Monetary Fund's Government
Finance Statistics Yearbook.

- *Evidence on subsidies.* Industrial and developing countries have spent
  public resources on subsidies. In the case of capital, they involve a
  variety of mechanisms including tax concessions, credit subsidies,
  and grants. These subsidies absorb a sizable share of government
  revenues, which in developing countries seem comparable to what
  is spent on education, health, and social sectors.
- *Impact of subsidies.* A finding in the literature is that capital subsidies have not contributed to increased productivity and have only
  modest effects on growth. Moreover, their effects on growth seem
  short-lived.

Reforms and Unbalanced Growth in 60 Countries

A review of 60 countries in the late 1980s and 1990s shows that about 16 of the countries were considered serious reformers in implementing a set of policy changes (table 2.2). The other 44 countries did not implement such a set of reforms over the period. Reformers already had higher rates of physical capital accumulation in the 1980s than the nonreformers.[7] Although a controlled experiment would better reveal counterfactuals, the contrast is suggestive. In the 1990s, the rates of physical capital accumulation increased by about 70 percent for reformers but declined for nonreformers. But the growth of human capital apparently has not increased much—for either reformers or nonreformers. Spending on education as a share of GDP was lower for reformers than for nonreformers, increasing modestly for both groups in the 1990s.[8]

Although deforestation rates, a rough proxy for natural resource degradation, were lower for reformers than for nonreformers in both periods, the deforestation by reformers almost doubled in the 1990s while that by nonreformers increased only slightly.

Thus, reformers have significantly accelerated economic growth over the 1990s. This growth seems to be based on an increase in physical capital accumulation while, relatively speaking, investments in human and natural capital lagged.

Table 2.2.   Review of Development Indicators for 60 Reformers and Nonreformers, Selected Years

Development indicator	Years	16 reformers	44 nonreformers
Per capita GDP growth rate (percent)	1984–89	2.8	−0.5
	1990s	3.5	0.1
Physical capital stock (per worker) growth rate (percent)	1984–89	2.1	0.0
	1990s	3.5	−0.5
Deforestation rate (percent)	1984–89	0.7	1.2
	1990s	1.1	1.4
Education spending as a percentage of GDP	1984–89	3.2	4.6
	1990s	3.5	4.7

Note: Reformers in this table are defined based on the speed of integration index (World Bank 1996a). Countries that implemented significant economic reforms (reformers) in the late 1980s or early 1990s by this measure are Argentina, Bolivia, Chile, China, Ghana, Indonesia, Korea, Malaysia, Mauritius, Mexico, Morocco, Nepal, Peru, Philippines, Sri Lanka, and Thailand.

Source: Author's calculations.

Are the increases in educational spending by reformers enough to sustain the new growth rates? Will the acceleration in degrading natural capital seriously hurt the sustainability of growth for reformers and nonreformers alike? To answer these questions we need to know how spending improves human capital, how deepening physical and human capital affects growth, and how losing natural capital can affect growth.

Econometric Evidence: 20 Middle-Income Countries

Country econometric analysis of growth in 20 mostly middle-income countries over 1970–92 shows the following (see annex table A2.1 and López, Thomas, and Wang 1998):[9]

- The marginal productivity of capital, given other asset levels, declines with increases in physical capital. Economies of scale and technological spillovers from investment in physical capital apparently may not be enough to offset the declining marginal productivity of physical capital. This suggests that growth based primarily on physical capital accumulation may not be sustained in the long run.
- Human capital, represented here by formal education, would seem to have a powerful positive effect on economic growth in reform episodes, but not in the absence of reforms. This implies that education would not contribute much to the productivity of physical capital in overregulated economies with little space for markets. But it could do much to boost the marginal productivity of physical capital and economic growth in a market-friendly framework. This confirms our hypothesis presented earlier that human capital accumulation at sufficient speed can induce sustained growth. At the same time, this evidence suggests that key market reforms are a necessary condition to achieve long-run sustained growth.
- In nonreforming economies and episodes, economic growth rates are not sustained, regardless of the additions to human capital, according to these results. Instead, they face stagnation after periods of moderate growth, triggered by favorable exogenous shocks that temporarily spur the returns to physical capital.
- The good economic growth rates in reform episodes can be sustained if human capital grows fast enough to offset the declining marginal returns to capital caused by physical capital accumulation. Per capita growth of about 4 percent a year, according to these estimates, can be sustained if per capita human capital expands at about 1.7–1.8 percent a year.

So the pace of growth based mostly on physical capital accumulation—to the neglect of human capital—would not seem to be sustained. Market reforms can accelerate growth. But if the reforms are not accompanied by investments in human capital, growth is likely to flag. Countries that implement market reforms have a chance of sustained growth. Nonreformers do not.

Econometric Evidence: 70 Developing Countries

The previous study did not consider natural capital as a determinant of growth, but few of the 20 countries analyzed earlier show a heavy dependence on natural capital as a source of income. A related study of 70 developing countries that includes both middle-income and poor countries, including several Sub-Saharan nations, considers natural, physical, and human capital as factors affecting growth (López, Thomas, and Thomas 1998; see also note 8).[10]

Unlike most previous studies, this one uses a flexible functional form (translog for the growth equations) that allows for nonlinear effects of the explanatory variables and for interactive effects across these variables. The interactive effects are extremely important in elucidating interasset substitution or complementarity in the growth process (see annex tables A2.2 and A2.3).

- According to these estimates, the rate of economic growth on average declines with increases in the stocks of physical capital—for constant human and natural capital—but not for all countries. Countries that have very low physical-capital-to-labor ratios tend to have their growth rates increase. So, in capital-poor countries, capital accumulation at first tends to speed growth even faster. But after reaching a certain capital intensity, further physical capital accumulation—for given human and natural capital—has a declining effect on economic growth.
- Human capital on average would seem to boost the rate of economic growth, though this link is smaller than in the previous study. As human capital increases, the positive link to economic growth becomes larger. At low levels of human capital, its link to economic growth is negligible, but at higher levels of human capital it becomes larger, with the marginal effect of the stock of human capital on growth always increasing.
- To sustain economic growth, human capital can to some extent substitute for natural capital, but physical capital may not. The growth rate of countries with high levels of human capital is much

less sensitive to losses of natural capital. But that of human-capital-poor countries is highly sensitive to those losses. For them, natural capital is crucial for sustaining rapid economic growth. They therefore need to invest in human capital to reduce their dependency on natural capital.

These results suggest that growth especially based on physical capital accumulation tends to be difficult to sustain. Economies of scale and technological spillover arising from physical capital accumulation exist, but may not be sufficient to sustain growth. Physical capital accumulation needs to be accompanied by an expansion of human capital to permit sustained growth.[11] Disinvestment in natural capital hurts the sustainability of growth, especially in human-capital-poor countries. This result, that physical capital accumulation alone may not sustain growth, is consistent with recent empirical studies (Barro and Sala-I-Martin 1996; Jones 1995; Mankiw, Romer, and Weil 1992; Young 1994, 1995).

Evidence on Subsidies

The evidence accumulated over the last decade indicates that government subsidies to industries, agriculture, and infrastructure worldwide are large. Table A2.4 in annex 2 presents some examples that illustrate both the size and impact of such subsidies. The data are fragmented and partial, making it difficult to put in perspective the real magnitude of these subsidies relative to GDP and relative to government expenditures. In addition, the available data only include direct subsidies involving financial outlays (or foregone tax revenues) for the public sector. The evidence on indirect subsidies, such as the giveaway of public lands and natural resources, is mostly anecdotal. The available evidence, however, permits us to derive lower-bound estimates of the financial subsidies, at least for some countries.

It is important to note that these remain *gross* estimates. They do not consider the net magnitude after accounting for taxes or other offsetting distortions. These estimates also do not differentiate between cases where such subsidies might be justified on social grounds and where they might not be. Together with taxes, they influence the implicit tax rates, introducing elements of nontransparency, discrimination across different activities, and pressures on scarce resources—rendering them distortionary.

During the early 1990s, industrial (OECD) countries spent an estimated US$490–$615 billion a year in subsidizing agriculture (US$335 billion), energy (US$70–$80 billion), and road transport (US$85–$200 billion) (de Moor and Calamai 1997). The total is about 2.5–3.0 percent of the total

GDP of OECD countries and about 7.6–9.1 percent of the total government expenditures. Developing countries spent US$220–$270 billion per year in subsidizing energy, road transportation, agriculture, and water during the early 1990s. These amount to some 4.3–5.2 percent of GDP and 19–24 percent of total government expenditures. These subsidy estimates point to possible distortions, and do not necessarily suggest overinvestment in these sectors in the aggregate.

On the one side, these are probably only a part of all subsidies, as subsidies to manufacturing are not included here. On the other, some of these subsidies (especially for energy) concern consumer demand and not corporate production, which is our primary focus. However, a significant part of the energy subsidies seem to be captured by corporate entities, and the above estimates might still be close to representing corporate subsidies.

From a different estimation, corporate subsidies in the United States in 1996 were US$170–$200 billion (Collins 1996), or 2.3–2.7 percent of GDP and 10–12 percent of total government expenditures. Government subsidies to Fortune 500 corporations, which in 1997 recorded profits of US$325 billion, were about US$75 billion—comprising government grants, cut-rate insurance, subsidized loans, and loan guarantees (Moore 1999).

Apart from the energy and agriculture subsidies, countries provide subsidies directly to manufacturing industries. The evidence suggests that these industrial subsidies may be larger than the energy and agriculture subsidies. Subsidies to foreign investors seem to be significant in a number of country cases. Preferential tax treatment for foreign firms sometimes costs the government in foregone tax revenues. Competition for foreign investments is, in some cases, a reason for these subsidies, which have gone to investors in mining and various industries ranging from automobile to steel (*Aviation Week and Space Technology* 1999; Castaneda 1997; *La Nacion* 1997, June 10; Sieh Lee 1998; Oman 2000; also table A2.4 in annex 2). They are essentially discriminatory in nature and raise the question of the effectiveness of favoring some over others.

These admittedly partial data suggest the significance of the corporate subsidies as a proportion of government expenditures—with implications for capital subsidies, although we have not been able to disentangle fully capital and corporate subsidies. In the previous sections we have emphasized a less distorted or a more neutral asset growth pattern that includes the expansion of human and natural assets along with physical. These subsidies compete for scarce public resources with alternative uses. The question is whether or not they could be better spent from a social viewpoint on the sector in question or in other areas such as building human capital and in preventing a rapid deterioration of the natural capital. It is also possible that the corporate subsidies contribute to a sustained expansion of investment in physical capital, increasing economic efficiency and productivity and generating positive social spillovers. If this is true, the case against subsidies would diminish.

The Impact of Subsidies

Recent studies based on industry or microfirm data have examined how corporate subsidies affect long-term economic growth and productivity. By and large they suggest that government subsidies to industries have a modest impact on firms' investment and growth in the first year, but over the medium run have little effect on growth. Capital subsidies also seem to induce a negative effect on total factor productivity of the industries that receive subsidies. Beason and Weinstein (1996) for Japan; Bergström (1998) for Sweden; Bregman, Fuss, and Regev (1999) for Israel; Fakin (1995) for Poland; Fournier and Rasmussen (1986) for the United States; Harris (1991) for Ireland; and Lee (1996) for Korea conclude that corporate subsidies are inappropriate if increasing national income and productivity is the goal (see also table A2.4 in annex 2).

The papers by Bregman, Fuss, and Regev (1999) and Bergström (1998) are particularly important because they use detailed firm-level panel data. Bregman, Fuss, and Regev (1999) found that capital subsidization induced efficiency losses ranging from 5 to 15 percent. They also show that the subsidies were basically incorporated into profits or rents, as the subsidized firms earned higher rates of return than those that were not subsidized. Similarly, Bergström (1998) found little evidence that subsidies affect productivity. Their effects on the growth rate of firms seemed temporary. This finding is consistent with the point in this chapter that capital subsidies could only offer a temporary relief to decreasing rates of economic growth associated with distorted asset growth.

Conclusions

This chapter presented a framework for the augmentation of three main assets: human, physical, and natural capital. Its main hypothesis: sustained growth and welfare improvement require the efficient expansion and use of all three assets. However, countries can be tempted to subsidize physical capital. The evidence is that such subsidies (tax exemptions, direct subsidies, easy access to natural resources, and so on) comprise large shares of government expenditures and of GDP. Such an approach is unlikely to produce sustained growth. It also neglects human and natural assets, which directly contribute to welfare. So, such growth may provide only a small contribution to welfare.

Investing a greater part of national savings in the expansion of human and social assets—and the sustainable use of natural assets—could contribute to more growth and better growth in the long run. This sustained growth, attending to all three assets, is more likely to increase welfare. This could be because investments in human and natural capital contribute to welfare directly and because investment in such assets helps to improve the distribution of income and reduces the instability of growth. That is why a relatively undistorted or balanced approach to the accumulation of all assets is likely to be superior to a primary focus on physical and financial capital.

Notes

1. Financial capital here does not refer to the development of financial institutions and the deepening of financial markets in a economy, which are desirable in supporting development (see chapter 5).

2. As discussed later, balanced asset growth does not imply that all assets should grow at the same rate. The focus of balanced growth, as the term is used in this chapter, is on the composition of assets, rather than on the sectoral composition of output, which is the common convention (Hirschman 1958; Nurkse 1953).

3. The lack of balance in asset growth arises as a consequence of externalities and market failures. Physical capital is perhaps less subject to externalities than human and natural capital. Imperfections in credit markets prevent the poor from investing in their education at desired levels even if they can obtain a high rate of return. Externalities affecting natural capital, including the environment, are extremely pervasive. Also, investments in human and natural capital require a long time to mature relative to most investments in physical capital. Capital market imperfections are likely to affect the financing of the former more negatively than the financing of the latter. Thus, the private market economy tends to concentrate more on the accumulation of physical capital than of the other two assets. Other reasons that could lead to unbalanced asset growth emphasized in the literature are coordination failures. These are caused by agent interactions that are not fully mediated by market prices (see, for example, Stiglitz 1975 for an early model of multiple equilibria arising from imperfect information concerning ability and education and Murphy, Shleifer, and Vishny 1989 and Rodriguez 1993 for intersectoral coordination failures).

4. Other examples of subsidies to capital are abundant. Argentina and Mexico provided monopoly rights to privatized telephone companies for prolonged periods. Brazil gave subsidies and tax concessions to invest in automobiles (*Financial Times*, July 21, 1999). Chile has subsidized tree planting by a few large

corporations to support the expansion of the private pulp and paper industry. Since the early 1980s, China has provided tax exemptions and tax reductions to foreign investors. In Central and Eastern Europe, direct government subsidies take the form of tax arrears that amount to 5–10 percent of GDP and increase by about 2 percent of GDP every year (Schaffer 1995). In Brazil, rubber producers received large subsidies from the government. Eight companies received R$5 billion (US$2 billion) (*Gazeta Mercantil*, May 21, 1999). In Korea, two major steel producers received US$6 billion in 1993–99 in government subsidies, according to the U.S. complaints filed with the World Trade Organization (*New Steel* 1998). Herrera (1992) discussed in detail the regressive impact of the lack of regulation in the privatized telephone system in Argentina. See table A2.4 in annex 2.

5. Because multiple equilibria and irreversible processes are likely outcomes, there is scope for public policy interventions aimed at avoiding vicious cycles of poverty and environmental degradation.

6. The distribution of education is measured by Gini coefficients and standard deviations of education (see chapter 3 for details of these measures and López, Thomas, and Wang 1998 for a statistical analysis).

7. The average growth rate in domestic investment among the most aggressive reformers was much higher during the 1990s, after the reforms had been implemented, than in the 1970s and 1980s. In Argentina, Bolivia, Chile, and Peru, four of the most aggressive reformers in Latin America, the growth of gross investment during 1990–97 was more than 9 percent a year, almost three times the historical rates (IDB 1998).

8. In table 2.2 we use expenditures on education as a percentage of GDP instead of per capita expenditures because the underlying stock of education is likely to be positively related to GDP. Thus, a change in the share of education expenditures in GDP is likely to be more closely related to the rate of growth in human capital than the level of expenditure per capita.

9. This study was based on an explicit growth theoretic behavioral model. This is important because the estimating empirical equations derived from such a model suggest a specification that is relatively free from the simultaneous equation bias that has affected some previous studies. In particular, the empirical model consists of explaining annual growth rates by lagged stocks of assets rather than by rates of change of assets as is usually done. This considerably reduces contemporaneous correlation with the error term that usually leads to serious difficulties in deriving causality from the results. Moreover, the fact that we use country fixed effects could decrease the possibility of bias due to omitted country-specific variables, another important source of difficulty in interpreting causal relationships. Controlling for omitted variable biases and simultaneous equation biases suggests that we are in large measure addressing causality problems. Finally, the study used a detailed analysis of the policy reforms of the various countries over the two decades considered, so that the coefficients estimated were allowed to vary systematically across policy regimes. This allowed

the study to show that the weak impacts of education on growth reported by other studies was right only under certain closed economy and distorted policy regimes, but not for market-friendly environments. For more details about the estimating procedure see annex 2.

10. This study used forest area as a proxy for natural capital. Loss of forest cover is usually associated with watershed deterioration, loss of commercial logging species, water depletion, and soil erosion, all crucial for production, and is likely to be a good proxy for the degradation of natural capital.

11. This finding is not necessarily inconsistent with the literature on growth convergence, which generally finds slow convergence across countries. In fact, we find that a stable growth rate can be maintained indefinitely if physical *and* human capital grow at balanced (not equal) rates. The problem is only that the rate of economic growth declines as the stock of physical capital increases for a *given* level of human capital, or if human capital expands at a speed below a minimum required rate.

CHAPTER 3

IMPROVING THE DISTRIBUTION OF OPPORTUNITIES

Wealth to us is not mere material, but an opportunity for achievement.
—Thucydides, 460–400 B.C.

The main asset of most poor people is their human capital. Investing in the human capital of the poor is a powerful way to augment their assets, redress asset inequality, and reduce poverty. This chapter examines the quality of education, associating the distribution of education with growth and poverty reduction. It then asks how to make education at all levels more productive. To be sure, access to good quality education is important in that it enhances people's capabilities to generate income. This is not enough, however. To be more productive, they need to be able to combine their human capital with other productive assets, such as land and equity capital, and with job opportunities in an open market.

Chapter 2 discussed the importance of undistorted or balanced asset augmentation. This chapter focuses on assets that the poor possess, primarily human capital, and those on which they rely most heavily, such as land. For growth to have an impact on poverty, the assets of the poor, especially their human capital, need to be augmented and distributed more equitably.[1] Yet inequality in education and health outcomes is staggeringly high, reflecting market failures and underinvestment in the human capital of the poor. Asset distribution represents the distribution of opportunities and is a precondition for individual productivity and income. While redistributing existing assets and incomes is politically difficult, building new assets such as human capital is widely accepted.

To be sustained, development must be equitable and inclusive. Ensuring adequate public spending in education and health care is important, but does not by itself guarantee progress. A multidimensional strategy to empower people is needed. Actions to highlight include the following:

- Augment assets of the poor by ensuring access to high-quality education and health services
- Increase attention to the distributive effect of public investment and reduce subsidies to the types of education and health care that benefit the rich
- Facilitate full use of human capital by empowering the poor with land, credit, training, and job opportunities
- Complement all human capital investments with economic reforms and market openness, which increase the productivity of education.

Potential Benefits of Education

Education and good health improve people's ability to shape their lives—strengthening their functioning in society and contributing to their welfare directly. Educating women, for example, not only increases their income-earning capacity, but also improves their reproductive health, lowers infant and child mortality, and benefits both current and future generations. Investing in human capital is therefore crucial for economic growth, poverty reduction, and environmental protection. The benefits of investing in human capital are well known, but some of the linkages with other dimensions of development—security, social justice, and sustainability—are better understood today than they were 10 years ago.[2]

Investing in people can protect workers and improve security—an important aspect of quality of life. Education and good health increase the poor's ability to cope with changes in their environment. They allow them to switch jobs and provide some protection against economic downturns and financial crises (chapter 5).

Social exclusion reduces an individual's incentive to attend school and to work (Bourguignon 1999; Loury 1999). Investment in human capital, if well distributed and targeted to the poor, can facilitate social inclusion. Better education and health services to vulnerable, often excluded groups, such as those who are illiterate, disabled, elderly, chronically ill, or separated by language barriers, can help them overcome social obstacles and increase their productivity.

Investing in people may also help protect the environment. Better-educated women have healthier and, in many cases, fewer children, thereby reducing demographic pressure on natural resources and the environment.

With more education, people can assimilate more information and employ instruments to protect the environment and better manage resources (chapter 4).

Investing in people improves human rights and social justice, which provides direct satisfaction. Basic education enables the poor to learn about their civil and political rights; to exercise those rights by voting and running for office; and to voice their concerns, seek legal redress, and exercise public oversight. That helps in building institutions, improving governance, and fighting corruption (chapter 6).

These benefits are far from automatic. Many studies show that additional years of education per person increase real output or growth rates. However, a few researchers suggest that human capital accumulation has an insignificant or negative impact on economic and productivity growth (Benhabib and Spiegel 1994; Griliches 1997; Islam 1995; Pritchett 1996). More government spending on education, if misallocated, might contribute little to poverty reduction and instead increase inequality and rent seeking. As Murphy, Shleifer, and Vishny (1991, p. 503) point out: "A country's most talented people typically organize production by others... When they start new firms, they innovate and foster growth, but when they become rent seekers, they only redistribute wealth and reduce growth."

Quantity Is Not Enough—Quality Matters

Since 1980, developing countries have invested substantial amounts of public resources in education services (see figure 1.11). In the 1990s, more than three-quarters of school-age children in developing countries were enrolled in schools, up from less than half in the 1960s. Illiteracy rates dropped from 39 to 30 percent between 1985 and 1995 (World Bank 1999a).

Progress has been uneven across regions. Enrollment rates fell in Sub-Saharan Africa: the proportion of 6–11 year olds enrolled in schools dropped from 59 percent in 1980 to 51 percent in 1992 (World Bank 1999a). Lack of access to basic education remains a major challenge in many countries. Increasing public spending is desirable, but not sufficient for the following reasons.

Public Spending Is Only Weakly Related to Outcomes

Cross-country analyses reveal a weak relationship between the generosity of education spending and education outcomes. Using cross-country data, Filmer and Pritchett (1999b) examined the correlation between government education spending per student and the percentage of people aged 15 through 19 who had completed grade five. The correlation appeared positive and significant at first, but after controlling for per capita income, the correlation was found to be fairly weak (figure 3.1). A similarly weak correlation

Public spending on education is only weakly related to education outcomes

Figure 3.1. Relationship between Public Spending Per Capita and Educational Attainment, Various Years

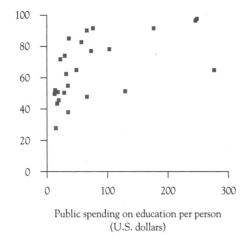

Percentage of 15–19-year-olds who have completed grade 5

Public spending on education per person
(U.S. dollars)

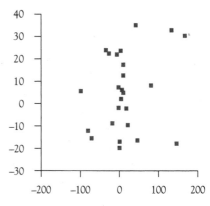

Percentage of 15–19-year-olds who have completed grade 5
(controlling for GNP per capita)

Public spending on education per person,
controlling for GNP per capita
(U.S. dollars)

Note: Expenditures refer to public spending on preprimary, primary, and secondary education only. Thirty-five developing countries were included in the study.

Sources: Education outcome data are updated from Filmer and Pritchett (1999b) combined with expenditure data from the United Nations Educational, Social, and Cultural Organization (UNESCO) database.

was found between government health spending and mortality rates for children under five years old (Filmer and Pritchett 1999c).

Why is public spending only weakly related to outcomes? What makes the difference is the quality and distribution of education services and the productivity of human capital. For developing countries that already allocate a substantial share of public resources to social services, further spending may not improve education outcomes for the poor. Reallocating public spending and improving its efficacy often can improve outcomes, especially when public resources are subsidizing education for the wealthy. Economywide strategies and policies also matter: subsidies to attract foreign capital may, under certain circumstances, bias the rate of return against human capital.[3] Labor market distortions create disincentives for investing in education. In addition, to be productive, people must have access to other productive assets, including land, credit, equity, and job opportunities in open and competitive markets.

Variability in School Quality

Despite progress on access to education, the quality of schooling varies considerably across countries and regions. An extensive literature explored how best to define and measure the quality of schooling: whether inputs, processes, or student achievements should be used in assessments (see, for example, Behrman and Birdsall 1983; Card and Krueger 1992; Greaney and Kellaghan 1996; Lockheed and Verspoor 1991). We measured quality as a combination of indicators that reflect inputs, defined by expenditure per student and the number and quality of teachers; processes, that is, the length of school terms and the curriculum content; and outputs, measured by cognitive achievements, attitudes, test scores, and dropout rates.

In high-income countries where these indicators are well developed, student achievement varies widely, even in countries with universal basic education. Functional literacy rates for young adults, 16–25 years old, in some industrial countries vary from 45 percent in the United States to 80 percent in Sweden, while the secondary net enrollment rates in these countries are all above 85 percent (World Bank 1999a).

In developing countries, where achievement indicators are scarce, less accurate indicators, such as repetition and dropout rates, have been used to assess education outcomes. Data generated by these imperfect measurements showed considerable variation in the quality of schools (table 3.1). Repetition and dropout rates for primary school are much lower and test scores higher in East Asia than in Latin American countries, where incomes are higher. While public education spending rose in some Latin American countries in the 1990s, average primary dropout rates also increased.[4] Other studies, based on the limited available data on internationally comparable test scores, also show that generous public spending did not guarantee high-quality education.

What explains the large variations in quality? Education outcomes depend on both demand and supply factors, and thus on policies and incentive structures that affect the whole economy. Macroeconomic stability, represented by international terms of trade and GDP volatility, for example, is found to be the most significant determinant of educational attainment in Latin America. Using data from 18 household surveys, Behrman, Duryea, and Szekely (1999) found that the debt crisis of the 1980s contributed to the slowdown in the accumulation of schooling in Latin American countries. Kaufmann and Wang (1995) found that macroeconomic policies affect social sector investment projects. As a country opens to international trade and investment, the rate of return to education rises. People demand higher quality education and are willing to pay more for it. Stronger demand, higher private

Repetition and dropout rates vary enormously across countries

Table 3.1. Primary School Repetition and Dropout Rates, Selected Years
(percent)

Country	Primary school repetition rate		Primary school dropout rates			Public spending on education (percentage of GNP)		
	1980s	1990s	1970	1980	1990	1970s	1980s	1990s
Argentina	—	6	36	34	34	1.65	1.79	3.07
Brazil	20	18	78	78	80	2.95	4.04	3.60
Chile	—	6	23	24	23	4.60	4.52	2.84
Colombia	17	9	43	43	44	2.05	2.75	3.43
Mexico	10	8	11	12	28	2.90	4.06	4.45
Peru	17	15	34	30	30	3.30	3.09	3.40
Venezuela, RB	10	11	41	32	52	4.30	5.09	4.56
Average Latin America	15	10	38	36	42	3.11	3.62	3.62
China	—	3	15	15	15	1.45	2.45	2.20
Indonesia	10	9	20	20	23	2.65	1.38	1.34
Korea, Republic of	—	—	5	6	1	2.80	3.89	3.92
Malaysia	—	—	1	1	4	5.10	6.61	5.37
Philippines	2	—	25	25	30	2.40	2.02	2.54
Thailand	8	—	57	23	13	3.35	3.58	3.88
Average East Asia	7	6	21	15	14	2.96	3.32	3.21

— Not available.

Sources: World Bank data; UNESCO for expenditure data.

investments, better-paid teachers, and more motivated students produce higher educational achievements, with differing time lags. The higher the demand for education, the higher its quality, and vice versa. If a country devotes public resources to subsidize physical capital instead of basic education, it can bias the rates of return against unskilled labor and hurt the poor (see table A2.4 on capital subsidies).

At the micro level, many studies have examined the links between schooling quality and student performance. Behrman and Knowles (1999) found a strong positive association between the quality of teaching staff, the quality of current inputs, and children's success at school. Hanushek and Kim (1995) found that conventional measures of school resources, that is, pupil-teacher ratios and educational spending, did not affect student test performance. In cross-country regressions, test scores were positively related to growth rates of real per capita GDP, indicating a potential feedback from growth to strong demand and good student performance. Lee and Barro

(1997) found that family background, strong communities, school inputs, and length of school terms are positively related to student performance; however, they cannot fully explain why East Asian countries experienced better education outcomes than did other developing countries. That suggests that other factors may be at play, including those associated with a more open and export-oriented economic environment.

Consequences of Poor Quality

Low-quality schooling disproportionately hurts the poor and limits their future earning opportunities. For example, Vietnamese students from high-income households enjoy greater access to high-quality education (Behrman and Knowles 1999). In Latin America, most students from low-income families attend public schools, which offer half the hours of instruction and cover only half the curriculum compared with the private schools. The higher the family's income, the greater the aversion to public schools (IDB 1998).

Estimates based on household surveys from Latin America show that students from lower-income deciles received an inferior primary education. Quality, measured by students' labor market performance, was 35 percent lower for low-income students than for those at the next-higher income decile (IDB 1998, p. 54). Figure 3.2 shows the enormous gaps in secondary school completion rates for the rich and poor. Because private education is feasible only for the wealthy, the poor quality of public schooling severely reduces the income-generating potential of children from poor families.

Quality and Quantity: A Tradeoff?

Improvements in quality complement the expansion of access to education. If poor children can go only to low-quality schools, they have few opportunities to obtain high-paying jobs and parents are disinclined to send them to school. When education coverage is not universal, the best strategy is to focus on policy interventions that raise demand for both the quantity and the quality of education. For example, programs to reduce child labor and keep children in school—such as school lunches and cash stipends—would go well with teacher training to improve quality.

However, with growing populations and tight budgets, the synergies of quantity and quality can turn into tradeoffs, especially if the quality measures selected are not closely linked with student learning. What quality measure should be used for intervention? Should it be student incentives, or length of school terms, or the quality of teaching staff? Evidence shows that reduction of pupil-teacher ratios, which is expensive, has little impact on

Figure 3.2. Secondary School Completion Rates for 20–25-Year-Olds by Household Income Level, Selected Latin American Countries and Years

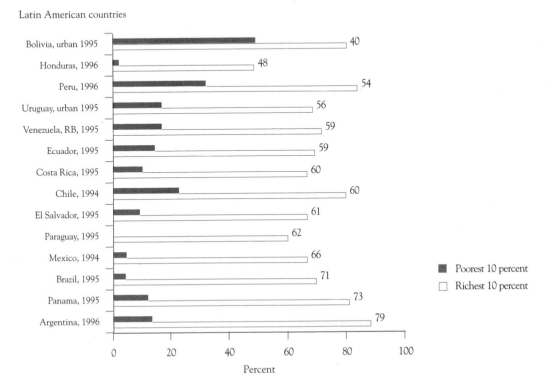

Latin American countries

Note: Numbers next to bars are gaps in completion rates (percent). The surveys for Argentina include only Greater Buenos Aires. *Source:* IDB (1998, p. 27).

student learning (Mingat and Tan 1998).[5] Despite the relatively high pupil-teacher ratio in the 1980s and 1990s, Korean students' average scores on international science and mathematics tests were among the highest. Spending more to hire more teachers might imply a tradeoff against wider coverage and broader distribution of education, which would be inefficient and inequitable, particularly where many children still have no access to basic education (Mingat and Tan 1998).

Achieving Equitable Education and Social Inclusion

Equal access to education and health services is among the basic human rights to which everyone is entitled. As with land and physical capital, an equitable distribution of human capital is important for broad-based growth and poverty reduction. Moreover, equitable distribution of opportunities is preferable to the redistribution of existing assets, because investing in people creates new assets and improves social welfare.[6] Ensuring access by the poor by distributing education services more equally is a win-win policy that is gaining support in both industrial and developing countries.

Why the focus on the distribution of education? This is because ensuring access to basic education by the poor is closely related to a better distribution of education. Given limited public resources for education, concentrating public investment on education for the poor usually implies a reallocation of public spending away from subsidies to the types of education services that benefit the rich. Such policies are politically unpopular, and many countries have been unable to implement them. However, as shown in this section, there are compelling reasons why a government should pursue such policies.

Measuring Dispersions in Education Outcomes

Since the days of Adam Smith, education has been linked to equitable social and economic progress. There is a small but growing literature on schooling inequality or the distribution of education (see, for example, Lam and Levinson 1991; Londoño 1990; Maas and Criel 1982; Ram 1990). As data became available for measuring the distribution of education, the disparities became more apparent. Using standard deviation of schooling attainment, Birdsall and Londoño (1997) investigated the impact of initial asset distributions on growth and poverty reduction and found a significant correlation between initial educational inequality and reduced income growth.

Later, researchers constructed education Gini coefficients, which are similar to the Gini coefficients widely used to measure distributions of income, wealth, and land. The Gini coefficient ranges from 0, which represents perfect equality, to 1, which represents perfect inequality (see annex 3 for the two methods used to calculate the Gini coefficient). Education Gini coefficients can be calculated using enrollment, financing, or attainment data, recognizing that different cohorts in a population were educated at different times. López, Thomas, and Wang (1998) estimated Gini coefficients of educational attainment for 20 countries and found significant differences in the distribution of schooling. Korea had the fastest expansion in education coverage and the fastest decline in the education Gini coefficient; it dropped from 0.51 to 0.22 in 20 years. India's education Gini coefficient declined moderately, from 0.80 in 1970 to 0.69 in 1990. Education Gini coefficients for Colombia, Costa Rica, Peru, and Venezuela have been increasing slowly since the 1980s, showing that inequality is on the rise (figure 3.3).

Figure 3.3. Gini Coefficients of Education, Selected Countries, 1960–90

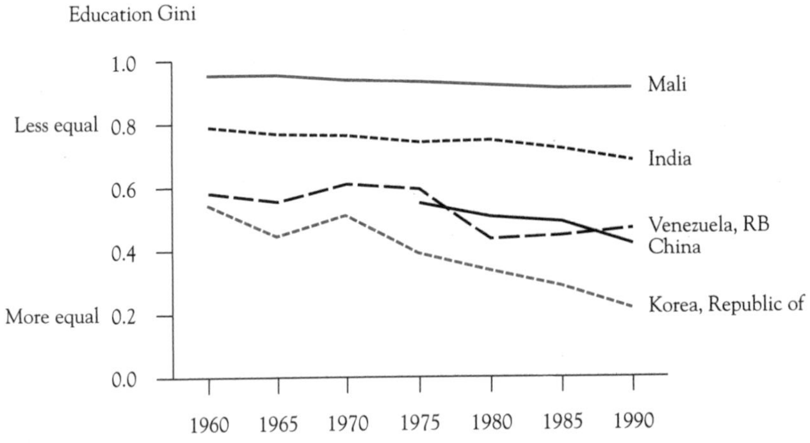

Source: López, Thomas, and Wang (1998).

An examination of education Lorenz curves for India and Korea in 1990 shows a great range among developing countries (figure 3.4). Despite progress in expanding primary and secondary enrollment in India, more than half of the population (age 15 and older) did not receive any education while 10 percent of the population received nearly 40 percent of total cumulated years of schooling. Providing universal access to basic education remains a huge challenge for the country.

Korea expanded its basic education program more rapidly, with a far more equitable distribution in educational attainment, as indicated by a flatter Lorenz curve and a smaller Gini coefficient. Even in 1960, when Korea's per capita income was similar to that of India, Korea's education Gini coefficient was 0.55, much lower than that of India in 1990. Note that the distribution of education in Korea was more equitable than that of income, but the distribution of education in India was much more skewed than that of income between 1970 and 1990.[7]

A distribution of education as skewed as that of India implies a huge social loss from the underutilization of potential human capital. Assuming that ability or talent is normally distributed across population groups, production increases to its optimum when the dispersion of education matches the distribution of human ability. When the distribution of education is too skewed to match the distribution of ability, there is a deadweight loss to the society of underdeveloped and underutilized talent. In this case, societies

The distribution of education varies enormously, from highly skewed to more equal

Figure 3.4. Education Lorenz Curves for India and Korea, 1990

Cumulative proportion of schooling, India
(percent)

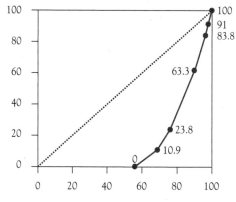

Cumulative proportion of schooling, Korea
(percent)

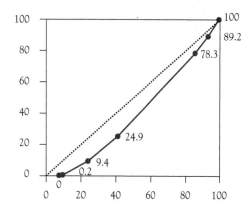

Cumulative proportion of population (15 and over) (percent)
Mean = 2.95 years   Education Gini = 0.69

Cumulative proportion of population (15 and over) (percent)
Mean = 10.04 years   Education Gini = 0.22

Source: Thomas, Wang, and Fan (2000).

would be better off to massively expand basic education, especially by improving access to education by the poor.

Examining the cross-country pattern of the distribution of education, we found that education Gini coefficients decline as the average education and income levels increase, although there clearly are other possibilities. Does the education Gini have to get worse before it gets better? As suggested by Londoño (1990) and Ram (1990), there is a "Kuznetsian tale" with distribution of education. That is, as a country moves from the zero to maximum level of education, the variance first increases and then declines. However, country analysis suggests that this may not be the case if Gini coefficients are used to measure inequality. In addition to the industrial countries, Argentina, Chile, and Ireland had relatively low education Gini coefficients from the 1960s to the 1990s. The Gini coefficient for education in Korea and some other countries declined dramatically. Only a few countries—Colombia, Costa Rica, Peru, and Venezuela—have seen a significant worsening of the education Gini coefficient. So worsening distribution of education is not inevitable (figure 3.5). Among 85 countries for which education Gini coefficients were calculated, Afghanistan and Mali had the

Education Ginis decline as average education level rises

Figure 3.5. Education Gini Coefficients for 85 Countries, 1990

Education Gini coefficient

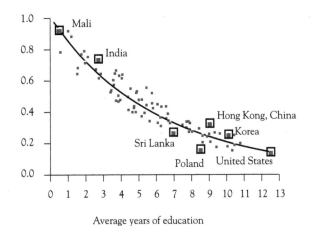

Average years of education

Source: Thomas, Wang, and Fan (2000).

least equitable distributions in the 1990s at approximately 0.90, while most industrial countries were at the lower end, with the United States and Poland having the most equitable distribution (Thomas, Wang, and Fan 2000). Similar to the large variations in the distribution of education, other studies found large variations in health outcomes across income groups (box 3.1).

Causes of Inequality in Education

Disparities in education is one of many aspects of poverty, but they are also associated with misallocation of public investment, war, wealth gaps, gender gaps, social exclusion, and economic crises. Numerous studies found that parents' education and household income, as well as wealth, affect children's education attainments.

Wealth Gaps. Using data from the National Family Health Survey collected in Indian states in 1992 and 1993, Filmer and Pritchett (1999a) found that the wealth gap, defined as the difference between the top 20 percent of an asset index and the bottom 40 percent, accounted for a large proportion of differences in enrollment rates. Enrollment rates varied from 4.6 percent in Kerala to 42.6 percent in Bihar.

Box 3.1. Health Gaps between the Rich and the Poor Are also Large

Health gaps between the rich and the poor are as large as education gaps, which reflects the difficulties of reaching the poorest people outside the mainstream of economic life. Many studies find that the poorest of the poor are in the worst health (Behrman and Deolalikar 1988), and they are often hit hardest by wars, external shocks, and social and political upheavals. Child mortality rates among the poorest of the poor are often much higher than those among people who have higher incomes. Figure 3.6 shows that in Brazil, child mortality rates were high among the poorest 10 percent of the population, and fell as wealth rose. It indicates that the poorest of the poor are in worse health than others. They suffer from infectious diseases much more than richer people do. Therefore, they are more dependent on good public policies than the rich (Bonilla-Chacin and Hammer 1999).

The poor are sicker than other people

Figure 3.6. Mortality of Children Two Years Old and Younger by Wealth, Brazil, 1996

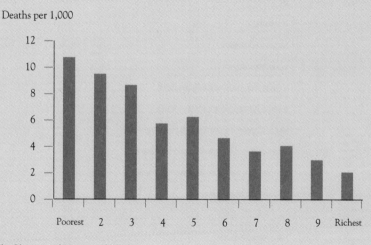

Deaths per 1,000

Source: Bonilla-Chacin and Hammer (1999).

In some countries, the differences in educational outcomes between the rich and the poor are staggering. A study of youths aged 15–19 in 20 countries showed that the poorest 40 percent of the population in five countries had a median of zero years of completed schooling; more than half of this group completed less than one year of school (figure 3.7). The education difference between the richest and poorest groups reached as high as 10 grades in India. Similar disparities in education attainment are found in Latin America (figure 3.8).

One implication of this large wealth gap is that demand for education is not independent of other endowments. Providing access to education

Differences in grade attainment for rich and poor households are enormous in some countries

Figure 3.7. Median Grade Attainment for 15–19-Year-Olds from Rich and Poor Households, Selected Countries and Years

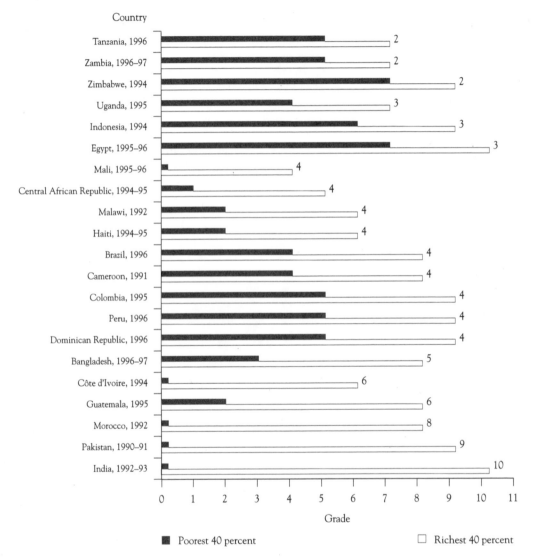

Note: Numbers next to bars are the gaps (in grades) between rich and poor.
Source: Filmer and Pritchett (1999b).

Figure 3.8. Years of Schooling for 25-Year-Olds from Rich and Poor Households in Latin America

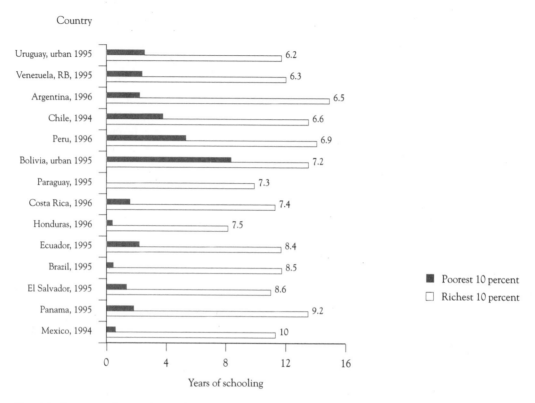

Note: Numbers next to bars are the gaps (in years of schooling) between rich and poor. The surveys for Argentina include only Greater Buenos Aries.
Source: IDB (1998, p.27).

(supply) is not sufficient. Addressing many structural and social inequalities influencing demand, such as gender gaps and the distribution of other productive assets such as land (discussed later), is important as well.

Social Exclusion. People who are excluded from mainstream society are less likely to be educated. Loury (1999) showed how social exclusion changes human behavior and reduces the demand for schooling in inner cities of the United States. One reason that students drop out of school is because their peers have dropped out. In Bolivia, the inability of parents to speak Spanish is associated with higher mortality rates for children under two years old. In India, members of scheduled castes have higher mortality rates than other groups (Bonilla-Chacin and Hammer 1999).

THE QUALITY OF GROWTH

Gender Gaps. In some countries gender gaps are an important cause of education inequality. Among many studies addressing gender gaps in education, Schultz (1998) found that some 65 percent of world inequality is between countries, 30 percent is between households in a country, and 5 percent is between gender inequality. Bouis and others (1998) found a significant difference in human capital investments, such as in nutrition, health care, and educational attainment, between boys and girls in the rural Philippines. In Bangladesh, which has the largest gender gap out of the countries reviewed, women's attitudes toward their daughters' education have been slow to change (Amin and Pebley 1994). However, recent efforts have resulted in encouraging progress (box 3.2). Knight and Shi (1991) found that educational opportunities were still unevenly distributed in China despite considerable progress. The pattern of educational attainment is affected by gender as well as by other factors, such as income of the provinces, rural-urban differences in income, and family background. Though on the decline, gender discrimination persists in China's rural areas (see Dubey and King 1996; King and Hill 1993; and World Bank 2000g for cross-country experiences).

The correlation is strong between inequality in education and gender gaps in literacy. Using a sample of 85 countries for which education Gini coefficients are available, Thomas, Wang, and Fan (2000) found that

---

Box 3.2. Supporting Girls' Education in Bangladesh

A revolution is taking place in schools across Bangladesh. Enrollment trends are changing and now more girls than boys can often be seen in schools.

The educational attainment of women in Bangladesh is among the lowest in the world, and the gender gap is among the largest. In 1997, the female-male illiteracy gap was as high as 23 percentage points. According to 1991 census data, only 20 percent of women could read and write, and only one in three students in secondary schools were girls.

In 1994, the government launched a program to increase support for female secondary education, to raise the female literacy rate from 16 to 25 percent, and to create employment opportunities for women. With support from the World Bank and other development partners, the program is being implemented successfully and has made Bangladesh a South Asia pioneer in this area.

The incentive program for girls, including fee exemptions and cash stipends, has generated tremendous enthusiasm for female education and has boosted the enrollment of girls in secondary schools. Girls' enrollment in the project districts is above expectations: enrollments rose every year and for every class. A total of 554,077 girls were awarded stipends in 1996, and the number was greater in 1997. In the Fulbaria Mohammad Ali High School in Savar, near Dhaka, girls outnumber boys four to one; a situation that was unthinkable a few years ago.

Source: Robboy (1999).

correlation coefficients between gender differences in illiteracy and education Gini coefficients increased significantly from 0.53 in the 1970s to 0.69 in the 1990s. While educational inequality declined, gender inequality accounted for much of the remaining disparities in educational attainment (figure 3.9). Reducing gender gaps in education is crucial to addressing the inequality in education.

Consequences of Large Dispersions in Education Outcomes

A society cares about the unequal distribution of education because it directly affects human welfare. Unequal distribution of education is both a source and a consequence of poverty and social exclusion. Poor children who drop out of school eventually form a core of disadvantaged citizens who will be left out of mainstream economic and social life. Unless such people can obtain training later in life to find a meaningful job, poverty reduction and social inclusion will remain out of reach.

A highly skewed distribution of education tends to be associated with reduced per capita income growth, even after controlling for labor and

While education inequality has been declining, gender inequality accounts for much of what remains

Figure 3.9.   Gender Gaps and the Inequality of Education, 1970 and 1990

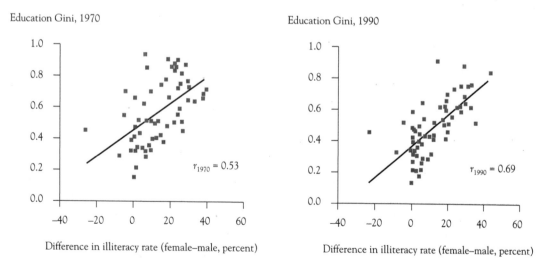

Note: The figures include data for 85 countries.
Sources: Education Gini coefficients from Thomas, Wang, and Fan (2000); gender gap in illiteracy from World Bank (1999d).

physical capital (López, Thomas, and Wang 1998). Unlike land and physical capital, which are tradable across firms and individuals, education and skills are not perfectly tradable. As a consequence, both the distribution and level of education enter the production function and affect the level and growth of output. Using panel data from 20 developing countries, López, Thomas, and Wang (1998) demonstrated the negative association between skewed distribution of education and economic growth. When a large part of the population is not educated, the low productivity of the labor force discourages investment in physical capital, and economic growth suffers (see regression analyses in table A2.1 and annex 3).

The distribution of education also holds strong implications for the poverty-reducing impact of growth. Ravallion and Datt (1999), using data from 15 Indian states between 1960 and 1994, found that the poverty-reducing association of growth varied according to initial conditions: growth contributed less to poverty reduction in states with initially lower literacy rates, farm productivity, and rural standard of living relative to urban areas. In Kerala, where basic education is well distributed and literacy rates are the highest, for males and females, a percentage point increase in the growth rate was more strongly associated with poverty reduction.

In Assam and Bihar, which had similar nonfarm growth rates to that of Kerala, but low literacy rates and higher inequality in basic education, growth contributed little to poverty reduction (figure 3.10). For example, Bihar, with the lowest female literacy rate among the states studied, 29 percent, showed a 32 percent gender gap in literacy rates, and 6 million children ages 6–10 were not enrolled in school between 1992 and 1993. Other states, such as Maharashtra and Madhya Pradesh, had higher growth rates but lower poverty reduction rates than that of Kerala. More than fast growth, pro-poor growth is needed for poverty reduction. If all Indian states had an elasticity of poverty reduction like Kerala, poverty, as measured by the headcount index, would have fallen at a rate of 3.5 percent, instead of 1.3 percent, a year since 1960.

Improving the Efficacy of Public Spending

Markets alone cannot provide equitable access to basic education by the poor. As partly a public good, education provides positive spillovers that are not fully captured by individuals and firms. However, the market fails mainly at the lower end of the income distribution: without public investment in the education of the poor, society's investment in education would be suboptimal. Yet, as we have seen, public spending is only weakly associated with education outcomes, partly because of a bias toward the better-off. Increasing public spending is desirable, but not enough to deal with the

Growth has a stronger poverty reducing impact in states with more equitable education such as Kerala

Figure 3.10. Trend Rates of Poverty Reduction and Nonfarm Output Economic Growth in India, 1960–94

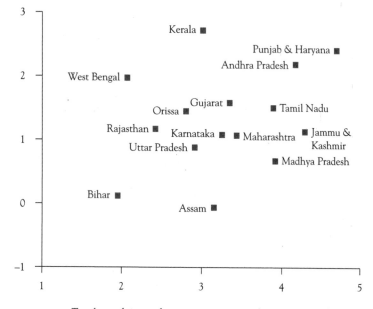

Trend rate of poverty reduction (headcount index; percent per year)

Trend growth in nonfarm output per person (percent per year)

Note: Trend rates of growth estimated by ordinary least squares regressions of the logarithms on time.
Source: Ravallion and Datt (1999).

inadequate human development outcome, therefore, we now turn to improving the allocation and efficacy of spending.

Allocate More Public Spending to the Education of the Poor

The composition of government expenditures on education and health influences human development outcomes. Public spending needs to concentrate on areas where market failure is pervasive and where positive spillover is largest: in primary and secondary schooling, especially for the poor. Given limited public resources, the balance needs to shift more toward investments in primary and secondary education. Additionally, the private sector and public-private partnerships should be encouraged to provide higher education where market failure is minimal.

Korea showed how a strong emphasis on primary and secondary education could eliminate illiteracy and reduce educational inequality. Korea allocated two-thirds of its public education spending to primary schooling in the 1960s and early 1970s (table 3.2). Public spending on secondary education rose from 22 percent in 1965 to 33 percent in 1990. Yet, public expenditures on higher education rarely exceeded 12 percent of the total public spending between 1965 and 1990. Tertiary education was mainly financed by private investments. Before the 1990s, India spent a larger share on higher education than did Korea and a smaller, but increasing, share on primary education. In the mid-1990s, India increased its spending on elementary schools and adult literacy programs from 20 to 31 percent of its total public spending on education, which was still far below that of Korea. To provide broader access to education and reduce the inequality, more remains to be done to improve the allocation of public investment in India.

Measured by public spending per student, public subsidies to higher education have been falling in many countries, but not fast enough to enable reallocation of public funds to basic education (table 3.3). Resource allocation is still biased against primary and secondary education in most countries. In the United States, the allocation of public spending has been balanced for more than 30 years, with subsidies to primary schooling at more than 20 percent of gross national product (GNP) per capita, the highest in the world. In Korea, due to the large number of students in primary schools, government support per student did not sufficiently emphasize primary education in the 1960s, even though more than 60 percent of total spending was allocated to primary education. This pattern was reversed in the 1980s, when public spending per primary school student exceeded that per college student. Associated with a strong emphasis on basic education, Korea was able to reduce education inequality rapidly. The United States has maintained the lowest education Gini coefficient in the world since 1965.

Venezuela, in contrast, has favored higher education over basic education for more than four decades. While total public spending on education

Table 3.2. Public Spending by Level of Education, Korea, Selected Years
(percentage of total expenditures on education)

Levels	1965	1970	1975	1980	1985	1990
Primary	64.7	67.4	52.2	47.9	44.5	43.2
Secondary	21.8	20.9	37.1	33.8	37.7	33.1
Higher education	13.3	8.2	10.7	11.4	11.5	9.6

Source: UNESCO database.

Table 3.3.   Public Expenditure Per Student by Level, 1960s to 1990s

Country	Level	Public expenditure per student (percent of GNP per capita)				Education Gini coefficient (national average, all levels)	
		1960s	1970s	1980s	1990s	1980	1990
Argentina	Primary	—	3.06	6.49	8.32	0.29	0.27
	Secondary	26.17	10.43	—	—		
	Tertiary	59.29	23.58	17.45	19.84		
Chile	Primary	6.92	6.08	12.53	9.20	0.32	0.31
	Secondary	—	12.01	12.58	8.80		
	Tertiary	151.71	67.46	79.69	23.36		
Korea, Republic of	Primary	6.21	7.86	12.79	14.86	0.34	0.22
	Secondary	8.64	7.39	10.76	11.88		
	Tertiary	36.67	28.02	10.49	5.83		
Mexico	Primary	4.34	—	3.97	7.18	0.50	0.38
	Secondary	—	—	8.61	13.93		
	Tertiary	70.72	—	32.43	35.66		
United States	Primary	22.05	28.45	26.28	19.83	0.12	0.15
	Secondary	—	—	18.77	23.86		
	Tertiary	73.73	58.84	37.85	22.91		
Venezuela, RB	Primary	8.50	7.37	4.80	2.39	0.39	0.42
	Secondary	21.26	17.60	18.34	7.07		
	Tertiary	121.76	100.00	65.74	37.38		

— Not available.

Sources: Public expenditure data are from the UNESCO database; education Gini coefficients are from Thomas, Wang, and Fan (2000).

has increased from 4.3 percent of GNP in the 1970s to 5.1 percent in the 1980s and 4.6 percent in the 1990s, its allocation has worsened. In fact, the subsidies to primary and secondary education were reduced in the 1990s. This misallocation of public resources might partially explain the worsening of the education Gini coefficient in the 1990s.

The Interaction between Demographics and Education

Public spending per primary-school-age student in Korea rose more than ten-fold between 1970 and 1995 as population growth rates slowed and the economy expanded (table 3.4). Public spending per secondary student also rose. Rapid economic growth, together with a stabilizing and even declining student base, meant that far more resources were being devoted to fewer children, allowing dramatic improvements in the quality of primary education.

Table 3.4. Public Current Expenditure Per Student, India and Korea, Selected Years

Country	Level	1965	1970	1975	1980	1985	1990	1995
Amount (1995 US$ per student)								
Korea, Republic of	Primary	92	207	182	386	701	955	1,890
	Secondary	—	223	134	339	541	786	1295
	Tertiary	545	757	622	589	546	460	599
India	Primary	8	10	20	23	29	39	39
	Secondary	—	54	35	34	38	—	43
	Tertiary	—	—	—	189	227	299	260
Percentage of GDP per capita								
Korea, Republic of	Primary	6.3	9.5	6.3	10.2	13.5	12.0	17.4
	Secondary	—	10.3	4.6	9.0	10.4	9.9	11.9
	Tertiary	37.2	35.0	21.5	15.6	10.5	5.8	5.5
India	Primary	4.3	4.8	9.2	9.7	10.6	11.8	9.9
	Secondary	—	24.9	15.8	14.8	13.9	—	11.0
	Tertiary	—	—	—	81.8	84.0	90.3	66.4

— Not available.

Note: Dollar amounts are not comparable across countries as they are not in PPP dollars, but are comparable over time.

Sources: Calculated from UNESCO and World Bank data.

In India, rapid population growth and constraints on public funding meant that a quantity-quality tradeoff was likely to occur. In 1995, India spent US$39 (in 1995 constant dollars) per pupil in primary schools, or 10 percent of its GDP per capita; Korea spent 17 percent (table 3.4). In Tamil Nadu, India, enrollment in primary and middle schools expanded 35 percent between 1977 and 1992, a major achievement, but the pupil-teacher ratio rose from 36 to 47 and school conditions worsened. Student achievement suffered as a result (Duraisamy and others 1998). These relationships point to a need to consider the interaction between demographics and education policy and a need for policies focusing on education of girls and women, education to improve reproductive health, and voluntary family planning as part of an overall development strategy centered on people (see also box 3.3).

Improve the Mix of Public and Private Spending

Korea also achieved a good mix of public and private financing in education. Since the mid-1960s, private colleges and universities have accounted

Box 3.3. Population and Development

The link between population growth and economic development is a subject of contentious debate. The 1960s and 1970s were dominated by pessimistic, and sometimes alarmist, predictions that rapid population growth would lead to famines, resource exhaustion, deficiencies in saving, irreversible environmental damage, and ecological collapse (Ehrlich 1968). The population optimists believed that rapid population growth would allow countries to capture economies of scale and promote technological and institutional innovation (Simon 1976). In the 1980s, the alarmist views were replaced by moderated, time- and country-specific assessments of the net negative impacts of rapid population growth, which were considered to be small. Only weak or inconclusive links were found between demographic changes and economic growth (Bloom and Freeman 1988; Kelley 1988).

More recent investigations revealed fairly large, negative effects of rapid population growth and related demographic components on per capita economic growth. Kelley and Schmidt (1999) found that rapid population growth exerted a fairly strong, adverse impact on the pace of economic growth in 89 countries between 1960 and 1995. The positive impacts of density, size of population, and labor force entry were dominated by the costs of rearing children and maintaining an enlarged youth dependency age structure. Declining mortality and fertility each

contributed approximately 22 percent to changes in output growth between 1960 and 1992, a figure that corresponds to approximately 21 percent of the average growth of per capita output, which was measured at 1.5 percent.

Various components of demographic change have been successfully introduced into growth models. Bloom and Williamson (1998) showed that rapid demographic transition in East Asia led to fast growth in the working-age population between 1965 and 1990, expanded the per capita productive capacity, and contributed to the East Asia economic miracle. Other economic policies also facilitated the East Asians to realize the growth potential of the demographic transition.

Less evidence was available on the link between demographic change and poverty until recently. However, if rapid population growth has a negative effect on economic and wage growth, it would negatively affect poverty as well. Eastwood and Lipton (1999) found that higher fertility increases poverty both by retarding growth and by skewing the distribution against the poor. In addition, evidence shows that public sector programs targeted at the poor, such as basic education and health care programs, have contributed to reduced poverty. Rapid population growth will dilute the intensity of public investment, and as a consequence make quality of service improvements more difficult to achieve.

Sources: Bloom and Williamson (1998); Eastwood and Lipton (1999); Kelley (1998); Kelley and Schmidt (1999).

for more than 70 percent of enrollments, private secondary institutions for more than 40 percent. Households assume a large share of educational costs, between 30 and 50 percent, depending on student education level. Tuition and related fees account for 40 percent of in-school expenditures for middle school, but rise sharply to 72 percent and more for high school and college students.

The most effective public-private mix depends on the extent of market failures and a variety of other factors. Higher education is crucial for technological progress and productivity growth, but it can be considered a private good, because most of the returns can be internalized by individuals and firms. Whereas primary and secondary education have large spillover effects that are not fully captured by individuals and firms. Thus while government has a direct role in primary and secondary education, it needs to encourage private investments and public-private partnerships in higher education. The United States, for example, provides valuable experiences in this regard.

The policy environment, which can be defined by the degree of openness to trade and investment, for example, affects the demand for skilled workers and as a consequence people's willingness to pay for education. The quality of service provision for education, which is related to institutional capacities, also affects the willingness to pay. Similarly, the public-private mix in health care also depends on the nature of services and the degree of market failures in particular subsectors (Filmer, Hammer, and Pritchett forthcoming).

One successful intervention is the Quetta Girls Fellowship Program in Pakistan. Launched in 1995, the pilot project aimed at determining whether establishing private schools in poor neighborhoods was a cost-effective way of expanding primary education for girls. The program encouraged private schools controlled by communities, ensuring them government support for three years. An evaluation analysis indicates that the program increased girls' enrollments by 33 percentage points, and boys' enrollment rose as well. Such programs offer promise for increasing enrollment rates in poor urban areas (Kim, Alderman, and Orazem 1999).

Decentralize Decisionmaking and Encourage Participation

How decisions are made also affects the efficacy of public services. Where institutional capacity is low, public spending on centrally planned and organized interventions is likely to be ineffective. Many countries are moving to decentralized decisionmaking to better match expenditures to local needs. Empirical evidence on the benefits of decentralized school management was rare until recently. A recent evaluation of El Salvador's EDUCO program (Community-Managed Schools Program) shows that enhanced community and parental involvement in EDUCO schools has improved students' language skills and diminished student absences, which may have long-term effects on achievement (Jimenez and Sawada 1999). Other studies have also shown that community-managed schools achieved better results in Indonesia and the Philippines (James, King, and Suryadi 1996; Jimenez and Paqueo 1996).

Several counties have been experimenting with voucher programs, which transfer resources to parents to help pay private school tuition. Colombia used a national voucher program from 1991 to 1997 to decentralize management and expand enrollment. The program was meant to address the deficiencies in the public education system, especially the low transition rate from primary to secondary schools by the poor. Only the poor were qualified for vouchers, which avoided subsidizing the wealthy as in previous voucher programs. Participation was a problem, however; only 25 percent of Colombia's municipalities joined the program, limiting the benefits. A careful evaluation of the program found that demand for secondary education and availability of space in private schools were key determinants of municipal participation (King, Orazem, and Wohlgemuth 1999). Such voucher programs are potentially beneficial to the poor.

In countries with corrupt and predatory governments, however, decentralizing decisionmaking may not be the answer. Corrupt officials are likely to reallocate public resources from the poor to elite interest groups, subsidizing the types of social services that benefit the rich. Empowering people to influence policy through democratization and a greater role for civil society, and encouraging greater participation of the community and families are steps in the right direction (see chapter 6 on the role of participation and civil society in anticorruption and better governance).

Making Education More Productive

Improving the productivity of education for the poor takes more than investments in their education. To be more productive, the poor must be able to combine their human capital with other productive assets such as land, equity capital, and job opportunities in open and competitive markets.

Distribute Land more Equitably

The poor are not just income poor; they also lack assets. In agrarian economies, disadvantaged households are usually landless or land poor. In South Asia, southern Africa, and much of Latin America, poverty is highly correlated with landlessness (figure 3.11a). Income inequality also seems to be associated with inequality in landholding (figure 3.11b), although data on land ownership is weak.

Land reform has many benefits for growth and poverty reduction, as suggested by empirical studies discussed later. In societies where a large segment of the population does not have access to the productive resources of the economy, strong demand for redistribution gives rise to civil unrest. Studies suggest that inequality in land ownership and income are correlated with subsequent lower economic growth (Alesina and Rodrik 1994); a one

Figure 3.11a. Poverty and Landholding, Bangladesh, 1988–89

Headcount index (percent)

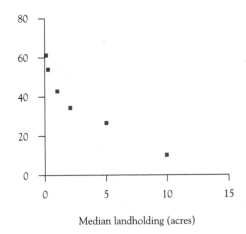

Median landholding (acres)

Source: Ravallion and Sen (1994).

Figure 3.11b. Income Share in the 1980s and Land Gini Coefficients in the 1960s

Income share of the lowest quintile in the 1980s

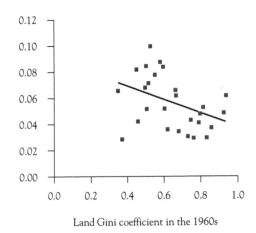

Land Gini coefficient in the 1960s

Note: Data are country-specific decade averages. $N = 27$. $r = -0.40$.
Source: Deininger and Squire (1996).

standard deviation increase in equality is associated with increases in growth of one-half to 1 percentage point (Persson and Tabellini 1994). Other studies showed that the initial inequality of assets, measured by land distribution, is more significant than income inequality in affecting subsequent growth (Deininger and Squire 1998; Li, Squire, and Zou 1998; Lundberg and Squire 1999). Still others have found initial land inequality, along with initial education inequality, to have strong negative links to economic growth and to the income growth of the poorest (Birdsall and Londoño 1998). In addition to being negatively correlated with growth, land inequality also appears to reduce the positive effect of human capital on growth through interaction effects (Deininger and Olinto 1999).

Redistributive land reform gives land to more efficient producers and reduces credit market imperfections, leading to improved investment decisions by the poor. Greater wealth, as measured by land ownership, also provides a safety net for the poor against external shocks and increases their ability to participate in the political process (Binswanger and Deininger 1997; Binswanger, Deininger, and Feder 1995). Ravallion and Sen (1994) noted that redistribution from land-rich to land-poor households would reduce aggregate poverty in rural Bangladesh. They also found that transfers from the budget would have the greatest impact on poverty if concentrated on landless and marginal farmers (see annex table A3.5 for a selective literature review).

Widespread ownership of land improves not just equity, but also productivity (Berry and Cline 1979) and efficiency (Banerjee 1999). Better land rights have facilitated investment in Ghana (Besley 1995), and possession of legal land ownership documents in Thailand has significantly impacted farmers' agricultural performances (Feder 1987, 1993). Many East Asian economies have widespread landholdings, a result of traditional ownership or land reform. In Korea, confiscated land at the end of World War II was first distributed to the tillers. Then in the 1950s the government distributed landlord properties, with nominal compensation, to 900,000 tenants, effectively eliminating tenancy. In Taiwan, China, the government obtained land from landlords in the early 1950s, compensated owners with shares in state enterprises, and then sold the land to tillers on favorable terms.

In China, the household responsibility system introduced in 1979 assigned collectively-owned land to households for up to 15 years. The system, which was renewed for another 30 years in 1998, tied rewards more closely to farming efforts. Together with price and other reforms, the initiative resulted in a 5.7 percent annual rise in average grain yields from 1978 to 1984 and 1.8 percent thereafter. Nearly half of the total output increase in the period can be attributed to the household responsibility system (Lin 1992). One study found that access to land can improve nutritional status in China, because it serves both as a means of generating income and as a source of cheap calories relative to the market (Burgess 2000). Another study found that in rural China, wealth, especially land, is distributed more equally (Gini coefficient of 0.31) than income (Gini coefficient of 0.34). The main source of rural income inequality is wage income rather than the returns from land, an atypical pattern for a developing country (McKinley 1996).

Land reform is contentious and politically difficult. Market-assisted land reform has emerged in recent years as an alternative to traditional land reform, and is being implemented by Brazil, Colombia, and South Africa. The basic idea is that the state gives qualified, landless people a grant or a subsidized loan to buy land. This market-assisted approach differs from fully compensated land reform in two ways: there are neither explicit targets for land distribution nor fixed time schedules. In addition, the reforms are demand driven; people who want the land most will come forward to buy it. Some researchers contend that market-assisted land reform has advantages, especially if combined with microcredit, extension programs, and complementary actions that facilitate agricultural cooperatives and contract farming (Banerjee 1999). The success of the programs can be enhanced if accompanied by efforts to make land markets more transparent and fluid and to involve the private sector (Deininger 1999). While it is still too soon to reach definitive conclusions on the costs and benefits of these reforms, some other studies have found that this approach benefits large landholders because land prices are likely to be bid up, requiring the poor to pay elevated prices (López and Valdes 2000).

Distribute Equity Capital and Foster Competition

A case can also be made for better distribution of equity through employee ownership plans. In industrial countries, employee stock ownership plans have been positively associated with firms' performances. Firms in the United States have used employee ownership plans in restructuring. For example, United Airlines negotiated significant wage concessions in return for a majority equity stake for employees. By communicating the benefits of the restructuring plan to its investors and employees, the company reduced the up-front restructuring cost, enhanced the effects of the restructuring, and thereby created additional shareholder value. Both investors and employees have benefited (Gilson 1995).

In countries hit by the recent financial crises, the sale of equity shares to employees may provide a way to recapitalize companies in desperate need of capital, and can also redistribute wealth and risks. Where restructuring leads to retrenchments, laid-off workers may be given equity shares in lieu of severance pay, and so benefit from the companies' restructuring and recovery. Employee ownership plans can also help reduce workers' resistance to restructuring (Claessens, Djankov, and Klingebiel 1999). Providing microfinancing to laid-off workers to establish small enterprises is another way to empower them to build physical and financial capital.

Privatization offers additional opportunities for redistributing equity. Because public enterprises were built using tax revenues, a certain proportion of the equity shares can justifiably be distributed or sold at a discount to taxpayers during privatization. Properly designed privatization programs can reduce asset inequality and poverty. For example, using proceeds from the privatization of the six largest state enterprises, Bolivia established a pool of financial assets to fund a minimum flat pension for everyone in the country. While the amount provided is small, the program will reach the most vulnerable in society: the elderly poor who are unable to save for retirement. Hungary used its receipts from privatization to repay foreign debt, which raised its sovereign debt rating, reduced its interest payments, and benefited all citizens (Kornai 2000).

Privatization entails efficiency gains as well as social losses, and society must maintain a balance between the efficiency gains and social losses (and compensate the losers), if the gains are to be sustainable. After privatization in Mexico, there was a 24 percentage point increase in the ratio of operating income to sales. Of those gains in profitability, 10 percent were due to higher product prices, 33 percent to a transfer from laid-off workers, and the remaining 57 percent to productivity gains (La Porta and Lopez-De-Silanes 1999). To compensate those who suffer losses as a result of privatization, equity shares in lieu of severance pay could be distributed to laid-off workers, or other forms of income transfers could be financed by taxation.

Competition and regulation are vital for a market economy. The efficiency of a market economy depends on both private property and competitive markets, but many developing and transition economies lack both. Before and during privatization, competition and a regulatory framework must be introduced (Stiglitz 1999). Evidence from the United Kingdom shows that when big public enterprises were privatized, antitrust regulations were crucial to ensure transparent, equitable, and efficient allocations of resources (see also Herrera 1992). Privatizing large public firms that have a natural monopoly without first setting up antitrust regulations, as was done in Russia, can worsen the distribution of wealth and income. And it could create powerful, entrenched interests that undermine the possibility of viable regulation and competition in the future, and block further broad-based reform measures (Kornai 2000).

Combine Human Capital with Opportunities in Open Markets

The urban poor must hire out their labor. Thus, the creation of job opportunities is critically important to the productive use of their human capital and to poverty reduction. The *World Development Report 1990* (World Bank 1990) proposed a strategy of broad-based, labor-intensive growth to generate income-earning opportunities for the poor. Some economies have pursued this strategy and more—they have combined investment in learning and education with openness, forming a virtuous circle. Examples include Japan in the 1950s and Hong Kong, China; Korea; Singapore; and Taiwan, China, from the 1960s through the 1980s.

The accumulation of knowledge influences a country's trade and competitiveness, and trade enhances the accumulation of knowledge, especially through imports. Lucas (1993) noted that to sustain knowledge accumulation, a nation must be outward oriented and a significant exporter. Young (1991) and Keller (1995) found that trade itself is not an engine of growth, but must operate through some mechanism, such as the formation of human capital, to affect growth.

Market openness facilitates technological progress and capacity building through various modes of learning, such as the importation of capital and intermediate goods, learning by doing, and on-the-job training. Foster and Rosenzweig (1995) found strong evidence of learning-by-doing and learning spillovers: farmers' own experiences and that of their neighbors with high-yield varieties significantly increased profitability. Farmers with experienced neighbors are significantly more profitable than others, and the spillover effects associated with learning from others are small, but not unimportant.

The link between overall economic policies and the impact of education is clear. The *World Development Report 1991* (World Bank 1991) found that among 60 developing countries from 1965 to 1987, economic growth rates were especially high for countries with high levels of education, macroeconomic stability, and market openness. The impact of trade openness on long-term growth thus depends on how well people can absorb and use the information and technology accompanying trade and foreign investment.

Increases in the stock of human capital tend to accelerate growth during market reforms and under an outward-oriented economic structure, but in their absence, education has no significant impact on growth. The growth effect of an interaction between openness and education was robust (López, Thomas, and Wang, 1998; see also chapter 2 and annex 2). Similarly, for 1,265 World Bank projects, Thomas and Wang (1997) found that the rate of return was 3 percentage points higher in countries with both a more educated labor force and a more open economy than in countries that had only one or the other (figure 3.12 and annex table A3.4).[8]

Protect Workers against Shocks

The urban poor usually lack adequate human capital for all but unskilled work. With increased openness and globalization, job opportunities for unskilled workers have become more scarce and incomes more volatile. Diwan (1999) found that labor shares in GDP have been falling for more than 20 years in most regions. Consistent with this evidence, unemployment rates in Latin America have risen since the end of the 1980s. In 1989, only 5 or 6 of every 100 Latin Americans willing to work were unemployed; by 1996, nearly 8 of every 100 were not working.

Unemployment rose in East Asian countries hit by the recent financial turmoil, from previously modest levels to 4.5 percent in Thailand, 5.5 percent in Indonesia, and 7.4 percent in urban Korea (World Bank 2000a, p. 59). Perhaps even worse was the fall in real wages, because the poor could not afford to remain unemployed. Real wages fell in 16 of 22 recessionary episodes in

Education and openness interact and increase investment returns

Figure 3.12. Education, Openness, and Economic Rates of Return in 1,265 World Bank Projects

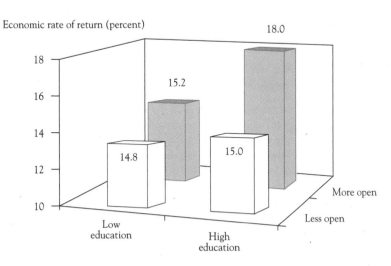

Note: Economic rates of return are from the evaluation database of the World Bank's Operations Evaluation Department. Education is measured by the average level of schooling of the labor force, and openness by the logarithm of the foreign exchange parallel-market premium.

Sources: Thomas and Wang (1997); annex 3.

Latin America during the 1980s and 1990s. In 18 cases, after two years real wages remained lower than their precrisis levels (Lustig 1999). In East Asia, manufacturing real wages fell by 4.5 percent in Thailand, 10.6 percent in Korea, and 44 percent in Indonesia between 1997 and 1998 (World Bank 2000a, p. 57). As a result of both a decline in real wages and in employment growth, labor shares in GDP fell sharply following the financial crises, perhaps because labor is less mobile than capital, and so is forced to bear a large share of the financial burden of crisis resolution (Diwan 1999).

Urban unskilled workers are most vulnerable to external shocks, structural adjustment, and economic downturns. Lacking adequate human capital, they are often unable to adjust to changes in labor market demand. The problem is exacerbated by labor market distortions and weak labor market institutions that further hamper labor market adjustments. Labor market distortions need to be checked: the existence of child labor and distorted wage structures discourage demand for education. Governments need to help build labor market institutions and provide the labor market information that the poor need.

There is also the need to train or retrain displaced workers and increase their mobility across sectors. Ghana trained more than 4,000 people in vocational schools or apprentice programs, which offered instruction in such skills as dressmaking, electrification, and carpentry. Participants received certificates and tools after completing the training, giving them the human and physical capital to begin work immediately as self-employed workers. Many labor exchange centers were established in China to retrain and redeploy displaced state sector workers in the private sector. Some of the proceeds from liquidating the assets of bankrupt state enterprises were used to redeploy unemployed workers. Such measures help to ease the rise in social tensions and inequality during transition periods.[9]

Conclusions

For growth to have an impact on poverty reduction, the assets of the poor must be augmented. This can be achieved either by investing in new assets, specifically, human capital, or by redistributing existing assets. This chapter has focused on investing in new assets by examining the quality and distribution of education and the causes and consequences of, and remedies for, large dispersions in educational attainment. When the quality of schooling is low and educational inequality is high, the poor are hurt most because human capital is often their main asset. Inadequate investment in the human capital of the poor exacerbates and perpetuates poverty and income inequality.

Improving the allocation of public expenditure in education is a key. Despite making efforts to this end, many countries have not been able to concentrate public investment on primary and secondary education. Inappropriate allocations of public expenditures have led to low average attainment per dollar spent on students, which affects mostly the poor. Governments need to reallocate public expenditure toward basic education, while at the same time enabling the private sector and public-private partnerships to increase efforts in higher education. Countries have compelling reasons to strengthen education at all levels. It can augment the poverty-reducing aspect of growth, in addition to improving welfare directly. It enables countries to participate effectively in the global economy.

Investing in education alone will not guarantee successful development or poverty reduction. Thus, this chapter went beyond education to issues related to the use of human capital, namely, the distribution of land and other productive assets and economywide policies. To reduce poverty, countries need a multidimensional strategy centered on people. There is the need to ensure access to education and health services and distribute them well; to facilitate fuller use of the human capital of the poor; and to empower the poor with land, equity capital, training, and job opportunities made possible by opening to international trade, investment, and ideas.

Notes

1. On the importance of asset distribution, see, for example, Ahluwalia (1976); Birdsall and Londoño (1997); Chenery and others (1974); Deininger and Squire (1998); Kanbur (2000); Knight and Sabot (1983); Lam and Levison (1991); Lanjouw and Stern (1989, 1998); Li, Squire, and Zou (1998); Ram (1990); Ravallion and Datt (1999); and Sen (1980, 1988). See annex table A3.5 for additional evidence.

2. Some arguments here apply to health, but due to space limits, this chapter focuses only on education.

3. Certain assumptions apply here. This conclusion holds if there is a competitive market and two factors of production: physical and human capital. It is also true if human capital is decomposed to skilled and unskilled labor.

4. These measures, however, are sensitive to national promotion policies. Scores on internationally comparable tests represent an improvement over traditional indicators, but they are available for only a few developing countries, and they are not comparable over time. Due to these problems they are not used here.

5. The same is true for industrial countries. A study estimated the cost of different kinds of national class size reduction policies in the United States and found

THE QUALITY OF GROWTH

the operational costs could be as large as US$2 billion to US$7 billion dollars a year (Brewer and others 1999).

6. There was heated debate over the "equity of what?" Sen (1980) sees individuals' levels of functionings, such as literacy and nutrition, as attributes to be equalized. Others see the opportunities people face as the attribute to be equalized (Arneson 1989; Cohen 1989; Roemer 1993). Yet others consider the amount of resources as the attribute to be equalized (Dworkin 1981).

7. Many studies have compared income, land, and wealth Gini coefficients (for example, Leipziger and others 1992 for Korea). However, no study has compared education Gini coefficients with those of income and land. Income Gini coefficients are available only for selected years (Deininger and Squire 1996):

	1970	1977	1983	1990	1992		1970	1976	1980	1985	1988
India	0.30	0.32	0.31	0.30	0.32	Korea	0.33	0.39	0.39	0.35	0.34

8. The cross-country, project-level data set included variables on education, per capita income, openness, government expenditure, and project performance. The project data covered 3,590 lending projects in 109 countries evaluated by the Operations Evaluation Department for 1974–94, with a rating of overall performance (satisfactory/not) and economic rates of return.

9. For more discussion on labor market and social protection issues, see Basu, Genicot, and Stiglitz 1999; Kanbur (2000); World Bank (1994) on old age crisis; and World Bank (2000i).

CHAPTER 4

SUSTAINING NATURAL CAPITAL

If we truly care about the future of our planet, we must stop leaving it to "them" out there to solve all the problems. It is up to us to save the world for tomorrow; it's up to you and me.

—Jane Goodall, *Reason for Hope*

Natural capital contributes enormously to human development and welfare. The term natural capital encompasses the sink functions, that is, air and water as receiving media for human-generated pollution and source functions, that is, production based on forests, fisheries, and mineral ores. Protecting sink functions is essential for human health. Protecting the productive or source functions is critical to the economic security of many who depend on these resources for their livelihoods. High-quality natural capital contributes to welfare indirectly as an essential part of the sustained production of economic goods and services. It also contributes to welfare directly as people derive enjoyment from pristine surroundings, old growth forests, and clean lakes and rivers in which to swim and fish.

Chapter 2 demonstrated the importance of human, natural, and physical capital to economic growth and welfare. Because of imperfect substitution, these assets need to grow at undistorted or fairly balanced rates to achieve sustainable economic growth. Distorted or unbalanced growth—signaled by especially rapid accumulation of physical capital, slow accumulation of human capital, and a draw down of natural capital—increases the volatility of growth, disproportionately hurting the poor. An economy fostering unbalanced growth is likely to suffer long-run stagnation (see annex 2).

Economies that derive much of their income from natural resources cannot sustain growth by substituting physical capital accumulation for deteriorating natural capital (López, Thomas, and Thomas 1998). Environmental degradation is likely to be most devastating for the poor, who often depend on natural resources for their income, with few possibilities for substituting other assets. Especially in the long run, growth approaches that pay attention to environmental quality and resource use efficiency contribute to accumulation, investment, economic growth, and human welfare (Munasinghe 2000).

Yet countries throughout the world have overexploited their forests, fisheries, and mineral wealth and polluted their water and air to accelerate short-term economic growth, with policymakers noting that their approach would increase the welfare of their citizens. While much natural capital has been sacrificed through deforestation, loss of biodiversity, soil degradation, and air and water pollution, access to safe water and sewage treatment and sanitation facilities has often shown improvements as economies grow. This chapter examines the reasons why natural capital tends to be abused and overexploited, especially during rapid economic growth, and what measures can be taken to correct the negative spiral of environmental decline.

The suitability of corrective actions will depend on the nature of the problem and the economic and institutional setting. For example, air quality may be improved by levying a pollution tax on industrial emissions, while production efficiency based on natural resources may be enhanced by such measures as assigning clear property rights to land or giving transferable quotas to fishers. Successful outcomes require active, yet selective, intervention by the state in collaboration with the private sector and civil society.

Extensive Losses

Air pollution from industrial emissions, car exhausts, and fossil fuels burned in homes kills more than 2.7 million people every year, mainly from respiratory damage, heart and lung diseases, and cancer (UNDP 1998). Of those who die prematurely, 2.2 million are rural poor exposed to indoor air pollution from the burning of traditional fuels. Air pollution also reduces economic output because of the loss of productive workdays. (See table 4.1 to understand the magnitude of the losses due to air pollution in different parts of the world. The numbers are simply meant to illustrate the possible impacts of environmental pollution; they are far from being noncontroversial estimates of environmental damage.)

Health costs associated with waterborne diseases and water pollution are also profound. In 1992, more than 2 million children under the age of five died from diseases caused by dirty water. Table 4.2 reports the findings of some studies on the health burden of water- and sanitation-related deficiencies and pollution effects.[1]

Table 4.1. Annual Health Costs Associated with Air Pollution

Region and city	Impact	Cost
China: 11 major cities	Economic costs of premature mortality and costs of illness	More than 20 percent of urban income
East Asia: Bangkok, Jakarta, Seoul, Kuala Lumpur, Manila	Number of premature deaths due to air pollution above WHO-defined safe limits	15,600
East Asia: Bangkok, Jakarta, Kuala Lumpur	Economic costs of premature mortality and costs of illness	More than 10 percent of urban income
Newly independent states: Russian Federation (Volgograd); Armenia (urban areas); Azerbaijan (national); Kazakhstan (national)	Number of premature deaths due to air pollution above WHO-defined safe limits	14,458

Note: The estimates are based on different studies applying different methodologies and are not comparable. In many cases, excess mortality is estimated using dose-response functions estimated for industrial economies for marginal changes in pollution, but then applied to nonmarginal changes, which tends to overestimate mortality reductions. Some studies use PPP-adjusted willingness to pay data from industrial economies; others use the cost of illness approach.
Sources: World Bank (1997a, 1999f).

Table 4.2. Annual Health Costs Associated with Waterborne Diseases and Pollution

Region or country	Impact	Cost
Vietnam	Infant deaths avoided yearly by providing access to clean water and sanitation	50,000
China	Premature deaths due to water-related diseases such as diarrhea, hepatitis, and intestinal nematodes	135,000
East Asia	Cost of waterborne diseases	US$30 billion a year
Moldova	Premature deaths	980–1,850
	Loss of workdays due to illness	2–4 million a year

Source: World Bank (1997a,c; 1999f).

Toxic effluents, such as dioxins, pesticides, organochlorines, grease, oil, acids, alkalis, and heavy metals such as cadmium and lead, from factories, mines, and chemical plants have contaminated major bodies of water in all parts of the world. Workers, farmers, and others who come in contact with the contaminants face severe health hazards. As with air pollution, the poor are hurt the most. As many as 25 million poor agricultural workers in the developing world (11 million in Africa alone) are poisoned by pesticides every year, and hundreds of thousands die (UNDP 1998). Fisheries, which provide a main source of protein for the poor, are also being destroyed by industrial discharges and water pollution. In Manila Bay, fish yields have declined 40 percent in the last 10 years (UNDP 1998). For a disturbing description of environmental degradation in India, as reported in the press, see box 4.1.

Recent estimates using DALYs suggest that premature death and illness due to major environmental health risks account for approximately one-fifth of the total burden of disease in the developing world (Murray and López 1996).[2] Of the main environmental risks, which include poor water supply, inadequate sanitation, indoor air pollution, urban air pollution, malaria, and agro-industrial chemicals and waste, 14 percent of the total disease burden is caused by poor water supplies, inadequate sanitation, and indoor air pollution. They affect predominantly children and women in poor families (Lvovsky and others 1999).

Overexploitation and degradation of natural resources are also enormous concerns. Soil degradation is a problem everywhere, especially in Asia and Africa. In China the costs may run as high as 5 percent of GDP (ADB 1997) and for several African countries the annual costs are 1–10 percent of agricultural GDP (Bojo 1996). While the annual losses are worrisome, the cumulative effects are alarming. Desertification, a direct consequence of soil degradation, is estimated to cost US$42 billion a year

---

Box 4.1. Environmental Degradation in India

In a special issue, *The Poisoning of India*, *India Today* (1999) reported the following information:

- Breathing urban India's air is equivalent to smoking 20 cigarettes a day. In the capital, New Delhi, the level of suspended particulate matter is more than twice the safe limit specified by the WHO. (Recent measurements of air pollution in New Delhi indicate that the level of total suspended particulates may be as high as five times the limit considered safe by the WHO.)
- Every year more than 40,000 people die prematurely from the effects of air pollution.
- More than 30 percent of garbage generated in cities is left unattended, becoming a fertile breeding ground for disease.
- Only 8 of India's 3,119 towns and cities have modern wastewater collection and treatment

facilities, another 209 have rudimentary facilities, and the rest have none at all.
- One-third of the urban population has no access to sanitation services. In Lucknow, 70 percent of the population sends its waste into the Gomti River.
- Most sewer lines date to colonial times. Thus, 93 percent of Mumbai's sewage is dumped untreated into the sea, killing virtually all large marine life along the coast.
- Dichlorodiphenyltrichloroethane, commonly known as DDT, and benzene hexachlorine, called BHC, account for as much as 40 percent of the total pesticides used in India. Both are neurotoxins that severely impair the central nervous system and cause muscular dystrophy. Chemical analysis reveals their presence in milk, vegetables, cereals, and fruits in increasing quantities.

in lost agricultural productivity alone. It directly puts some 250 million poor people at risk of starvation from reduced crop yields (UNDP 1998).

At least 10–12 million hectares of forest land disappear each year. Unsustainable logging practices and forest conversion to agriculture and pasturelands account for the bulk of the losses (Brown, Flavin, and French 1998; World Bank 1999d). Declining yields of timber and nontimber forest products, reduced soil and water conservation services, and loss of carbon sequestration functions translate into net economic losses of US$1 billion to US$2 billion a year to the global economy (calculated from World Bank data). In 1997, forest fires caused haze and smoke-related damage of US$4 billion in Indonesia and extensive damage in neighboring Malaysia and Singapore (EEPSEA 1998). Future generations will bear the cost of the associated, if hard to quantify, loss of biodiversity.

Like the forest fires in Indonesia, the impacts of local environmental neglect are not confined to political boundaries. Witness the increasing desertification, coastal zone degradation, global climate change, transboundary acid rain, and depletion of the ozone layer (GEF 1998; Watson and others 1998). Global climate change during the 21st century could result in increases in the intensity and frequency of floods and droughts, inundation of low-lying coastal areas, more frequent outbreaks of infectious diseases, and accelerated dieback of forests. Climate change will also hurt food security by reducing agricultural output in developing countries and poses a threat to human health and safety. It could cost the world economy as much as US$550 billion a year and developing countries are likely to bear an inequitable proportion of the burden (Furtado and others 1999).

"Genuine savings" provides a useful concept to capture the degradation of natural capital that can be used to assess the environmental health of countries. Genuine savings equal gross domestic savings minus depreciation of physical capital, minus depletion of minerals and energy, minus net depletion of forests, minus pollution damage, plus investments in human capital. For the developing world as a whole, in 1997 gross domestic savings were 25 percent of GDP. Net domestic savings (after correcting for the depreciation of physical capital) were about 16 percent of GDP, but corrected further for depletion of natural capital (such as forest, energy, and minerals) and damage from carbon dioxide emissions, the domestic savings were a little more than 10 percent of GDP (World Bank 1999e). After including human capital investment, the genuine savings rose to about 14 percent. This includes Nepal, where forest depletion alone was estimated at 10.3 percent, overwhelming the country's gross domestic savings of 10 percent, and the Russian Federation, where depletion of energy resources (oil, coal, and natural gas) reduced savings by more than 9 percent per year.

Significant Benefits of Environmental Action

From an economic point of view, not all pollution is to be fully controlled nor all natural resource degradation is to be fully reversed. Pollution and natural resource degradation are to be controlled to the point where the marginal (social) damages equal the marginal (social) costs of abatement or control, that is, the optimal level of environmental protection.

The present discounted cost of providing everyone in China with access to clean water within 10 years, for example, is US$40 billion, and the present value of benefits is US$80 billion to US$100 billion (World Bank 1997a). Doing the same in Indonesia would cost an estimated US$12 billion to US$15 billion, with corresponding benefits of US$25 billion to US$30 billion. In Moldova piped water of adequate quality would cost US$23 million to US$38 million a year to provide, but would bring benefits of US$70 million to US$120 million (World Bank 1999f). Controlling air pollution in China would cost an estimated US$50 billion, but would yield benefits of about US$200 billion in reduced illness and death (World Bank 1997a).

With the payoffs so large, why do environmental degradation and destruction continue?[3] The main reason is that private returns on investment in environmental protection are significantly smaller than private costs (Dasgupta and Mäler 1994; Hammer and Shetty 1995). Many of the benefits are distributed to society at large, now and in the future, rather than to the private agent making the investments. Thus, individuals, who see only their own private, short-term gains, seldom factor the cost of degradation—spread inequitably across the current generation and affecting future generations as well—into their decisionmaking. This classic case of externalities and market failure provides strong justification for public policy actions to create markets or marketlike conditions that align private incentives with the social costs and benefits of providing environmental services.

Policy distortions reflecting undervaluation of the environment contribute to pollution and degradation (Dasgupta and Mäler 1994). For example, agricultural subsidies on inputs and price supports for outputs make forest management noncompetitive and create pressures to convert forests to pastures. Energy subsidies to keep consumer prices low contribute to overconsumption and excessive pollution. Tax exemptions, subsidies to firms operating on frontier land, road construction in ecologically fragile areas, and a host of other short-sighted policies also lead to degradation and mismanagement of resources and threaten vulnerable populations who live in these areas (Chomitz and Gray 1996; Cropper, Griffiths, and Mani 1997). By removing subsidies and imposing environmental taxes, policy reforms can alleviate distortions and allow prices to reach their optimal level.

Several other contributory factors and false notions stand in the way of efficient management of natural capital: the grow-now-and-clean-up-later mind-set, corruption, ill-defined property rights, and inadequate funds for environmental management. Often, information gaps prevent a full understanding of the causes and consequences of environmental degradation, and public indifference hinders their resolution. Fostering international action is difficult despite existing momentum for environmental protection (box 4.2). The relative contribution of these factors differs from country to country and needs to be assessed before effective public actions can be determined.

The Growth–Natural Capital–Welfare Nexus

After dispelling the idea that environmental degradation can wait for redress after other pressing reforms have been addressed (the grow-now-and-clean-up-later mind-set), we will explore empirical evidence that links growth to the quality of natural capital.

Grow Now and Clean Up Later

The growing evidence to the contrary has not dispelled the perception that the environment is a luxury good that will be demanded as incomes rise with economic growth. As a result, developing countries tend to ignore environmental concerns as policymakers focus almost exclusively on accelerating economic growth. They support their position by citing examples of industrial countries that paid scant attention to environmental degradation in the early phases of their growth and arrested and reversed the problem later. However, they ignore the potential enormity of economic, social, and ecological costs and the reality that sometimes the damage is irreversible.

While air and water pollution levels appear to be reversible, their impacts on human well-being often are not. Promises of future remedial action can hardly compensate for welfare losses by the present generation. Only a policy of clean growth is consistent with intergenerational equity. Furthermore, investing in pollution control up-front will yield positive returns in other areas. For example, improved health outcomes can lead to a more favorable accumulation of human capital and more sustained growth.[4]

A grow-now-and-clean-up-later approach also tends to be inequitable; the poor and disadvantaged suffer the brunt of environmental pollution and resource degradation. For instance, when industrial toxic effluents and

Box 4.2. Worldwide Efforts for Environmental Action

In June 1992, representatives of 178 nations met in Rio de Janeiro to agree on measures for ensuring environmentally and socially sustainable development. The Earth Summit captured government interest in translating broad policy goals into concrete actions. The commitment of leaders from around the world to sustainable development was enshrined in Agenda 21, the key document of the summit. Agenda 21 activities are organized under environmental and development themes: quality of life, efficient use of natural resources, protection of the global commons, management of human settlements, and sustainable economic growth. Agenda 21 recognizes that the persistence of severe poverty in several parts of the world alongside a standard of living based on wasteful consumption of resources in other parts is incompatible with sustainability, and that environmental management needs to be practiced by developing and industrial countries alike. A consensus was reached that, to implement Agenda 21, countries should prepare a national sustainable development strategy.

In 1987, donors of the International Development Agency initiated national environmental action plans for all agency borrowers. Before receiving funds, borrowers were required to present a long-term strategy for maintaining the country's natural environment, the health and safety of its population, and its cultural heritage during economic development efforts. This practice spread to other countries, and 100 nations have prepared national sustainable development strategies or national environmental action plans to guide their thinking on environmental management. These plans have been useful in identifying environmental problems, fostering national ownership of environmental planning, and creating the political climate necessary to encourage effective action for policy reforms. They have also been useful in identifying country policy frameworks and designing a strategic vision for the environment (Bojo and Segnestam 1999).

While essential for highlighting important environmental issues, the strategies and plans are less effective in identifying priorities for action and making explicit the process of policy reform to achieve desirable outcomes. The documentation and dissemination of successful cases and specific experiences in environmental management becomes crucial. The World Bank has been playing an important facilitating role through its efforts at integrating the environment in Bank policy dialog (Warford and others 1994; Warford, Munasinghe, and Cruz 1997).

Source: World Bank (1997d).

other pollutants degrade water quality, the poor often lack access to purified municipal water supplies and the resources to invest in water filters and other purification systems. Air pollution also disproportionately hurts the poor, as they tend to live closer to roads where pollution levels are highest and cannot afford to switch to cleaner fuels for indoor use (UNDP 1998). These distributional impacts aggravate income inequalities and can lead to serious social conflicts. Thus, paying attention to the environment while accelerating growth is fully consistent with a poverty reduction strategy.

The irreversible loss of genetic material and the potential threat of ecosystem collapse provide other compelling reasons for rejecting a grow-now-and-clean-up-later approach. Some damage can never be undone. Habitat destruction has resulted in the irreversible loss of terrestrial and aquatic biodiversity worldwide. Marine pollution and destructive fishing techniques have damaged a large proportion of coral reefs in East Asia and threaten much of the ocean's animal and plant life (Loh and others 1998).

The experiences of high-income countries show that the health costs of delayed pollution control can exceed the prevention costs, although in comparing them, the difference in the time of their occurrence and resulting uncertainty should ideally be accounted for. For example, the cost of cleanup and compensation to victims of itai-itai disease, caused by cadmium poisoning; Yokkaichi asthma, the result of excessive exposure to sulfur emissions; and Minamata disease, or mercury poisoning, are from 1.4 to 102 times the cost of prevention (Kato 1996). In addition to the impacts on human health, the high cleanup costs of widespread dumping of toxic wastes by U.S. industrial firms illustrate another limitation of the grow-now-and-clean-up-later approach (Harr 1995).

Does Faster or Slower Economic Growth Ensure Protection of Natural Capital?

Both fast- and slow-growing economies have experienced environmental degradation, but to different degrees. Analysis of GDP growth and an index of natural capital quality show a negative correlation coefficient (see figure 1.5). By looking at the link between rapid growth and various components of natural capital degradation at a more disaggregated level, one can get a better idea of the strength and direction of the relationships.

Belying East Asia's phenomenal record of economic growth and poverty reduction is its poor environmental record. In 1995, China was home to 15 of the 20 most polluted cities in the world, as measured by the concentration of total suspended particulates (World Bank 1999e). Air pollution, especially high levels of total suspended particulates, has resulted in premature deaths and severe health damage in urban areas such as Bangkok, Jakarta, Manila, and several cities in China (see table 4.1). Countries that experienced rapid growth in the context of economic reforms in the 1980s—China, Korea, Malaysia, and Thailand—saw carbon dioxide emissions per capita that doubled or tripled after the reforms and growth acceleration (table 4.3).

Natural resources fared poorly as well. Deforestation rates have been high and remain so in most countries (table 4.3). About 20 percent of vegetated land in East Asia suffers soil degradation from waterlogging, erosion, and overgrazing. Severe land degradation in China, Thailand, and Vietnam threatens several ecosystems with irreversible damage

Table 4.3.   Trade, Growth, Poverty, and Environmental Degradation, Selected Years
(percent, unless otherwise indicated)

Region and economy	Trade Annual growth of merchandise export volume, 1980–94	Growth Annual growth of GNP per capita, 1970–95	Poverty Percentage of population living on less than US$1 a day (PPP) various years	Indicators of natural capital Annual deforestation (percent change) 1990–95	Total suspended particulates in capital cities (micrograms per cubic meter)	Percentage increase in carbon dioxide emissions per capita, 1980–96
East Asia						
China	12.2	6.9	29.4 (1993)	0.1	377	86.7
Hong Kong, China	15.4	5.7	< 1	0.0	—	15.6
Indonesia	9.9	4.7	14.5 (1993)	1.0	271	100.0
Korea, Rep. of	11.9	10.0	< 1	0.2	84	172.7
Malaysia	13.3	4.0	5.6 (1989)	2.4	85	180.0
Philippines	5.0	0.6	27.5 (1988)	3.5	200	12.5
Singapore	13.3	5.7	< 1	0.0	—	63.6
Thailand	16.4	5.2	< 1	2.6	223	277.8
Latin America						
Argentina	1.9	–0.4	—	0.3	97 (Cordoba city)	–2.0
Bolivia	–0.3	–0.7	7.1 (1989)	1.2	—	62.5
Brazil	6.2	—	28.7 (1989)	0.5	86 (Rio = 139)	13.3
Chile	7.3	1.8	15.0 (1992)	0.4	—	36.0
Costa Rica	6.6	0.7	18.9 (1989)	3.0	—	27.3
Mexico	13.0	0.9	14.9 (1992)	0.9	279	2.7
Peru	2.4	–1.1	49.4 (1994)	0.3	—	–21.4
Uruguay	0.9	0.2	—	0.0	—	–15.0
Venezuela, RB	1.1	–1.1	11.8 (1991)	1.1	53	10.7

— Not available.

Sources: World Bank (1997a, 1999e); see also annex 4.

(World Bank 1999b). Biodiversity in 50 to 75 percent of coastlines and protected marine areas in East Asia is classified as highly threatened.

Not all indicators show worsening environmental conditions among the fast-growing economies in Asia. Access to clean water and sanitation increased rapidly in China, Korea, Malaysia, and Thailand. In 1995, the share of the population with access to safe water rose from 71 percent in 1982 to 89 percent in Malaysia, from 66 to 89 percent in Thailand, from 39 to 65 percent in Indonesia, and from 65 to 83 percent in the Philippines. Sanitation service availability rose from 46 to 96 percent in Thailand, from 30 to 55 percent in Indonesia, and from 57 to 77 percent in the Philippines (World Bank 1999e). Though still at low levels in Cambodia, the Lao People's Democratic Republic, and Vietnam, access to safe water and sanitation has been steadily increasing with economic growth (World Bank 1999b,e).

However, it is not just fast growth that leads to problems of natural capital degradation. Like East Asian countries, slow-growing Latin American countries have seen improvements in access to clean water and sanitation (World Bank 1999e), but have also suffered environmental deterioration. Most have experienced extensive deforestation, especially of ecologically sensitive areas and steep slopes; widespread soil degradation; overfishing and water pollution in coastal zones; water contamination from agrochemicals; and pesticide poisoning of people and livestock. While air pollution is not as widespread a problem as in Asia, in part because of the relatively low growth of industrialization (table 4.3), it is a serious concern in Mexico City, Rio de Janeiro, and Santiago. Because of low growth, highly skewed income distributions, inadequate investments in education and health, and political instability, poverty has remained stubbornly high, creating vicious cycles of increasing natural resource degradation and further loss of income (see also box 4.3).

Thus, neither rapid nor slow growth is an automatic ally of natural capital (Thomas and Belt 1997). For example, in the 1980s, differences in air pollution and traffic congestion between slow-growing Manila and fast-growing Bangkok were minimal (Hammer and Shetty 1995). However, fast growth, with increasing urbanization, industrial expansion, and exploitation of renewable and nonrenewable resources, places pressure on the environment such that many indicators show a decline in the quality of natural capital during growth periods.

Yet, growth creates conditions for environmental improvement by creating demand for better environmental quality and making resources available for supplying it. Does this imply the existence of an environmental Kuznets curve? As incomes rise, does environmental quality first deteriorate and then start to improve? If environmental goods are normal consumer goods with positive income elasticity of demand that is greater than unity at certain income levels, then quality will improve beyond the threshold income level. López (1997) suggests that environmental goods, such as clean air and water and sewage treatment, which directly affect health and generate local externalities, are likely to be normal goods with a high income elasticity of demand. Thus, they are likely to improve after a period of decline during a growth period.

Most empirical studies have focused on indicators of the sink function of environmental quality, such as the concentration of suspended particulates in air, the biochemical oxygen demand of water, the level of carbon dioxide and sulfur dioxide emissions, and the prevalence of inorganic industrial pollutants

Box 4.3. Population, Poverty, and the Environment

Analysis of the poverty-population-environment nexus is complex. Population growth has often been blamed for poverty and for environmental degradation (Cropper and Griffiths 1994; Pearce and Warford 1993). However, the converse argument contends that poverty and environmental degradation are the causes of population growth, not the consequences of it. Both views are partial; it needs to be recognized that the three factors are interlinked (Cleaver and Schreiber 1994; Dasgupta 1995; Ekbom and Bojo 1999; Mink 1993). The strength of these linkages will differ from situation to situation, and the policy recommendations will depend on a host of factors, including type of resource, density and rate of growth of population, institutional arrangements, and laws regulating the use of the resource (López 1998b). As a result, no general conclusions about the linkages between population, environment, and poverty are available.

The following example from Dasgupta (1995) gives some insight into the complicated nature of the nexus. In rural settings much labor is needed even for simple tasks, such as collecting clean water or fuelwood for cooking. In addition, members of rural households devote time to growing food, caring for livestock, and producing simple marketable products. Children are needed as extra workers, even when parents are in their prime. Small households are simply not viable; each one needs many hands. As the community's resources are depleted, more hands are necessary to gather fuel and water for daily use. More children are produced, further damaging the environment and providing an incentive to enlarge the household even more.

Factors that influence the parental demand for children can reverse this destructive spiral. The most potent policy will use many of the factors simultaneously. Good economic policies, secure tenure rights, and political stability can all alleviate the population pressures. Providing cheap fuel and potable water will reduce the need for extra hands and lower the demand for children. Family planning services allied to reproductive health services will help bridge the unmet needs for contraception, and a literacy and employment drive for women that empowers them in decisions of family size becomes crucial.

(Galeotti and Lanza 1999; Grossman and Krueger 1995; Ravallion, Heil, and Jalan 1997; Roberts and Grimes 1997; Selden and Song 1994; Shafik 1994; Stern, Common, and Barbier 1996), finding some support for an environmental Kuznets curve.

Hettige, Mani, and Wheeler (1998), using international data, measured the relationship between water pollution from industrial discharges and per capita income. The study showed that pollution first increases with development, peaking at a per capita income of about US$12,000, and then levels off for all observable values. The study concluded, "economic development remains far short of a Kuznets-style happy ending in the water sector" (p. 26) and suggests that total emissions will remain constant with income growth unless other factors intervene.[5]

The quality of natural resources is less likely to follow a Kuznets-curve pattern than pollution, because they are typically factors of production rather than consumer goods. Furthermore, the externalities associated with the destruction of natural resources are mainly global and less likely to be internalized in local demand (López 1997). As a consequence, a growing economy imposes even greater demands on natural resources and makes management interventions crucial.[6]

Countries do not need to wait until incomes reach the Kuznets-curve turning point. São Paulo curbed severe pollution within a generation, even while millions remained poor. Fast-growing Shanghai, the largest industrial base in China, has produced lower sulfur dioxide loads than slow-growing Sichuan (World Bank 2000d). These and other cases illustrate methods— which include characteristics such as appropriate regulatory regimes, centralized and market-based instruments—for environmental conservation, policy and legislative frameworks, institutional capacity, and technological options that help prevent pollution and protect resources (Panayotou 1997).

Evidence suggests that flexing of the Kuznets curve is both possible and necessary.[7] Whether economies are fast or slow growing, many indicators of natural resources—deforestation, fisheries depletion, soil degradation, coastal zone pollution—have been deteriorating. Because natural resources are important as factors of production, increasing growth tends to put increasing demands on them. Many of the externalities associated with their overexploitation, such as carbon sequestration and biodiversity loss, are global. As a consequence, local governments often do not consider the repercussions of misusing or exhausting their resources.

Other components of natural capital, such as air and water quality and access to sewage and sanitation services, are typically normal consumer goods. For these goods with an income elasticity greater than unity, income growth is likely to be associated with improvements in quality. Though some empirical evidence suggests the existence of environmental Kuznets curves for a limited set of indicators, the costs of inaction can be extremely high, because many developing countries cannot reach the turnaround income level for decades.

Two indicators, access to clean water and sanitation, appear to improve in both fast- and slow-growth scenarios and testify to the efficacy of interventions, but a careful look at the benefits and costs is required to determine whether the pace of improvements is optimum.

Asset-Income Inequality and the Quality of Natural Capital

A more equitable distribution of income and assets might be associated with improvements in key indicators of environmental quality, such as deforestation and water pollution. For example, if small-scale farmers must use marginal land because large-scale landowners occupy the best land, the inequitable land distribution may drive deforestation (Ekbom and Bojo 1999). Adoption of clean fuels and more energy efficient technologies implies that the marginal propensity to emit carbon dioxide declines as income rises. Thus income redistribution can speed emissions reduction (Holtz-Eakin and Selden 1995). In a study of 42 countries, Ravallion, Heil, and Jalan (1997) estimated a large positive coefficient between carbon dioxide emissions per capita and the Gini coefficient of income inequality. This study suggests that growth that reduces income inequality and poverty could lead to a decline in emission rates.

Growth Can Complement Protection of Natural Capital

A diagram can help to show that growth and protection of natural capital complement each other (figure 4.1). Consider a preindustrial economy with a low rate of growth and a pristine environment, represented as point A. The country attempts to accelerate economic growth by investing in industry and exploiting the potential of globalization. In an ideal situation, it would seek to balance accelerated growth with high environmental quality, which can be graphically represented as a vertical move toward point E or to one to its right. However, even a well-managed environmental strategy, which could be shown as a move from point A to point F, may not totally

Many combinations of growth and environmental quality are possible

Figure 4.1. Growth Paths and Environmental Quality

Per capita income

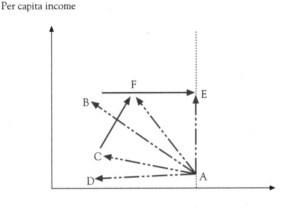

Environmental quality

Source: Author.

eliminate quality deterioration in both sink and source functions, although the negative impact on natural capital would be relatively small and reversible.[8] While countries embarking on a path of sustainable development can incorporate environmental policies directly into their economic strategy at any time, most countries have followed the grow-now-and-clean-up-later approach (table 4.4).

The fast growers among developing countries, such as China, Indonesia, Korea, and Thailand, experienced a situation that could be represented by a move from point A to point B, where they paid severely in terms of deteriorating environmental quality. Many of the slower growers, such as Ghana and Nepal, showed a move from point A to point C on figure 4.1 and also suffered considerable environmental damage. Still others in Central and South America and Africa followed policies that failed to stimulate growth while still harming the environment; their actions would be simulated by an arrow from point A to point D.[9]

The economies represented at points B, C, and D have incurred serious losses from ecosystem damage: disease, death, degraded forests and bodies of water, polluted air, and more. Industrial and developing economies that ignored the degradation of their natural capital have learned that the grow-now-and-clean-up later strategy created costs that are difficult or impossible to recoup. For example, the United States will need to spend tens of billions

Table 4.4. Classification of Selected Countries by Growth-Environment Trajectory

A to B: High growth and environmental degradation		A to C: Medium growth and environmental degradation		A to D: Low growth with environmental degradation		A to F: Growth with environmental protection	
Deforestation	Carbon dioxide emissions	Deforestation	Carbon dioxide emissions	Deforestation	Carbon dioxide emissions	Deforestation	Carbon dioxide emissions
Indonesia	China	El Salvador	El Salvador	Algeria	Mexico	Botswana	
Malaysia	India	Ghana	Pakistan	Cameroon			
Sri Lanka	Indonesia	Guatemala	Panama	Haiti			
Thailand	Korea,	Mozambique		Mexico			
	Republic of	Nepal		Nicaragua			
	Malaysia	Pakistan		Zambia			
	Thailand	Panama					

Note: Deforestation rates depicted by annual averages for 1990–95, carbon dioxide emissions are from 1980 through 1996. High growth is defined as per capita income growth of more than 2.3 percent a year in both the 1980s and the 1990s; medium growth includes countries that maintained a positive growth of per capita income in both decades, or improved growth of at least 2 percentage points a year higher in the 1990s than the 1980s; the rest are classified as low-growth countries.

Source: World Bank (2000c).

of dollars to restore the damage caused to the Florida Everglades by the development of irrigation canals for sugarcane cultivation.

Incorporating Environmental Sustainability in Growth Policies

Many countries have integrated environmental concerns and growth policies. The following four cases show how this can be done. The cases were chosen to illustrate success stories in pollution management and natural resource preservation and to highlight the types of interventions required to achieve specific environmental goals. For more case studies of instruments successfully suited to particular settings, see Thomas, Kishor, and Belt (1998), World Bank (1997e, 2000d).

Costa Rica: Conserving Forests and Mitigating Climate Change

The rich biodiversity of Costa Rica attracts wealthy ecotourists from around the world. Yet in the 1980s deforestation rates climbed to more than 3 percent a year. To protect this valuable natural resource, Costa Rica designed one of the most innovative and workable systems of forest protection in the world. It surveyed the marketed and nonmarketed benefits of the environmental services of the forests and identified who bears the costs and who derives the benefits (table 4.5). It calculated annual values per hectare of US$29 to US$87 for primary forest and US$21 to US$63 for secondary forest. The survey showed that landowners or the government (in the case of national parks) bore the costs of habitat preservation, while

Table 4.5. Environmental Services of Costa Rican Forests and Their Beneficiaries

Type of benefit	Beneficiaries		
	Landowner	Country	World
Sustainable wood production	X		
Hydropower production potential		X	
Water supply purification		X	
Soil stabilization and regulation of hydrologic flow		X	
Scenic beauty, ecotourism uses, and "existence" value		X	X
Carbon sequestration			X
Biodiversity preservation			X

Source: Castro and others (1997).

substantial benefits went to foreign interests. Thus, Costa Rica decided to create markets for some environmental benefits (Castro and others 1997).

Of the several environmental benefits forests provide, Costa Rica has been most successful in capturing carbon sequestration and watershed protection. The government acts as an intermediary in the sale of these services to international and domestic buyers. Funds from the sales (and from an earmarked fuel tax of 5 percent) go to the landowners for preserving the forest cover on their lands. Contracts for more than 50,000 hectares of forest protection were established in 1997. Before that time, cumulative protected areas had encompassed only 79,000 hectares.

Costa Rica has also attracted international investments to compensate landowners who promote carbon sequestration by maintaining forests. Certifiable tradable offsets can be used to sell greenhouse gas offsets in the international marketplace. The first batch was sold in July 1996. Between 1996 and 1998, sales were negotiated bilaterally, but recently Costa Rica started working with brokerage firms in Chicago and New York to establish the certifiable trade offset as a freely tradable commodity, similar to emissions trading in sulfur dioxide in the United States (Chomitz, Constantino, and Brenes 1998).

Costa Rica demonstrates the practical success of creating green markets and implementing green taxes to reduce environmental damage. The potential for replication elsewhere is good, but it depends to a large extent on completion of an international agreement on carbon offsets and acceptance by all parties of the Clean Development Mechanism of the Framework Convention on Climate Change.

China: Controlling Water Pollution with a Levy

The pollution levy, an emissions charge covering thousands of factories in China, is one of the few economic instruments with a long, documented history in a developing country. Although the levy has been used for several decades, serious studies of its efficacy have appeared only recently (Wang and Wheeler 1996).

The system, which has been expanded since 1982, has been implemented in most of China's counties and cities and includes 300,000 factories that are charged for their emissions. The National Environment Protection Agency's regulations specify variations in effluent standards by sector and fees by pollutant. Any enterprise whose effluent discharge exceeds a legal standard must pay a levy. Levies are charged only on the most polluting emission from each source. The levy differs from a tax, which would cover each unit of pollutant, not just those in excess of a certain standard.

Between 1987 and 1993 total organic water pollution fell for the state-regulated industries that reported discharges to the National Environment Protection Agency (Wang and Wheeler 1996). With output growth of 10 percent a year, China experienced an especially impressive decline in pollution per unit of output. While provincial total discharges declined at a median rate of 22 percent, pollution intensities fell at a median rate of 50 percent. Econometric analysis shows that much of the decline was attributable to the levy.

Significant variation in effective levy rates across provinces is explained by local assessments of pollution impacts and local capacities to enforce national standards. Allowing for such regional differences enhanced the feasibility and effectiveness of the pollution levy system.

Since 1991, the authorities have collected more than US$240 million per year in levies.[10] Approximately 60 percent of the funds finance industrial pollution prevention and control and represent some 15 percent of total investment in these activities, providing an additional incentive for firms to abate. The remainder goes to local agencies for institutional development and administrative costs (Wang and Chen 1999). In addition to helping regulate pollution, the levies help build the monitoring and regulation capacities of local enforcement agencies and reinforce the incentives for effective regulation.

Indonesia: Fighting Pollution with Information

The government can set standards for maximum allowable pollution levels relatively easily, but monitoring and enforcing compliance can be difficult. Indonesia's Environment Impact Management Agency faced compliance challenges in the late 1980s and resorted to voluntary agreements, out-of-court settlements, and other ad hoc approaches that had a limited impact on pollution control.

Seeking a more sustainable approach, the agency developed the Program for Pollution Control, Evaluation, and Rating (PROPER), which receives pollution data from factories, analyzes and rates their environmental performance, and disseminates the ratings to the public (Wheeler and Afsah 1996; World Bank 2000d). The agency hoped that publicizing the performance ratings would encourage local communities to pressure nearby factories that scored poor ratings to clean up their operations. It also hoped to influence polluters through financial markets, which were expected to react to the ratings. To encourage firms to improve their performance, it also established a program for recognizing excellent environmental pollution control practices.

The agency decided to focus on water pollution first. It gathered data on water pollution from factories through questionnaires and rigorous on-site inspections. The government compiled information on 187 highly polluting factories and ranked the companies by level of emissions. The data were combined into a single performance rating keyed to five categories: gold, green, and blue signified compliance; red and black represented noncompliance.

The agency disclosed the results in stages, first publicly recognizing the best performers and giving the others six months to clean up before their bad ratings would be revealed. This phased approach gave factories time to adjust to the program and increased the likelihood of compliance. Between June and September 1995, half the firms that had been rated noncompliant observed the new mandates. This suggests that PROPER created powerful incentives for pollution control. In many instances firms have realized that better environmental management reduces the costs of production, creating additional incentives for them to clean up their production practices. Encouraged by these initial efforts, the agency planned to rate 2,000 plants by 2000.

Indonesia's PROPER program goes beyond the command-and-control approach traditionally used with limited success to regulate polluters. The rating system is unique in that it allows for multiple outcomes. The final choice lies with the firm and depends on its resources for pollution control, the perceived benefits to cleaning up, and its overall corporate strategy. PROPER relies on public disclosure and public pressure to bring polluting firms in line with environmental regulations. By involving the people affected by pollution, PROPER ensures a bargaining equilibrium between firms and stakeholders. The government's role is to set the rules of the game, monitor the level of discharges, take punitive action when necessary, and act as the final arbiter.

Europe's Blue Flag Campaign: Increasing Awareness of the Coastal Environments

The European Blue Flag Campaign, operating through a network of national organizations, is coordinated by the Foundation for Environmental Education in Europe (Thomas, Kishor, and Belt 1998). It encourages citizen understanding and appreciation of the coastal environment and the incorporation of environmental concerns into the decisionmaking of coastal authorities. The European Commission finances approximately 25 percent of the campaign's budget, which now amounts to more than US$1 million, and private sponsors finance the remainder.

A beach or marina receives a Blue Flag if it meets three sets of criteria relating to the environmental quality of the locality, management and safety, and environmental education and information. Recipients must meet mandatory and guideline criteria.

Based on maps, photographs, water samples, and a completed questionnaire, a national jury nominates sites for a European jury, which makes the final selection of Blue Flag recipients by unanimous vote. The results are announced at the beginning of June before the main holiday season commences. The campaign has attracted several commercial sponsors in addition to schoolchildren, who have cleaned local beaches to maintain the high standards required by the Blue Flag judges. Over the years the standards of environmental quality needed to win the award have been successively raised to provide dynamic incentives for better environmental management. More than 1,000 coastal localities, most of them in Denmark, Greece, and Spain, have been awarded the Blue Flag.

Governments see the Blue Flag program as an efficient way to promote environmental awareness and increase tourism revenues. Private sponsors view it as an opportunity to attract more tourists. The initiative brings the government, the private sector, and the public into partnership and generates competition between jurisdictions, which pushes environmental standards higher.

Rethinking the State's Role

Attributing environmental degradation to distorted policies, damaging subsidies, missing markets, externalities, and incomplete public knowledge puts the state in the position of a catalyst for environmental protection and management. However, the mixed record on government interventions has motivated extensive rethinking of the policies the state should foster. To achieve the greatest impact, government should intervene selectively (see box 4.4).

Streamline Subsidies and Implement Environmental Taxes

In principle, subsidies support the incomes of the poor; in practice, they often increase inequalities, drain the public budget, accelerate the depletion of natural resources, and degrade the environment. The global cost of subsidies in agriculture, energy, road transport, and water is estimated at US$800 billion a year, with about two-thirds of the expenses incurred in OECD countries (de Moor and Calamai 1997). In recent years subsidies have been coming down remarkably rapidly, especially in developing countries. In China, coal subsidies fell from US$750 million in 1993 to US$250 million in 1995 (UNDP 1998). Subsidy rates fell from 61 percent in 1984 to 11 percent in 1995 (World Bank 1997e). Removal of perverse

Box 4.4. Development and the Environment

World Development Report 1992 (World Bank 1992, p. 2) addressed the challenge of finding the right balance between development and environment.

> *The protection of the environment is an essential part of development. Without adequate environmental protection, development is undermined; without development, resources will be inadequate for needed investments, and environmental protection will fail...growth brings with it the risk of appalling environmental damage. Alternatively, it could bring with it better environmental protection, cleaner air and water, and the virtual elimination of acute poverty. Policy choices will make the difference.*

The report highlighted two sets of policies for sustainable development. The first builds on positive, win-win links, such as removing environmentally damaging subsidies; clarifying property rights; accelerating the provision of sanitation; providing clean water; providing education, especially for girls; and empowering local people. The second seeks to break the negative links between environment and development by such means as establishing standards, using market-based instruments such as green taxes, and taking collaborative approaches to pollution management.

The report emphasized that although the costs of adequately protecting the environment were large, the costs of inaction would be monumental. It is rational to act sooner rather than later.

Eight years later, the prescriptions of the report are still valid. Experience in natural resource management and environmental protection shows that finding the right mix of policies for environmentally sustainable development is even more feasible today if it is given a high priority.

subsidies has three benefits: reducing environmental degradation, promoting equality, and conserving budgetary resources.

Not all subsidies result in bad outcomes, and good subsidies should be encouraged. Inaccessibility to water and sanitation services accounts for a significant loss of life, especially among women and children in poor households. Studies show that these households have a high willingness to pay for reliable and adequate supplies of these services. Subsidies targeted to these households to purchase water and sanitation services, perhaps from the private sector, is probably a cost-effective intervention to mitigate negative health impacts and reduce poverty by promoting human capital accumulation.

On the other side of the ledger, green taxes on activities that cause environmental degradation provide a powerful way to fight pollution and resource depletion. Green taxes can be particularly useful in managing emissions that contribute to air and water pollution. Taxing the use of coal by industry or the use of gasoline in motor vehicles will reduce excessive resource use and emissions and raise tax revenues; thus, green taxes can provide a win-win approach to managing environmental quality with growth (World Bank 1997d). Pollution taxes are most effective when a well-established regulatory framework with emissions norms and an efficient system of monitoring and enforcement are in place. Effective green taxes also encourage the use of cleaner energy sources, such as solar power.

A switch from income to consumption taxes can also benefit the environment and growth. The production and consumption of luxury goods often make heavy demands on environmental and natural resources. Consumption taxes can curb the overexploitation of these goods. Progressive consumption taxes also promote equity, and by encouraging savings, they promote economic growth (Frank 1998).

In addition, green taxes can generate the funds needed to promote environmental management. The public sector needs money for its facilitating role, but funds often fall short of needs. Any strategy for environmental management must identify sources of adequate financing. Many developing countries now rely more on green taxes to create funds for environmental improvements than they have done in the past (World Bank 1999f).

Move from Central Control to Partnerships

In the past, governments relied too much on central control, which required extensive monitoring of compliance, for environmental management. The combination of command-and-control policy and inadequate resources for monitoring and enforcement ensured program failure. Policymakers are learning that community members affected by pollution can complement regulation. The involvement of local communities and civil society has other advantages. In rural areas, especially, they are both the source of key environmental information and the custodians of traditional environmental knowhow. Thus, they can identify and implement strategies that balance growth with environmental protection.

Where undervaluation of a resource can lead to its degradation, proper valuation of its economic and social benefits can ensure that its contribution is fully considered in decisionmaking (Dixon and Sherman 1990; Pearce and Warford 1993; Ruitenbeek 1989). Measurements of "green gross national product" and genuine savings are gaining prominence as a way to incorporate sustainability in traditional economic planning (Hamilton and Lutz 1996; World Bank 1997d). The gap between estimated total economic value and actual private valuation cannot be easily bridged, but evidence suggests that the state can do it by creating markets or by setting up appropriate institutions and legal statutes that create marketlike conditions and by generating adequate financial flows (see the illustrative case of Costa Rica).

Based on data for 77 developing countries, a significant positive association between educational spending and increase in forest cover was found (correlation matrix available upon request). This suggests that added impetus to environmental sustainability can come from state and private sector cooperation to raise the educational attainment of the population.

Recognizing the limitations of state intervention and the need for active partnerships in environmental management, governments are looking for new ways to promote environmental management. Spreading knowledge about the full consequences of environmental neglect to all stakeholders, together with a clear framework of accountability and environmental liabilities, can have a powerful impact (Thomas, Kishor, and Belt 1998). Alliances between state regulatory agencies and industrial firms are helping to control pollution in many countries (Hanrahan and others 1998; Schmidheiny and Zorraquin 1996). In Zimbabwe, the CAMPFIRE program promotes alliances between provincial governments, the private sector, and local inhabitants in managing wildlife for profit and biodiversity conservation within a legal framework laid down by the central government (Thomas, Kishor, and Belt 1998).

In Africa, East Asia, and Latin America the conventional wisdom that the slash-and-burn agricultural practices of the poor are a cause of large-scale deforestation has given way to a realization that macroeconomic change, commercial enterprises, and infrastructure development often have far greater impacts on deforestation (Chomitz and Gray 1996; Deininger and Minten 1996; Mamingi and others 1996). As unsustainable timber extraction by large commercial logging companies leads to deforestation, poor indigenous communities lose their sources of fuelwood, fodder, medicinal plants, and even their means of livelihood. The poor communities that depend on forests should be the focus of public action that ensures improved and sustainable use of forests. The best chance of a negotiated agreement lies with a three-party partnership of the state, local communities, and the logging companies. The challenge for developing countries is to scale up such partnerships as quickly as possible.

Clarify Property Rights, Resource Ownership, and Environmental Liabilities

The empirical relationship between clear property rights and environmental quality is strong (Dasgupta and others 1995). Farmers with secure title to land are more likely to invest in soil conservation, sustainable cultivation techniques, and other environmental protection practices (Feder 1987). Vested with ownership rights, local communities have reforested degraded lands in India and Nepal (Lynch and Talbott 1995). Establishing use rights for water, fisheries, and logging provides a clear incentive and means for resource management (World Bank 1997e).

Without enforced property rights to natural resources, outside interests take advantage of open access and, with no accountability for their actions, overexploit the natural capital by overfishing, overgrazing, overusing village woodlots, and extracting excessive amounts of groundwater. While experience varies, vesting communal property rights in these resources seems to relieve the pressures for overexploitation. The communal group develops mechanisms for restricting access by outsiders, distributing management responsibilities, allocating use rights among group members, and monitoring and compliance. Examples of communal management systems include those for forests in Japan; fisheries in Turkey; irrigation water in south India; and pastures in the Swiss Alps, the Himalayas, and the Andes (World Bank 1992).[11]

Security of tenure for urban dwellers can also improve the quality of the environment by simplifying the identification and enforcement of environmental liabilities for air and water pollution and solid, hazardous, and toxic chemical disposal (World Bank 1997e). A study of the relationship between property rights and the urban environment found that when people moved from squatter status to moderate security, the probability of purchasing garbage collection services increased by 32 percent, while moving to high tenure security (high tenure security is characterized by land tenure accompanied by a certificate of legal title) increased the probability of buying trash removal by 44 percent (Hoy and Jimenez 1997). Thus, establishing clear property rights and ownership and identifying environmental liabilities could be the state's most important contributions toward achieving environmental sustainability.

Improve Governance and Reduce Corruption

Rent-seeking and corruption hurt economic efficiency and prevent desirable outcomes even when good policies for environmental management exist on paper (Bhagwati 1982; Krueger 1974; Rose-Ackerman 1997a). Corrupt officials undermine efforts to monitor and enforce environmental measures, from industrial effluent discharges and automobile emissions inspections to allowable cuts for timber (box 4.5). It is found that controlling corruption is significantly associated with, for example, a reduction in water pollution (annex 1, figure A1.1). Collecting knowledge and sharing it widely can combat corruption and foster good governance, with beneficial outcomes for economic growth and environmental management. Specifically, the corruption diagnostics approach has shown promise to reduce corruption and promote integrity in several countries (chapter 6 in this volume; Kaufmann, Pradhan, and Ryterman 1998).

> **Box 4.5.   Private Profit at Public Expense: Corruption in the Forest Sector**
>
> Corruption is rampant in the logging and timber trade at all levels of forest-related decision-making. Most damaging to forest resources is the misuse of public resources for private gain by the political elite. In addition to the degradation and misuse of forests, corruption deprives governments and local communities of resources that could be used for development or improved forest management. Corrupt practices include the concealed or secret sale of harvesting permits, illegal underpricing of wood by companies (transfer pricing), false certification of species or volumes cut in public forests, and illegal logging. Examples from around the world are prevalent.
>
> - Transfer pricing was so prevalent in Papua New Guinea that until 1986 not a single company declared a profit despite the booming timber trade.
> - In Ghana, 11 foreign companies were implicated in fraud and other malpractices, costing the economy about US$50 million.
>
> - In the 1980s, the Philippines lost about US$1.8 billion a year from illegal logging.
> - In 1994 the Indonesian Department of Forestry admitted that the country was losing about US$3.5 billion a year, or a third of its potential revenues, because of illegal logging.
> - In 1994, the Russian government collected only 3–20 percent of the estimated potential revenues from logging fees; that is, US$184 million instead of US$900 million to US$5.5 billion.
>
> The World Commission on Forestry and Sustainable Development emphasized the need for mechanisms for public participation and conflict resolution to expose cases of corruption and penalize offending corporations and individuals. Acting on this recommendation, the World Bank started a forest law enforcement program, focused mainly on Southeast Asia, to address corruption.
>
> *Source:* World Commission on Forestry and Sustainable Development (1999).

Thus, developing countries should give high priority to stamping out corruption and improving governance.

Global Environmental Issues Must Be Confronted

Many environmental management issues are global in scale, though local in cause.[12] The greenhouse effect and global climate change are clearly connected to human activities (see box 4.6). Fossil fuel combustion is the biggest source of greenhouse gases. Deforestation contributes to the problem because of the loss of forest sink functions, which transform gaseous carbon dioxide into biomass. Farm activities, coal mining, and leakages from natural gas transmission pipes also add to greenhouse gases by releasing methane.

Because the problem originates with a large number of economic activities considered essential to growth, controlling them raises difficulties. Most developing nations depend on fossil fuel combustion for economic production and are unlikely to switch to cleaner, but more expensive, fuels.

Box 4.6.   International Cooperation to Mitigate Global Climate Change

The first World Climate Conference, held in 1979, recognized climate change as a serious problem and explored how it might affect human activities. The conference declaration called on the world's governments to predict and prevent potential manmade changes in climate that might have adverse impacts on the well-being of humanity. The Intergovernmental Panel on Climate Change, established by the World Meteorological Organization and United Nations Environment Programme, released its first assessment report in 1990 and confirmed the scientific evidence for climate change. The Second World Climate Conference in 1990 called for a framework treaty on climate change. The United Nations Framework Convention on Climate Change, which was opened for signature at the Rio Earth Summit in June 1992 and entered into force in March 1994, provides the context for a concerted international effort to respond to climate change. There are 166 signatories and 167 parties to the convention.

The Conference of Parties, which replaced the Intergovernmental Negotiating Committee for the Framework Convention, became the convention's ultimate authority. It held its first session in Berlin in 1995. The second, held in Geneva in 1996, took stock of progress and other issues. Participating officials stressed the need to accelerate talks on how to strengthen the Climate Change Convention. The Geneva Declaration endorsed the second assessment report of the Intergovernmental Panel on Climate Change as the most comprehensive and authoritative assessment of the science of climate change, of its impacts, and of the response options available.

The Kyoto protocol adopted at the Third Conference of Parties in December 1997 is acknowledged as a historic step toward binding emissions limitations in 39 industrial and transition economies. These parties agreed to ensure that their greenhouse gas emissions are reduced by at least 5.2 percent below 1990 levels in the commitment period 2008–12. This is a significant development, because projections for the United States, for example, indicate that without such binding commitments its emissions could be 30 percent above 1990 levels by 2010.

Despite the significant progress, the details of joint implementation, emissions trading, and developing country obligations still remain to be resolved.

Yet, switching to cleaner fuels can lead to better health outcomes, which is good for national economic objectives. As a consequence, a natural tension exists between the two goals, and many countries opt for more growth over better health (Munasinghe 2000). Financial and technical assistance from the international community, in return for reaping the benefits of switching to cleaner fuels, can enable the joint realization of both national and global interests.

Cooperation between rich and poor countries can also help control deforestation. Despite the externalities that it generates, developing countries see deforestation as an unavoidable consequence of their economic development. As with clean fuels, the international community needs to deal with the threat of global climate change by transferring resources, including technology, to control deforestation (Kishor and Constantino 1994; López 1997). Under the Joint Implementation Initiative of the

United Nations Framework Convention on Climate Change, several bilateral schemes of forest conservation are being tested in different parts of the world. Successful pilots will be replicated on a larger scale.

The Global Environment Facility is the main institution addressing global environmental concerns. As the interim financial mechanism of the Convention on Biological Diversity and Climate Change, it addresses global environmental problems through collaboration between industrial and developing countries that benefit both parties. For example, industrial countries can mitigate greenhouse gas emissions cheaply, and developing countries can benefit from financial and technological transfers in protecting their resource base and promoting economic development.

Preventing global climate change and managing its consequences will be one of the biggest challenges of the 21st century. Global conventions, treaties, and agreements have been important in identifying common problems, developing solutions, and allocating responsibilities. National awareness and commitment are increasing, and implementation must be encouraged to secure national and global objectives. Successful examples of this marriage of national and global objectives need to be replicated widely (Castro and others 1997; Watson and others 1998).

Conclusions

For the developing world, depletion of natural capital (forest, energy, and minerals) and damage from carbon dioxide emissions is estimated to be 5.8 percent of GDP. Environmental health risks account for 20 percent of the total global burden of disease. In addition, the huge costs of global environmental problems need to be factored into domestic development policies. The poor, especially women and young children, often bear much of the burden of environmental degradation. Thus, natural capital is crucial for sustained growth, and its conservation and augmentation are crucial to national and international development strategies.

Three key findings emerge from the evidence presented in the chapter, namely:

- Several indicators of the quality of natural capital, with the notable exception of access to clean water and sanitation facilities in some countries, tend to worsen in both slow- and fast-growth economies, imposing heavy costs and diminished prospects for future growth. However, faster growth makes more resources available to invest in the improvement of natural capital. Thus, the grow-now-and-clean-up-later approach espoused by many industrial and developing countries needs to give way to one of growth with sustainability of natural capital.

- The state performs a crucial role in environmental management, but it needs to be selective and efficient in its interventions. It should focus on collaborative approaches with local communities and the private sector.
- Global environmental problems are huge, but they offer opportunities to simultaneously address national problems if international cooperation can be secured. The development of transfer mechanisms for resources to pay for global externalities is key.

Countries need to focus on strategies to achieve high-quality growth that is sustainable and compatible with domestic and external financial stability, that is, growth that supports the poor and vulnerable and does not excessively degrade the atmosphere, rivers, forests, oceans, or any other part of humanity's common heritage. Cost-benefit estimates support a strategy of growing clean, and the examples in this chapter show that such a strategy is feasible.

Notes

1. Some World Bank studies attributed 100 percent of all waterborne illnesses to the lack of piped water connections and sanitation facilities. However, epidemiological studies rarely showed declines of more than 40 percent in sickness due to water access interventions (Esrey and others 1990). Thus, health benefits related to a cleaned up water supply and improved sanitation services may be overstated in table 4.2.

2. Work done under the Global Burden of Disease Initiative uses a standardized measure of health outcomes, DALYs, across various causes of illness and death, giving a standard way to quantify some of the losses described here (Murray and López 1996).

3. Most estimates use discount rates in the range of 6–10 percent to calculate the present value of benefits. If actual discount rates are higher, say 20–25 percent, as evidence from some developing countries suggests, then the present value of benefits will be much lower. Similarly, the opportunity cost of capital available to finance environmental improvements is assumed to be much lower than that developing countries actually face. The net result of applying the "true" values would be to reduce the gap of benefits over costs, thereby reducing the investment required for optimal environmental management, or even reduce benefits below costs, making such investments unprofitable. This points to the need to carry out a sensitivity analysis with respect to discount rate changes to reliably identify the priority areas for intervention (Kishor and Constantino 1994).

4. Protecting the environment while accelerating growth can also have beneficial impacts on the accumulation of physical capital. If the authorities announce more stringent environmental standards in advance of the date when they become binding, investments embodying the improved standards can be made over a period of time, thereby reducing capital obsolescence or the need for costly retrofitting to meet environmental standards, for example, the experience with emissions standards and catalytic converters for cars.

5. Even where an environmental Kuznets curve seems to be supported, this does not imply that environmental management is unnecessary. Take the case of sulfur dioxide emissions, where Grossman and Krueger (1995) estimated the turning point for emissions to decline at a per capita income level of US$4,053. Even with a high growth rate of 5 percent a year, India, for example, will take several decades to reach this income level. India and much of the rest of the developing world cannot continue to suffer the consequences of this type of pollution while hoping to "grow out of the problem."

6. Deforestation appears to follow a Kuznets curve path (Cropper and Griffiths 1994), but with a turning point of US$5,420 per capita income for Latin America, proactive polices are absolutely necessary.

7. Clearly, the links between pollution and growth depend on many factors, and a case-by-case analysis is necessary. In China, for example, the development of private town and village industrial enterprises was the prime engine of growth in the 1990s, lifting more than a 100 million people out of poverty. These enterprises are often more efficient, with better pollution control technologies, than state-owned enterprises. Therefore, as a result of the expansion of private enterprises, accelerated growth is likely to be associated with declining pollution intensities.

8. Moving from A to F implies that environmental quality deteriorated from its pristine state. This corresponds to the optimal rate of environmental protection referred to earlier. For the sink function of environment, this may be justified on the ground that "small" amounts of air pollution, water pollution, and so forth neither pose health risks nor impair the ability of the resource to "renew" itself; and the economic gains resulting from the pollution-generating activities are large. For the source function, a certain amount of forest clearing, for example, is justified as long as the alternative use of land provides greater social returns and forest clearing does not occur in the "wrong" places, such as steep slopes, along river basins, and so forth.

9. East Asia provides an interesting case. The recent economic crisis has plunged Thailand and Indonesia from B to C. As a consequence, they have the tough task of implementing policies to clean up the environment as they raise economic growth, that is, move from C to F.

10. Some Y 2 billion, converted at the rate of Y 8.3 to the dollar. China unified its dual exchange rate regime in 1994; hence, this amount should be viewed as approximate.

11. Protected areas, national parks, and other public lands that provide critical environmental services typically do not enjoy the advantages of community management. As a result, migration, encroachment, illegal extraction, and other forces continue to degrade government-managed lands in many areas.

12. Watson and others (1998) classify global environmental issues into two categories: those involving the global commons (atmosphere, water, and so on) and those of worldwide importance, but not directly involving the global commons (biodiversity, land degradation, and so forth). On the basis of current scientific assessment, the most important global environmental issues for this century requiring urgent action are global climate change, stratospheric ozone depletion, loss of biological diversity, deforestation and unsustainable use of forests, desertification and land degradation, freshwater degradation, marine environment and resource degradation, and persistent organic pollutants. The interlinkages among these issues and the need to address them simultaneously is also emphasized. Without downplaying the importance of other global environmental issues, this section focuses on global climate change mitigation and forest management to illustrate the challenges that we face in this area.

CHAPTER 5

DEALING WITH GLOBAL FINANCIAL RISKS

Times of trouble prompt us to recall the ideals by which we live.

—Michael J. Sandel, *Democracy's Discontent: America in Search of a Public Philosophy*

The financial crisis of 1997–99 that affected most severely Brazil, the Russian Federation, and several countries in East Asia underscored the importance of financial stability as a contributor to the quality of growth. As with environmental sustainability, education, and good governance, managing the risks of financial instability, especially those of cross-country capital flows, can stimulate sustainable growth by reducing economic inequality, enhancing social stability, and strengthening democratic trends and institutions. Without social and political stability, "no amount of money put together in financial packages will give us financial stability" (Wolfensohn 1998).

Global financial integration has undeniable benefits for developing and industrial countries, but it also exposes countries to the vicissitudes of international capital markets, such as volatility in currency values, interest rates, liquidity, and volumes of capital flows, with important macroeconomic and growth consequences. These risks are pronounced and costly, as demonstrated recently by lost output and jobs, corporate and banking distress, and increased poverty in crisis-hit countries, especially in countries where the institutional and regulatory frameworks for open capital markets are not fully in place.

The high social and economic costs associated with financial instability are unacceptable and make a strong case for devising better ways to deal with financial risks and to ensure stable growth. Chapter 2 shows how policy distortions, subsidies, and unnumerated guarantees can cause overinvestment in certain physical and financial capital, but underinvestment in other assets. This chapter turns to the factors that influence the volatility in capital flows to developing countries and the associated suboptimal investments that could lead to an increased vulnerability to financial turbulence. After a brief review of the benefits and risks of financial market integration, the chapter examines the causes and consequences of capital flow volatility and its implications for the poor. It then reviews the evolution of policy and institutional arrangements for managing risk and suggests a broad framework for risk management that integrates insights from the theory and practice of modern financial risk management with the political economy of open capital markets.

For growth to be relatively stable, governments can consider a spectrum of actions as follows:

- Remove distortionary policies and implicit or explicit subsidized guarantees that provide incentives for short-term foreign capital inflows, which may accentuate vulnerability to financial shocks.
- Strengthen domestic regulation and supervision of banks and other financial intermediaries and improve corporate governance and transparency.
- Build a broad framework for risk management, based on an orderly opening of capital markets combined with measures for controlling short-term capital flows.
- Maintain public support for open capital markets by providing cushions against risks, either through the marketplace or through redistributive policies and a social safety net.

Expansion of Capital Markets and Volatility of Capital Flows

By any measure, the growth in international financial markets throughout the 1990s was astounding. International lending in new medium- and long-term bonds and bank loans reached US$1.2 trillion in 1997, up from US$0.5 trillion in 1988 (BIS various years). World trade in goods and services, though growing significantly since the early 1970s, is now dwarfed by international financial transactions of more than five times the value of world trade (figure 5.1).

OECD cross-border transactions in bonds and equities, less than 10 percent of GDP in 1980, reached more than 100 percent of GDP in 1995. Average daily turnover in foreign exchange markets reached US$1.6 trillion in 1995, up from US$0.2 trillion in 1986, and annual trade in goods and

Figure 5.1. Global Financial Market Size and World Trade, 1980–96

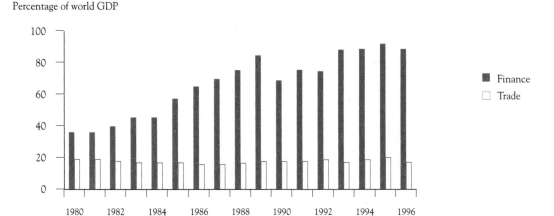

Percentage of world GDP

Note: Financial market size refers to world stock market capitalization plus stock of international bonds and loans outstanding. Trade figures are averages of imports and exports.
Sources: BIS (1997, 1998); International Finance Corporation (various years).

services reached US$6.7 trillion in 1998. Global market capitalization of stock markets relative to world GDP rose from 23:1 in 1986 to 68:1 in 1996, while derivative markets expanded from US$7.9 trillion in 1991 to US$40.9 trillion in 1997 (table 5.1).

The net flow of foreign private capital to developing countries also rose dramatically, from US$43.9 billion in 1990 to US$299 billion in 1997. Most of the capital came from foreign direct investment (FDI) and international capital markets, which include portfolio equity flows, commercial bank lending, and equity and bond issues in offshore markets. Flows of FDI to developing countries increased more than sixfold between 1990 and 1998, and the share of global FDI flows to developing countries rose from 18 percent in the mid-1980s to 24 percent in 1991 and 36 percent in 1997. However, when the financial crisis struck Asia beginning in 1997, capital flows from international capital markets to emerging market economies took a heavy hit, falling to their lowest point since 1992 at US$72.1 billion, while FDI remained resilient (figure 5.2) (World Bank 1999c).

Causes and Consequences of Capital Flow Volatility

The large expansion in private capital flows to developing countries from 1990 to 1997 was positively affected by advances in communication and

Table 5.1.   Growth of Derivatives Markets, 1991–97
(notional values in billions of US$)

| Year | Instruments traded on exchanges | | | | | Over-the-counter (OTC) instruments | | | | Total |
	Interest rate futures	Interest rate options	Currency futures and options	Stock market index futures and options	Total exchange traded	Interest rate options	Interest rate swaps	Currency swaps	Total	
1991	2,157	1,073	81	109	3,420	577	3,065	807	4,449	7,869
1992	2,913	1,385	98	238	4,635	635	3,851	860	5,346	9,980
1993	4,959	2,362	110	340	7,771	1,398	6,177	900	8,475	16,246
1994	5,778	2,624	96	366	8,863	1,573	8,816	915	11,303	20,166
1995	5,863	2,742	82	502	9,189	3,705	12,811	1,197	17,713	26,901
1996	5,931	3,278	97	574	9,880	4,723	19,171	1,560	25,453	35,333
1997	7,489	3,640	85	993	12,207	5,033	22,116	1,585	28,733	40,940

Source: BIS (various years).

Figure 5.2. The Rise and Fall of International Capital Flows, 1990–99

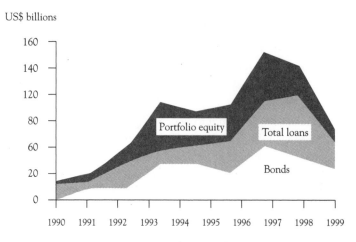

Note: International capital market flows to developing countries (including Korea) consist of portfolio equity, international private bonds, and loans.
Source: World Bank (2000g).

information technologies, which reduced cross-border transaction costs.[1] The advances facilitating cross-border capital flows have included the creation of the Euro-currency money market, the spread of derivatives, and the rapid expansion of hedge funds. In addition, both industrial and developing countries have opened their financial markets by removing barriers to cross-border capital flows.[2] However, various implicit or explicit government guarantees provided to banks, corporations, and investors in liberalized, but inadequately regulated, financial sectors, fueled overinvestment in certain industrial sectors in East Asian countries, on the one hand, and creating moral hazard and excessive risk-taking behavior among investors on the other hand.[3] The accumulation of contingent government liabilities and overleverged corporate indebtedness may have contributed to vulnerability, to the loss of investor confidence, and to the eruption of the recent financial crisis. Historically, shifts in the supply of foreign capital to developing countries have been caused by exogenous factors, such as the increase in oil prices in the 1970s, low interest rates, deregulation of institutional investors in industrial countries, and institutional innovation and competition in the 1990s.

The dismantling of barriers to capital flows across national boundaries, such as capital controls and foreign exchange restrictions, accelerated in OECD countries in the 1980s and spread to emerging markets. OECD countries liberalized almost all capital movements, including short-term transactions by enterprises and individuals, in compliance with the OECD Code of Liberalization of Capital Movements. The United Kingdom achieved full capital account convertibility in 1979, and in 1992 Greece, Ireland, Portugal, and Spain became the last OECD countries to fully abolish their capital controls (OECD 1990). By the early 1990s, the capital accounts of OECD countries were open to a wide range of cross-border financial transactions in capital market securities, money market operations, forward operations, swaps, and other derivatives.[4]

Many emerging market economies have also reformed their financial markets and liberalized cross-border capital movements. Based on an index of financial openness constructed for 96 countries, as of 1977, 46 can be classified as open and 10 as semi-open (box 5.1 and annex 5). As countries liberalized, banks and corporate borrowers gained access to a broader menu of foreign financing. The desirability of long-term capital, especially for funding infrastructure projects, provided a strong competitive advantage for foreign capital, particularly in countries with an exchange rate pegged to the U.S. dollar. Greater access to foreign capital in developing countries opens up possibilities for financing a broader set of investment projects, both sound and risky ones.

Despite the positive potential of foreign capital, weaknesses in domestic policy and liberalization measures, including subsidized guarantees, created incentives for imprudent behavior by banks, corporations, and investors that led to overinvestment in physical capital (for examples, see Demirgüç-Kunt and Detragiache 1998; Williamson and Mahar 1998).

Box 5.1. Openness to International Capital Flows

Evidence about the openness of emerging market economies to cross-border capital flows is scanty and fragmented. Information and methodology problems impede the development of proper quantitative measures. Most studies measure the incidence of capital controls rather than the intensity of restrictions and controls (see, for instance, Alesina, Grilli, and Milesi-Ferretti 1994; Razin and Rose 1994). However, not all transactions are subject to all controls, and most measures are intended to influence the incentives for certain activities. Controls range from direct quantitative limits on certain transactions or associated transfers, to such indirect measures as tax withholding or reserve requirements on external assets and liabilities. Such controls could also apply to transfers of funds associated with financial transactions or to the business activities themselves.

No single measure of openness exists. Any viable measure of financial openness needs to incorporate distinctions between the severity of controls and the types of transactions. The financial openness index, shown in annex 5 (table A5.5), addresses the relationships between types of control and transactions. It uses disaggregated measures of capital controls based on the classifications and information contained in the International Monetary Fund's *Annual Report on Exchange Arrangements and Exchange Restrictions*. Drawing on the coding methodology developed by Quinn and Toyoda (1997), the measure is a composite index of rules, regulations, and administrative procedures that affect capital flows for 27 transactions in the current and capital accounts of balance of payments for 96 countries.

Government guarantees took many forms, such as pegged exchange rates, directed lending, too-big-to-fail policies, and deposit insurance. Implicit or explicit government guarantees on liabilities encouraged excessive risk taking, influencing both domestic and international investors (see McKinnon and Pill 1997 for an analytical model). In essence, such weakness resulted in an underpricing of risk and lowering of margins on foreign currency denominated debt to emerging market economies, until just before the beginning of the East Asian crisis.

The Bangkok International Banking Facility, established in 1993 during financial liberalization, enabled Thai banks and firms to borrow in foreign currency at short maturities, which is a process called out-in lending. Because of bilateral tax treaties between Japan and Thailand, Japanese banks were willing to absorb the withholding tax and lend at very low spread to Thai companies. This infusion of Japanese money resulted in rapid growth of Bangkok International Banking Facility out-in lending: The foreign currency loans of Thai commercial banks rose to US$31.5 billion, 17 percent of private sector loans, by the end of 1996 (Alba and others 1998).

The Korean government directed lending to *chaebols*, which led to overinvestment in favored industries such as semiconductors, automobiles, steel, and shipbuilding. In Korea, the average debt-to-equity ratio of the top 30 *chaebols* was more than 500 percent by the end of 1996, and return on invested capital was below the cost of capital for two-thirds of the top *chaebols* (Park 2000).

With excessive foreign short-term borrowing induced in part by subsidized guarantees, government contingent liabilities accumulated. Once investors realized that the government was no longer able to meet its obligations, they took the exit route. Once a crisis began in one country, investor herdlike behavior and contagion spread through international trade and financial linkages, which resulted in private capital flow reversals and considerable widening of spreads for almost all emerging market economies (see Calvo 1999; Reinhart and Kaminsky 1999; Van Rijckeghem and Weder 1999).

Benefits and Risks of Open Capital Markets

The benefits of open capital markets are indisputable; the policy debate concerns whether the benefits outweigh the risks. Governments can also consider employing instruments to minimize such risks.

Open capital markets bring many benefits to both borrowing and creditor countries. They offer developing countries broader sources of investment finance to complement domestic savings. They also result in increased efficiency in domestic financial institutions and more disciplined conduct of macroeconomic policy. In addition, by easing financing constraints, open capital markets provide time for countries to make payment adjustments to correct imbalances that were created in response to external shocks.[5] Open capital markets offer creditor countries broader investment- and risk-diversification opportunities, particularly as their aging populations with growing pension funds seek higher and safer returns on their investments.

Open capital accounts also support the multilateral trading system, expanding the opportunities for portfolio diversification and for the efficient allocation of global savings and investment (Fischer 1998). An important property rights issue with regard to international finance also has attracted the attention of scholars and policymakers. Cooper (1998, p. 12) notes the view that embodies the thinking behind a liberal world order: "Individuals should be free to dispose of their income and wealth as they see fit, provided their doing so does not harm others." Others argue that openness to international capital flows is highly correlated with measures of political and civil liberty. The empirical evidence on the importance of financial openness and democratic governance is compelling, although the direction and nature of the link need study (see figure A5.1 in annex 5).

Openness also brings with it increased risks. Volatility in capital flows creates uncertainty in economic conditions, raises the cost of capital, may adversely affect long-term investment and growth, and slows poverty reduction efforts. Based on data from 90 developing countries, a strong correlation exists between the volatility of capital flows and the volatility of growth, as measured by the standard deviation of annual growth rates in real GDP (figure 5.3). In addition, using data from 130 countries between 1960 and 1995, Easterly and Kraay (1999) found that growth volatility, based on the standard deviation of GDP growth, has a negative effect (–0.18) on average per capita growth.

Two broad risk categories, those related to distorted domestic policies and those associated with external factors, can create economic problems for foreign investors and policymakers. Distorted domestic policies and weak regulatory and institutional environments provide incentives for banks and corporations to build up excessive short-term external liabilities relative to their short-term assets or unhedged foreign exchange positions. Examples of domestic sources of such risks include explicit and implicit government guarantees, pegged exchange rates, directed lending to investment projects, and mounting contingent liabilities. Dooley (1996) argued that the adoption of fixed exchange rates and deposit guarantees, in the context of a liberalized but poorly regulated financial sector, may induce foreign investors to reap

Figure 5.3. Relationship between Economic Growth Variability and Volatility in Private Foreign Capital Flows, 1975–96

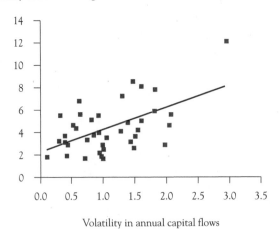

Votality in annual GDP growth rates

Volatility in annual capital flows

Note: y = 2.02x + 2.15, r = 0.57.
Source: See annex 5 for definitions and sources.

high private rates of return that do not benefit the borrowing countries. This underpricing of the true risks of underlying investments must be addressed to ensure balanced investment that could stimulate long-term growth and poverty reduction in borrowing countries.

The second category of risk relates to the functioning of international financial markets, external factors, and foreign lender and investor shifts in sentiment, belief, and confidence that are not necessarily related to a country's long-term creditworthiness. Thus, Calvo, Leiderman, and Reinhart (1994) found that external factors, such as U.S. interest rates and volatility in OECD growth could explain 30–60 percent of the variance in capital flows to Latin America. Shifts in investors' sentiment and beliefs, as reflected in a sharp turnaround in capital flows and/or a spike in emerging market economies' borrowing costs, can be caused by coordination failures on the part of creditors. This coordination problem could happen because of incomplete information between creditors that could render their decision to run or flee from a particular country dependent on the behavior of others. This dependence can generate a run, analogous to a bank run in domestic settings, adding a noncooperation premium on top of other country risk premiums (see Haldane 1999 for further elaboration of this point).

Countries need to be prepared to deal with the risks associated with financial integration and capital flow volatility. Because countries' preparedness varies and institution building takes time, governments can consider a spectrum of policy and regulatory actions as they open up to international capital flows in an orderly fashion.

Growth Volatility and the Poor

Financial crises are extremely costly. Latin America lost a decade of economic and social progress following the debt crisis of the early 1980s. East Asian countries lost an estimated US$500 billion, based on 1996 prices and exchange rates, in aggregate domestic output between 1997 and 1999, as measured by deviation from historical trends, or nearly 1.3 times the external debt of those countries in 1996 (see annex 5 for the method of calculation). In addition, the international financial community extended substantial financial assistance through multilateral and bilateral rescue loans to crisis-affected countries in the 1990s.

In particular, growth volatility has severe consequences for the poor, who lack assets to smooth their consumption during economic downturns.[6] The social costs associated with the crises in emerging market economies have been substantial. In just one year, unemployment doubled in Thailand

and tripled in Korea, while standards of living fell 14 percent and 22 percent, respectively. Indonesia also experienced a 25 percent decline in its standard of living (Stiglitz and Bhattacharya 1999) and a sharp increase in the number of poor. By the third quarter of 1998, Thai workers' real-wage income had fallen 24.8 percent from the noncrisis, trend rate (Krongkaew 1999). Levinsohn, Berry, and Friedman (1999) examined the impact of price hikes on the cost of living of poor households and found that in Indonesia, the poor were indeed hit the hardest compared with other groups. Because of a dramatic rise in food prices, the cost of living for the poorest income decile rose more than 130 percent after the crisis. The urban poor, who lack access to land and do not own their homes, were the most adversely affected by the crisis. Thus, as a result of the crises, East Asian countries experienced sharp reversals of their previous achievements in poverty reduction (see World Bank 2000a).

Past and Present Risk Management

To protect their growth and gains in poverty reduction, developing countries must be better prepared to deal with the risks associated with financial integration and capital flow volatility. Global financial risk and the strategies for managing it have changed substantially over the past 50 years, and new approaches are needed to deal with the new risks.

Early Mechanisms and Arrangements for Managing Risk

Viewed from the perspective of financial risk management, the Bretton Woods period (1945–73) exhibited a high degree of stability by judiciously combining fixed exchange rates with capital controls on the external side, and Keynesian macroeconomics and welfare state positions on the domestic side.[7] The Bretton Woods approach gave priority to fixed exchange rates and national policy autonomy. Capital controls were an accepted norm of the international monetary system in the 1950s and 1960s. Not until September 1997 did the Interim Committee of the International Monetary Fund agree that the Fund's Articles of Agreement "should be amended to make the promotion of capital account liberalization a specific purpose of the Fund and to give the Fund appropriate jurisdiction over capital movements" (Fischer and others 1998, p. 47).[8] With economies relatively closed to capital flows, governments could exercise fiscal and monetary policy in pursuit of national objectives, such as full employment and social equity, without fear of capital flight. This high degree of policy autonomy also served the cause of democracy, particularly in Western Europe.[9]

In the 1970s, once Western European countries had achieved currency convertibility in their current accounts, the free movement of capital across national boundaries began to emerge as an important policy priority. The collapse of the Bretton Woods system between 1971 and 1973, the move toward a floating exchange rate regime, rising oil prices, chronic inflation, and slumping global economic conditions intensified currency- and interest-rate risks in global financial markets. The responses were principally market-based solutions, exemplified by the drive toward the international diversification of capital and the rapid expansion of derivatives markets (interest and currency forwards, options, and swaps). Macroeconomic policy in OECD countries shifted from an emphasis on full employment to greater attention to macroeconomic stability, defined as smaller fiscal deficits and lower inflation and interest rates.

Financial Risk Management in the 1990s

In the 1990s, numerous liquidity and currency crises erupted in both industrial and developing countries: the European Monetary System during 1992 and 1993, Mexico between 1994 and 1995, East Asia in 1997, the Russian Federation in 1998, and Brazil and Ecuador in 1999. All these emerging market economies first experienced a surge in capital flows (from the early to mid-1990s) and then fell victim to sudden reversals; East Asia experienced reversals on the order of 10 percent of GDP. The crises of the 1990s exposed several weaknesses in international financial markets, namely:

- World capital markets failed at several levels. Borrowing countries were not monitoring the high exposure of their domestic banks and corporations to foreign currency risk. Credit rating agencies and other major international players failed to properly assess country risk in the globalizing financial environment of the 1990s. Regulators failed because of weak regulatory and supervisory frameworks. Financial risk management specialists underestimated the positive correlations between the quality of private sector credit and the quality of sovereign credit, and so failed to identify the causes of contagion in emerging market economies.
- Capital flows into many developing countries were channeled through short-term banking instruments because of implicit government guarantees for banks. Many market participants succumbed to the moral hazard in these perceived government guarantees. Credit standards and prudent project appraisals were often compromised, leading to overinvestment in sectors with surplus

capacity or declining demand. The result was simultaneous domestic banking system collapse and foreign exchange liquidity crises in countries with fixed exchange rates.

- The primary sources of instability were in the capital account, not in the current account, a situation that the Bretton Woods institutions were designed to prevent. In today's global financial environment, a country's total balance sheet, defined by its assets and its debt and equity liabilities, should be the measure of its external payments position.

These weaknesses reflect major shifts in the global financial landscape, which can be characterized by the internationalization of the banking business; the breakdown of traditional boundaries between financial and insurance functions; the new investment opportunities in emerging markets; and the broader investor bases in emerging market economies, such as commercial banks, pension funds, hedge funds, and insurance industries. These shifts put new demands on risk management; governments must employ more judicious strategies at international, institutional (corporate and financial institutions), and national levels.

A Broad Framework of Risk Management

Much current activity in risk management concerns how best to handle, through better crisis prevention, the risks of capital flows to developing countries, and through containment and orderly resolutions when crises do occur.

We present a broad, two-part framework for risk management that favors a moderate view. An appropriate regulatory framework and related instruments for controlling short-term capital flows should accompany an orderly opening up of financial markets. Public support for openness should be maintained by government provision of cushions against risks, such as social safety nets and well-designed and cost-effective redistribution policies.

International Policy and Regulatory Responses

With the memory of the 1980s debt crisis and its prolonged resolution still fresh, governments promptly implemented international policy and regulatory responses to the 1997–99 crises. In major industrial countries, they eased monetary policy, extended large rescue loans, developed international standards of good practice and disclosure, and established high-level committees to strengthen the soundness of banks and other financial institutions (see Drage and Mann 1999 for more examples of crisis resolution).

In February 1999, the G-7 (which comprises Canada, France, Germany, Italy, Japan, the United Kingdom, and the United States) finance ministers and central bank governors endorsed the creation of the Financial Stability Forum. At the new roundtable, the G-7 convened monetary authorities, principal regulatory agencies, and multilateral institutions to assess vulnerabilities in the global financial system and identify responses.

Institutional Responses

Financial risk management at the institutional level advanced significantly in the late 1990s. Today, financial and nonfinancial institutions use quantitative risk measurement techniques such as value at risk, volatility and beta measures, option pricing models, and Sharpe ratios. Using these tools, financial institutions have the ability to systematically measure and control market-related risk under normal volatility. In addition, the rapid expansion in the credit derivatives market is fundamentally altering the banking business by providing opportunities to trade credit risk. Risk management at the corporate level is moving toward a companywide integrated approach that encompasses credit, market, and liquidity risks.

National Responses: Reconciling Financial Integration and National Policy Autonomy

The integration of financial markets imposes a much more severe constraint on national policy choice than do other aspects of globalization, such as trade in goods and services, on which liberalization efforts had concentrated since World War II. Capital market integration reduces the ability of national governments to conduct policy, especially macroeconomic policy, because of the risk of capital exit. Those holding this view, which is based on the Robert Mundel and J. Marcus Fleming model of an open macroeconomy, argue that countries can attain only two of the following three conditions: capital mobility, fixed exchange rates, and monetary policy autonomy.

Redistribution to Mitigate Risk. Democratic societies need to resolve the tension between financial market integration and national policy autonomy to pursue their democratically defined economic and social goals. This tension relates to the ability of national governments to regulate, tax for redistributive purposes, and share risk while following the discipline needed in a global setting. In a world of high international mobility of capital, open democratic societies must balance the threat of capital exit, made easier by the open capital markets, with political demands for voice and government intervention to cushion market dislocations. Investors dissatisfied with the host countries' policies or prevailing investment climate find it easier to shift their financial resources to other countries and regions, with a subsequent disproportionate distribution of costs borne by less mobile factors of production, that is, labor and land. Thus, the motivation for redistribution as income insurance—distinct from altruism and other motives related to poverty reduction—is induced by volatility and insecurity in underlying economic conditions and when citizens are risk averse. The risk of capital exit intensifies economic insecurity and risk for a broad section of society. Because the rich are likely to benefit relatively from capital market liberalization, at least initially, while the poor may bear the costs, the political dimension of capital market liberalization is important and requires careful attention.

Social Sector Spending, Openness, and Political Liberty. The counterbalance to the threat of exit of capital is the political voice of citizens demanding protection against external risks through redistribution, social safety net programs, and other insurance-like measures.[10] In the absence of a market for such risk insurance, rational citizens will structure nonmarket institutions to reduce the welfare losses incurred from volatility in economic conditions. Thus, in this interpretation voice belongs to the political sphere, and how it is exercised is a function of the underlying political institutions and, in particular, the strength of democracy and the corresponding degree of political and civil liberty: the higher the degree of democracy, the greater the need to balance the threat of capital flight with political demands, which include political incentives to increase government intervention in cushioning market dislocation. It is fair to say that the political voice of citizens, who demand protection through redistribution, social safety nets, and other insurance-like measures, has been critical in easing the tension between politics and financial openness in OECD countries. Government spending on health, education, social security, and welfare in high-income countries between 1991 and 1997 averaged about 25 percent of GDP, with relatively small, open European countries such as Denmark, Norway, and Sweden spending as much as 30 percent.[11] A positive association exists among redistribution, financial openness, and civil and political liberty for a large sample of countries (table 5.2). Statistical analysis confirms that financial openness, democracy (as defined by political and civil liberties),[12] and government social spending go hand in hand (table 5.3, figures 5.4, 5.5, and 5.6).

Yet, because redistribution often needs to be financed through discretionary taxation, policymakers need to assess the associated fiscal and macroeconomic costs.

Almost all modern, advanced democracies are open to international capital movements. The relationship between financial openness and democracy appears to be primarily a function of per capita income: with few exceptions, rich countries have democratic governments and are

Table 5.2. Country Grouping by Financial Openness

Category	Open	Largely open	Largely closed	Closed
1 Democracy index[a]	0.81	0.71	0.63	0.48
2 Civil liberties[b]	2.28	3.30	3.38	4.55
3 GDP per capita, 1990–97	13,147	3,051	2,317	1,557
4 Social expenditure (percentage of GDP)[c]	22.30	23.50	12.50	6.70
5 Total government expenditure (percentage of GDP)[d]	26.00	19.90	23.40	27.70
6 General government consumption (percentage of GDP)[e]	16.10	17.90	15.50	14.70
Number of countries	46	10	34	11

Note: Table displays the group averages computed for countries with data. Definition of variables:

a. Ranges from 0 (lowest) to 1 (highest), computed on the bases of political rights and civil liberties indices, see endnote 11 for details.

b. A measure of respect for and protection of a country's citizens' religious, ethnic, economic, linguistic, and other rights, including gender and family rights, personal freedoms, and freedoms of the press, belief, and association.

c. Sum of health, education, and social security and welfare; average 1991–97.

d. Average of central government and budgetary accounts plus state or provincial government, 1990–97.

e. All current expenditures for purchases of goods and services by all levels of government, excluding most government enterprises, 1990–97.

Source: Annex 5.

Table 5.3. Estimation Results of the Binomial Logit Model on the Likelihood of Countries Belonging to the High Democracy and High Financial Openness Categories

Independent variable	Coefficient	Standard error	Marginal effect[a]
Constant	−11.234**	2.7500	−2.0296
Log (ratio of social expenditure to GDP)	1.534*	0.6146	0.2772
Log of GDP per capita	0.795*	0.3156	0.1436
Actual number of countries in the target group	28		
Predicted number of countries in the target group[b]	20		
Actual number of countries in other groups	39		
Predicted number of countries in other groups	32		
Log likelihood	−27.744		

*$p \leq 0.05$.

**$p \leq 0.01$.

Note: The dependent variable is coded 1 if the country falls into the financial openness–high democracy, and 0 otherwise.

a. Marginal change in the probability resulting from an infinitesimal change in the explanatory variable.

b. Target group refers to countries with high level of political rights and high financial openness.

Source: Annex 5.

open to international capital movement because they have a high degree of financial sector development and enjoy macroeconomic stability, stable expectations of peaceful regime change, domestic rule of law, and stable institutions that guarantee civil and political liberties (for a more

Transfers and social spending ease the tension between financial openness and politics

Figure 5.4. Relationships among Democracy, Financial Openness, Capital Mobility, and Government Social Expenditures

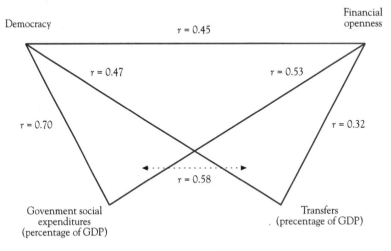

Note: The cross-country data, with sample sizes ranging from 70 to 140, show statistically significant results at 1 percent (except for the correlation between transfers and financial openness, which is siginificant at 5 percent) for all relationships.
Source: Annex 5 (table A5.5).

Figure 5.5. Relationship between Financial Openness and Social Expenditure
(controlling for per capita income)

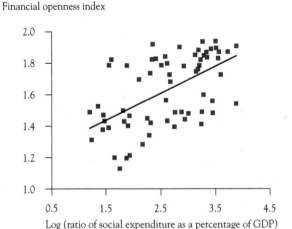

Note: y = 0.17x + 1.17
$R^2 = 0.32$
Source: See annex 5 for a description of the data.

Figure 5.6. Country Classification: Political Rights and Financial Openness

Financial openness

		Low	High
	Low	23	9
Democracy			
	High	32	37

Note: The level of democracy is derived from the political rights and civil liberties indexes from the Freedom House survey of Freedom in the World. The level of financial openness is defined by a score of >1.6 in the financial openness index (see table A5.2 in annex 5).

Source: Author's calculation.

detailed discussion of the link between democracy and financial openness, see Dailami 2000).

However, the link between democracy and financial openness proves to be more complex; analysis reveals that more than just income influences this link. International policy coordination in macroeconomic policy and financial regulation and supervision is part of the answer. It has been instrumental in reducing payment imbalances, in stabilizing expectations for currency and interest rate movements, and in lessening the volatility of capital flows across borders. The coordination of international banking regulation in industrial countries, such as the Basel Capital Accord of 1992 and the subsequent Core Principles for Effective Banking Supervision, has also been a significant factor in providing economic stability to OECD democracies.[13]

Empirical investigations of country classifications along the two axes of democracy and financial openness support the view that distribution policy contributes to democracies and open markets (figure 5.6 and table 5.3). Using logit analysis it can be shown that both per capita income and the ratio of social expenditures to GDP are statistically related to the likelihood that a country will be both financially open and democratic (see annex 5 for model specification and estimation, and Dailami 2000 for a more detailed analysis). After controlling for income in the analysis, redistributive policy, which includes programs for public expenditure on social security, health, housing, welfare, education, and transfers, figures prominently in the link between democracy and financial openness.

Capital Controls as Instruments of Risk Management. Capital controls can be employed as an alternative approach for resolving the tension between capital market integration and national policy autonomy. Interest in this approach has been rekindled by the 1997–99 financial crises in Asia and Latin America. Capital controls, particularly on short-term flows, are desirable to reduce volatility under some circumstances, such as weakness in local financial markets, euphoric or panic behavior by foreign investors, and structural balance of payments problems.

Many policy interventions are available for managing capital flows, including taxes and market-based instruments, such as contingent liquidity facilities and remunerated or nonremunerated reserve requirements on risky short-term flows. Argentina and Mexico have used contingent liquidity facilities and remunerable liquidity requirement for banks, and Chile used nonremunerable reserve requirements on risky short-term capital inflows between 1991 and 1998.

Controls on short-term capital in Chile have attracted considerable interest, partly because they are market based, transparent, and easier to phase out than quantitative controls (box 5.2). The controls were effective

---

Box 5.2. Chile: Openness, Capital Controls, and Social Protection

With the reestablishment of democracy in 1990, Chile has pursued an explicit strategy of growth with equity, while maintaining a market-oriented policy framework. The government has taken many measures for risk management in an open trade and investment regime.

Chile's social investments were extremely low during the late 1980s. They did not measure up to the spending levels of the premilitary regimes. However, since 1990, Chile has implemented a highly targeted system of social assistance in areas such as health, education, and housing. It has also used income transfers to improve conditions affecting human capital. Social investments increased by 75 percent between 1987 and 1994, which contributed positively to poverty reduction.

In response to the rapid expansion of capital inflows between 1988 and 1990, in 1991 the Central Bank of Chile imposed an unremunerated reserve requirement on selective inflows. At the same time, the government lifted several administrative controls on outflows, including ceilings on foreign asset holdings by banks, insurance companies, and pension funds, and the requirement that exporters surrender their export proceeds to the central bank. The unremunerated reserve requirement has increased the scope for an independent monetary policy. The reserve requirement contributed to changing the composition of inflows toward long-term maturities. However, the drop in short-term flows was only partly compensated for by the increase in long-term inflows. The reserve requirement does not seem to have affected the pattern of real exchange rates: to increase short-term interest rates, thereby adversely affecting the investment that it has directly contributed to. Furthermore, it involved transaction costs in monitoring commercial banks.

Sources: Ferreira and Litchfield (1999); Gallego, Hernandez, and Schmidt-Hebbel (1999); World Bank (1997b). See also Ariyoshi and others (1999) and Edwards (1999) for a survey of country experiences on capital controls.

in changing the composition of debt by reducing short-term capital inflows while increasing long-term flows and allowing for a larger wedge between domestic and foreign interest rates. The measures were countercyclical; they were imposed in 1991 after a growing tide of capital inflows, between 1988 and 1990, and phased out in September 1998 when they were no longer needed during the global financial crises.

Conclusions

Countries face two challenges in integrating their capital markets. The first is the pace at which countries dismantle administrative controls over capital flows and move toward capital account convertibility. The second is the incentive system and regulation of international financial flows to minimize risks and panics. Countries need suitable mechanisms to balance both the benefits and the risks of financial integration. Technological advances and the sheer size of financial markets make the risk of panic and crisis ever present. However, governments have various options for significantly reducing that risk.

Pursuing sound macroeconomic policies is an obvious first step, but not sufficient. Recent experience shows that macroeconomic stability is not enough to guarantee enduring results and sustainable growth. To ensure sustainable growth it must be reinforced by actions that remove distortionary policies that provide incentives for short-term foreign capital inflows that could lead to heightened financial vulnerability. Domestic regulation and supervision of banks and other intermediaries need to be strengthened and corporate governance improved.

With the move toward democracy worldwide, mechanisms for providing citizens with insurance against the risks of capital mobility, through either the marketplace or redistributive policies, are equally important if political pressure for capital controls is to be averted. In the long run, the globalization of capital requires an open institutional framework to ensure transparent accounts; secure property rights; and permit enforceable contracts, regulations, and mechanisms to manage risks. Establishing such a framework enhances assurance that open financial markets will contribute fully to stable growth and poverty reduction.

The remarkable economic turnaround in crisis-hit countries over the past months, reinforced by measures already taken at the international level to strengthen the architecture of international financial markets, bodes well for the prospects of greater financial stability and collective commitment to an open and liberal international financial system in the new millennium.

Notes

1. A large body of literature has developed over the last few years discussing the causes and consequences of recent financial crises in emerging market economies. See Calvo and Mendoza (1996); Corsetti, Pesenti, and Roubini (1998); Krugman (1998); Obstfeld (1996); Radelet and Sachs (1998); and Sachs, Tornell, and Velasco (1996). On causes of capital flow volatility, see Dooley (1996), Lopez-Mejia (1999), Montiel (1998), and World Bank (1997f).

2. From a historical perspective, the globalization of finance in the 1990s is equivalent to the level reached during the gold standard period of 1870–1914. However, during the gold standard only a few industrial countries were involved in capital flows (see Verdier 1998).

3. Moral hazard is a key concept in the economics of asymmetric information. Moral hazard occurs when economic actors covered by some form of insurance take more risks than they would otherwise take. Typical examples include an insured driver driving recklessly or an insured banker engaging in imprudent lending practices.

4. See also Helleiner (1994) for an account of how in 1974 the United States lifted the temporary capital restrictions of the mid-1960s.

5. Markets will provide leeway only if lenders perceive that countries are undertaking adjustments that fundamentally address existing and prospective imbalances. Otherwise, markets will eventually exert discipline that may brutally shorten the time allowed for readjustment (Dailami and ul Haque 1998).

6. See, for example, Diwan (1999); Krongkaew (1999); Levinsohn, Berry, and Friedman (1999); Lustig (1999).

7. This policy mix was referred to by Ruggie (1983) as "a compromise of embedded liberalism." It connotes a commitment to a liberal order different from both the economic nationalism of the 1930s and the liberalism of the gold standard. For further elaboration, see Garrett (1998). Sally (1998) also referred to embedded liberalism as "mixed system thinking." Also see Dailami (2000).

8. Reflecting the understanding of the time, Keynes expressed the issue succinctly in his often quoted 1944 speech to Parliament, stating: "Not merely as a feature of the transition, but as a permanent arrangement, the plan accords to every member government the explicit right to control all capital movements. What used to be heresy is now endorsed as orthodox... It follows that our right to control the domestic capital market is secured on firmer foundations than ever before, and is formally accepted as a part of agreed international agreements" (Gold 1977, p. 11).

9. However, in the Bretton Woods era there were periodic balance of payments crises, exchange rate devaluations, and stop-go growth episodes.

10. The idea of distribution as insurance has a long tradition in welfare economics going back to Harsanyi (1953), Lerner (1944), and Rawls (1971).

More recently this issue has been analyzed from the perspective of constitutional political economy (see Mueller 1998; Wessels 1993).

11. Focusing on globalization through trade, Rodrick (1997b) also emphasizes the relationship between redistribution and openness.

12. More precisely, one measure of democracy, following the recent literature exploring the role of democracy on economic growth, income levels, and wages, defines democracy as a composite index and draws on the Freedom House measures of political and civil liberty; that is:

$$\text{Democracy} = \frac{14 - \text{civil rights} - \text{political rights}}{12}$$

This index will be defined from 0 to 1, with 0 indicating low democracy and 1 indicating high democracy. Political and civil liberty indexes are from the *Comparative Survey of Freedom* that Freedom House has provided on an annual basis since 1973.

13. See Bryant and Hodgkinson (1989) and Webb (1994) for a discussion of international policy coordination in macroeconomic terms and Kapstein (1989) for information on international coordination of banking regulation. For selected readings in the voluminous literature on the need for better regulation and supervision, see Alba and others (1998); Caprio and Honohan (1999); Claessens, Djankov, and Klingebiel (1999); and Stiglitz 1993.

GOVERNANCE AND ANTICORRUPTION

Just as it is impossible not to taste honey or poison that one may find at the tip of one's tongue, so it is impossible for one dealing with government funds not to taste, at least a little bit, of the King's wealth.

—Kautilya, *The Arthashastra*

Written in ancient India more than 2,000 years ago, the *Arthashastra* is a detailed vision of a society that weaves together socioeconomic, institutional, and political variables. In contemporary development writing, such notables as Hirschmann, Myrdal, Coase, Stiglitz, North, Olson, and Williamson provided a broad view of the interplay of institutions and conventional economic variables. In recent years, increasing attention has turned to corruption, starting with Rose-Ackerman and Klitgaard, in some measure due to the growing awareness of its dire consequences for development. However, most contemporary economic development work

---

The work in this chapter draws from a number of collaborative initiatives between the chapter's author and World Bank staff on governance issues, including Aart Kraay, Sanjay Pradhan, Randi Ryterman, and Pablo Zoido; as well as collaboration with Joel Hellman and Geraint Jones at the European Bank for Reconstruction and Development and Luis Moreno Ocampo of Transparency International, and the invaluable inputs of the World Bank Institute's Governance Team and the Bank's Public Sector Group. The data used in this chapter originate from various research projects and surveys (as well as outside expert rating agencies) and are subject to a margin of error. Their purpose is not to present precise comparative rankings across countries, but to illustrate characteristics of government performance. Hence, no ranking of countries is intended by either the chapter author, the World Bank, or its Board of Directors. For further details on the empirical "unbundling" of governance and corruption, the data, and methodological issues, see annex 6 and visit http://www.worldbank.org/wbi/governance.

has underestimated the primacy of governance, broadly defined, for growth and development. Missing too often is the recognition that an effective and transparent government, operating within a framework of civil liberties and good governance, is vital for sustained welfare gains and poverty alleviation. Also missing is an integrated view of governance and corruption. Indeed, corruption ought to be seen as a symptom of the state's fundamental weaknesses, not some basic or single determinant of society's ills.

This chapter does not present an all-encompassing approach to the study of governance and corruption. Instead, we dissect the notions of governance—and of corruption and state capture—and present aspects relevant to the growth and development of nations to derive insights for strategies to improve governance. We lack many of the answers; the emerging lessons of success and failure are being distilled. Nonetheless, advances have been made in the conceptual, empirical, and practical understanding of these issues. Some of this progress pertains to the sharpening and "unbundling" of the notions and measurements of governance and corruption. This unbundling permits a better understanding of the causes and consequences of misgovernance, helping provide improved policy advice.

Governance Affects the Quality of Growth

Worldwide evidence suggests that a capable state with good and transparent government institutions is associated with higher income growth, national wealth, and social achievements. Higher incomes, investment, and growth, as well as longer life expectancy, are found in countries with effective, honest, and meritocratic government institutions with streamlined and clear regulations, and also where the rule of law is enforced fairly, where the policies and legal framework has not been captured by the vested interests of the elite, and where civil society and the media have an independent voice enhancing the accountability of their governments. International and historical experience also tells us that capable and clean government does not first require a country to become fully modernized and wealthy. The experience of such industrializing countries as Botswana, Chile, Costa Rica, Estonia, Poland, and Slovenia, as well as evidence over the past 20 years from economies like Singapore and Spain, illustrate this lesson.

Previous chapters emphasized the need for policies, regulations, and public resources to promote market-oriented development and to mitigate the negative impacts of externalities and market failures. With an emphasis on poverty and income distribution, they examined those factors that adversely affect human capital and the environment. A key role for the state involves delivery of public services and goods vital to achieving sustained growth and thus reducing poverty. Also, governments need to set up effective policymaking structures, market-friendly policies, and efficient and streamlined regulatory frameworks, as well as eliminate unnecessary regulations on enterprises, such as price controls, trade restrictions, enterprise licensing, and bureaucratic harassment.

Often, however, governments have paid insufficient attention to regulations governing child labor, worker safety, infrastructure monopolies, financial sector supervision, and the environment. Moreover, in many settings there has been a bias in the size, composition, and delivery of public expenditures and investments to benefit elite interests, frequently resulting in underinvestment in human capital and in outcomes harming the poor. Such elite interests often also lead to legal, regulatory, and policy anticompetitive capture. The study of governance and inadequate institution building is essential to understand these outcomes.

A political process determines public policies and the allocation of public benefits and expenditures. Its success depends on accountable government, community participation, and a strong voice for people and competitive enterprises. Effective adoption and use of policies and expenditures requires good governance. Enterprises need to operate within a legal and contractual framework that protects property rights, facilitates transactions, deters attempts by elite enterprises to capture the state, allows competitive market forces to determine prices and wages, and lets firms enter and exit the market. The public sector can do much to lower the transaction costs for farms and firms by supporting them with information and institutions and by rooting out misgovernance and corruption.

Defining and Unbundling Corruption and Governance

Corruption is commonly defined as the abuse of public office for private gain. Notwithstanding the debates about whether certain activities can be classified as corrupt or not and the need to unbundle corruption, the vivid day-to-day illustrations in the press and in conversation circumscribe the discussion of what constitutes corruption. However, governance is a much broader concept than corruption. We define governance as the exercise of authority through formal and informal traditions and institutions for the common good. Governance encompasses the process of selecting, monitoring, and replacing governments. It also includes the capacity to formulate and implement sound policies, and the respect of citizens and the state for the institutions that govern economic and social interactions among them.

From this notion, we can divide governance into *six* components, organized around three broad categories as follows (a) *voice and accountability*, which includes civil liberties and freedom of the press, and *political* stability; (b) *government effectiveness*, which includes the quality of policymaking and public service delivery, and the *lack of regulatory burden*; and (c) *rule of law*, which includes protection of property rights and independence of the judiciary, and *control of corruption* (Kaufmann, Kraay, and Zoido-Lobatón 1999a,b).

Therefore, in unbundundling governance, we posit that corruption is one among six closely intertwined governance components. Governance affects welfare and the quality of life through complex direct and indirect channels that we do not yet fully understand. An improvement in one governance component, such as civil liberties, *directly* enhances the quality of life for a country's people even when all other socioeconomic factors remain constant. Thus, governance can be a direct input into the well-being of the population.

However, important *indirect* effects are also at play. For example, misgovernance can hurt the growth rate of incomes and human capital, and increase the rate of natural resource depletion—often the result of the vested interests of politicians and the elite. Furthermore, misgoverned states tend to exhibit a distorted set of economic and institutional policies that blunt factor productivity, growth, and poverty alleviation. Therefore, via complex direct and indirect mechanisms, effective and clean government is vital for implementing and sustaining sound economic and institutional policies and for promoting human capital development and poverty alleviation.

Empirical Measures of Governance

Recent empirical studies suggest the importance of institutions and governance for development outcomes. Knack and Keefer (1997) found that the institutional environment for economic activity determines, in large measure, the ability of poor countries to converge to industrialized country standards. In turn, La Porta and others (1999) investigate the determinants of the quality of governments and, inter alia, find that the type of legal regime matters, as well as other historical factors.

The definition of governance, as presented in the previous section, is broad enough that a wide variety of cross-country indicators might shed light on its various aspects. Applying such a broad definition, Kaufmann, Kraay, and Zoido-Lobatón analyzed hundreds of cross-country indicators as proxies for various aspects of governance. These indicators came from a variety of organizations, including commercial risk-rating agencies, multilateral organizations, think tanks, and other nongovernmental organizations (NGOs). They are based on surveys of experts, firms, and citizens and cover a wide range of topics: perceptions of political stability and the business climate, views on the efficacy of public service provision, opinions on respect for the rule of law, and reporting on the incidence of corruption.[1] (See annex 6 for a description of Kaufmann, Kraay, and Zoido-Lobatón's methodology.)

Skeptical reactions naturally arise regarding the wealth of data on governance. Are the data informative? What can business analysts on Wall Street possibly know about corruption in Azerbaijan, Cameroon, Moldova, Myanmar, or Niger? Are the data coherent? Do reported ratings by enterprises about pressures from civil servants and their waiting times for customs clearances tell us something about the government's effectiveness in general, or do they measure totally different things? Are the data comparable? Can a score of 3 (out of 4) in transition economies be compared with a score of 7 (out of 10) in Asian countries? In addition to meeting these criteria, can the data be useful for rigorous econometric analysis of corruption or for policy advice purposes?

These questions, addressed in detail in the two references and in annex 6, motivate the empirical strategy for measuring governance: the data are mapped to the six subcomponents of governance and expressed in common units. The data are informative, within measurable limits, but the imprecision in the estimates requires care in their presentation and use for policy advice. These six distinct aggregate governance indicators are then developed, imposing some structure on available variables and improving the reliability of the measured governance component, which significantly exceeds the accuracy of any single governance measure.

For illustration, we first consider the measurement issues for one of the six composite governance components: rule of law. In figure 6.1, the vertical bars depict country-specific confidence intervals for the estimated ("point estimate") levels of governance. The confidence intervals (vertical lines) reflect the disagreement, or margin of error (among the original individual sources provided by the various external organizations) about the application of rule of law.[2]

The differences among more than 160 countries are large for rule of law, as well as for the other five measures. Countries are ordered along the horizontal axis according to their (admittedly imprecise) rankings, while the vertical axis indicates the estimates of governance for each country. The margins of error for each country, depicted by each thin vertical line, can be considerable. Thus, it is misleading having countries "run" in seemingly precise worldwide "horse races" to ascertain their ranking on various governance indicators. Instead, the following approach that groups countries into three broad categories akin to a traffic light for each governance dimension is more appropriate and statistically warranted:

- *Red light*: Countries in this category could be considered to be in governance crisis in that particular component. In fact, despite the

Figure 6.1. Quality of Rule of Law Indicator: The "Traffic Lights" Presentational Approach

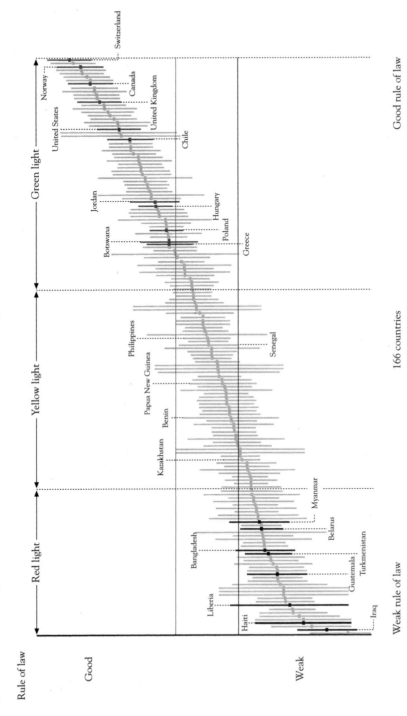

Note: This figure shows estimates of the quality in the application of rule of law for 166 countries based on 1997–98 data, with selected countries indicated for illustrative purposes only. The vertical bars show the likely range of the governance indicator for each country, and the mid-points of these bars show the most likely value. The length of these ranges varies with the amount of available information for each country and on the extent to which different sources' perceptions of corruption coincide. Countries with solid black vertical bars (in the red light area) or dark green vertical bars (in the green light area) are those for which the governance indictor is statistically significantly in either the bottom third (right light) or the top third (green light) of all countries. Countries with light green vertical bars (in the yellow light area) fall into neither of the two previous groups. Countries' relative positions are subject to significant margins of error and reflect the perceptions of a variety of public and private sector organizations worldwide. Thus, no precise ranking can be preformed. The country ratings in no way reflect the official views of the World Bank.

Source: Kaufmann, Kraay, and Zoido-Lobatón (1999a,b). For details, including the overall data set and methodology, see http://www.worldbank.org/wbi/governance. For a synthesis paper, see Kaufmann, Kraay, and Zoido-Lobatón (2000) at http://www.imf.org/fandd.

margins of error in the available data, it is still the case that a group of approximately 30 to 40 countries exhibit an extremely high probability of being in crisis where rule of law (or other governance measures) is assessed.

- *Yellow light:* Countries are vulnerable or at risk of falling into a governance crisis in a particular governance component.
- *Green light:* Countries have better governance and are not at risk

In moving away from a false sense of precision common in indexes that rank countries internationally (which are subject to considerable margins of error), this alternative approach of broad categorical groupings can flag vulnerabilities where a country falls into the red light or yellow light groups. For another governance component, in this case measuring control of corruption (also based on data from the late 1990s), selected countries are presented within such an illustrative traffic light framework in figure 6.2.

Effects of Governance

The cross-country data indicate a significant simple correlation between governance and socioeconomic outcomes. To explore the effect of governance on socioeconomic variables, we estimated a two-stage least squares regression of a socioeconomic variable (for example, per capita income) on a constant and on the governance component, using historical indicators as instruments (following the approach of Hall and Jones 1999). Within such an approach, concerns about measurement error and omitted variables were also addressed (see Kaufmann, Kraay, and Zoido-Lobatón 1999b for details). The evidence challenges the argument that only rich countries can afford the luxury of good governance.

The empirical analysis suggests a large direct effect going from better governance to better development outcomes. Consider an improvement (of one standard deviation) in the rule of law from the low levels in the Russian Federation today to the middling levels in the Czech Republic or a similar reduction in corruption from that in Indonesia to that in Korea. In this framework, it increases per capita incomes two to four times, it reduces infant mortality by a similar magnitude, and it improves literacy by 15 to 25 percentage points in the long run. And consider that the differences in governance for these two pairs of countries are not very large. Much larger improvements in government effectiveness from the levels in Tajikistan (in the red light group) to those in Chile (in the green light group) in this framework would nearly double the development impacts just mentioned.

The relationships between development outcomes and four measures of governance are illustrated in figure 6.3. The heights of the vertical bars show

Figure 6.2. Control of Corruption: The "Traffic Lights" Presentation Approach

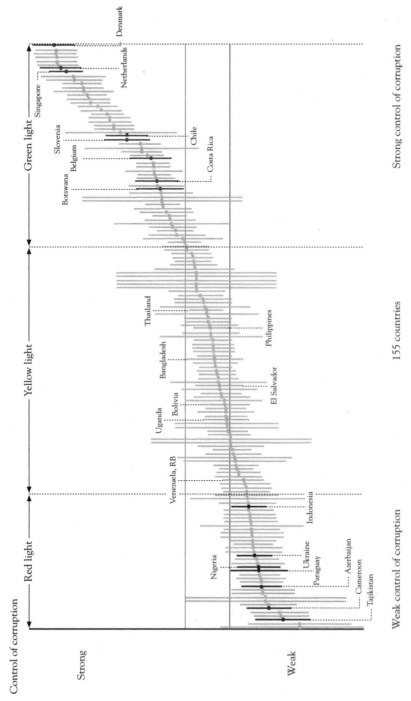

Note: This figure shows estimates of control of corruption for 155 countries based on data from 1997–98, with selected countries indicated for illustrative purposes. The vertical bars show the likely range of the governance indicator for each country, and the mid-points of these bars show the most likely value. The length of these ranges varies with the amount of available information for each country and on the extent to which different sources' perceptions of corruption coincide. Countries with solid black vertical bars (in the red light area) or dark green vertical bars (in the green light area) are those for which the governance indictor is statistically significantly in either the bottom third (right light) or the top third (green light) of all countries. Countries with light green vertical bars (in the yellow light area) fall into neither of the two previous groups. Countries' relative positions are subject to significant margins of error and reflect the perceptions of a variety of public and private sector organizations worldwide. Thus, no precise ranking can be preformed. The country ratings in no way reflect the official views of the World Bank.

Source: Kaufmann, Kraay, and Zoido-Lobatón (1999a,b). Details of the overall governance dataset in Kaufmann, Kraay, and Zoido-Lobatón (2000), http://www.imf.org/fandd/2000/06/Kauf.htm; and http://www.worldbank.org/wbi/governance.

Figure 6.3. The Development Dividend of Good Governance

Infant mortality and corruption

Infant mortality (deaths per 1,000)

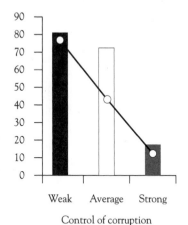

Control of corruption

Per capita income and regulatory burden

Per capita income (US$)

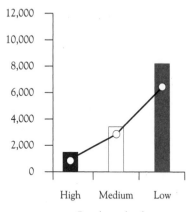

Regulatory burden

Literacy and rule of law

Literacy (percent)

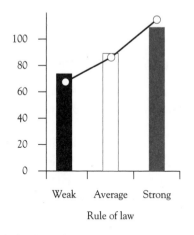

Rule of law

Life expectancy and voice and accountability

Life expectancy (years)

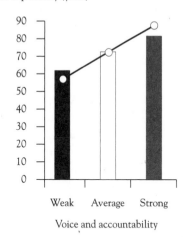

Voice and accountability

Note: The heights of the vertical bars show the differences in average development outcomes in countries with weak, average, and strong governance. The solid lines show the estimated effect of governance on development outcomes. See endnote 3 in this chapter and table A6.1 in annex 6 for details on econometric tests (synthesized in the solid lines).

Source: Kaufmann, Kraay, and Zoido-Lobatón (1999b, 2000); http://www.imf.org/fandd.

the differences in development outcomes in countries with weak, average, and strong governance and illustrate the strong correlation between good outcomes and good governance. After controlling for reverse causality and for the effects of other, nongovernance factors on development, the solid

143

lines represent the estimated impact of governance on development outcomes: the "development dividend" of improved governance.[3]

Composite indicators of governance, based on multiple, outside sources of data, powerfully draw attention to governance issues. They are also indispensable for cross-country research into the causes and consequences of misgovernance.

For instance, this large data set debunks the notion that larger countries are more corrupt (a statistical construct resulting from tests with a smaller number of countries). However, these new governance indicators provide only a first and rough benchmark of where countries stand relative to each other on governance issues and make a blunt tool for informed action to improve governance. To make composite indicators more specific and useful within a country, one needs to know much more about how perceptions of and data about misgovernance are reflected in policy and institutional failures. In-depth governance diagnostic tools are needed within a country to provide meaningful data and information for formulation of governance reforms. Against this background, the rest of the chapter addresses the following questions: How do corruption and misgovernance undermine development? What are the underlying causes of corruption? What kind of insights can be derived by unbundling corruption into distinct components? What kinds of diagnostic tools and strategic approaches can best serve a country intent on making progress toward good and clean government?

Corruption Undermines Growth and Development

Many studies have shown the pernicious effect of corruption on development. Mauro (1997) showed that corruption slows the growth rate of countries. He found that if Bangladesh reduced corruption to equal the level in Singapore and the growth rate was 4 percent a year, Bangladesh's average annual per capita GDP growth rate between 1960 and 1985 would have been 1.8 percentage points higher, a potential gain of 50 percent in per capita income.

The following are some of the many channels whereby corruption can weaken economic growth:

- Misallocation of talent (Murphy, Shleifer, and Vishny 1991), including underutilization of key segments of society, such as women
- Lower levels of domestic and foreign investment (Mauro 1997; Wei 1997)
- Distorted enterprise development and growth of the unofficial economy (Johnson, Kaufmann, and Zoido-Lobatón (1998)
- Distorted public expenditures and investments and deteriorated physical infrastructure (Tanzi and Davoodi 1997)

- Lower public revenues and less provision of the rule of law as a public good (Johnson, Kaufmann, and Shleifer 1997)
- Overly centralized government (Fisman and Gatti 2000)
- State capture by the corporate elite of the ("purchased") laws and polices of the state, thereby undermining growth of output and investment of the enterprise sector (Hellman, Jones, and Kaufmann 2000a; see annex 6 for details).

Lower Investment

Evidence from a large cross-section of countries suggests that corruption significantly reduces domestic and foreign investment. If the Philippines could reduce its corruption to the much lower level of that in Singapore, it would raise its investment-to-GDP ratio by 6.6 percentage points (Mauro 1997). By looking at bilateral FDI in the early 1990s from 14 source countries to 41 host countries, Wei (1997) found evidence that corruption discourages investment. Reducing corruption to the low level in Singapore would have the same effect on foreign investment for a corrupt country as reducing the marginal corporate tax rate by more than 20 percentage points. Many countries afflicted by corruption also offer substantial tax incentives to lure multinational firms. By controlling corruption, they could attract at least as much foreign investment without such tax incentives.

Misallocation of Public Expenditures

Some of the pioneers in the study of the economics of corruption have highlighted corruption's effect on the allocation of public finances (Klitgaard 1988; Rose-Ackerman 1989). Tanzi and Davoodi (1997) found that corruption increases public investment because it creates opportunities for manipulation by dishonest high-level officials. It also skews the composition of public expenditure away from needed operations and maintenance spending and directs it toward new equipment purchases, thereby reducing the productivity of public investment, especially in infrastructure. Under a corrupt regime, public officials shun health programs because they offer less scope for rent-seeking. Corruption may also reduce tax revenue, because it compromises the government's ability to collect taxes and tariffs.

Drawing on the findings of Tanzi and Davoodi, Wei (1997) showed that an increase in corruption, comparable to the corruption level of Singapore rising to that in Pakistan, would increase the public expenditure-to-GDP ratio by 1.6 percentage points and reduce the government revenue-to-GDP ratio by 10 percentage points. In addition, an increase in corruption would reduce the quality of roads and increase the incidence of power outages, telecommunication failures, and water losses.

Johnson, Kaufmann, and Zoido-Lobatón (1998) also showed that corruption reduces tax revenue, mainly through the growth of the unofficial economy. Overburdened by red tape and associated rent-seeking in the official economy, firms move to the unofficial economy and pay fewer taxes. Such reduced tax revenue is associated with a lower provision of key public goods, such as rule of law, further increasing the unofficial economy and impairing public finances.

Impact on the Poor

Where corruption prevails, growth is impaired, and this has an enormous effect on poverty. Furthermore, the poor receive fewer social services, such as health and education. Corruption biases infrastructure investment against projects that aid the poor and impairs the use of small-scale entrepreneurial means to escape poverty. Worse, corrupt regimes often prefer defense contracts over rural health clinics and schools, a policy bias that worsens income distribution and diverts resources from the countryside to the cities.

Gupta, Davoodi, and Alonso-Terme (1998) show that corruption increases income inequality and poverty through channels such as lower growth, regressive taxes, less effective targeting of social programs, unequal access to education, policy biases favoring inequality in asset ownership, reduced social spending, and higher investment risks for the poor. As suggested in figure 6.3, Kaufmann, Kraay, and Zoido-Lobatón (1999b) also found that corruption increases infant mortality and reduces life expectancy and literacy. Furthermore, when analyzing the UNDP's Human Poverty Index, the data suggest that it is negatively associated with the various indexes of governance and corruption even after controlling for GDP per capita. The mechanisms through which governance affects poverty are varied, complex, and still not fully understood. The matrix in table 6.1 suggests some of the complex effects of corruption on poverty through a variety of channels.

Country analyses using new governance diagnostic tools illustrate how regressive corruption is as a tax. For instance, poor households in Ecuador must spend three times more in bribes as a share of their incomes than higher income households for access to public services (figure 6.4). Similarly, in various diagnostic surveys of public officials in Latin America in the late 1990s, bureaucrats in those agencies rife with corruption and lacking in meritocracy were found to discriminate against the poor by limiting access to basic services and by failing to pursue poverty alleviation—in contrast with the better access to the poor by agencies with less corruption and meritocracy (figure 6.5).

Table 6.1. A Synthesis Matrix: Corruption and Poverty

"Immediate" causes of poverty	How corruption affects "immediate" cause of poverty
Lower investment and growth	Unsound economic/institutional policies due to vested interests Distorted allocation of public expenditures/investments Low human capital accumulation Elite corporate interests capture laws and distort policymaking Absence of rule of law and property rights Governance obstacles to private sector development
Poor have smaller share in growth	State capture by elite of government policies and resource allocation Regressiveness of bribery "tax" on small firms and the poor Regressiveness in public expenditures and investments Unequal income distribution
Impaired access to public services	Bribery imposes regressive tax and impairs access and quality of basic services for health, education, and justice Political capture by elites of access to particular services
Lack of health and education	Low human capital accumulation Lower quality of education and health care

Source: Author.

Impact of Corruption on Commerce and Corporate Influence on National Governance

A common argument found in the literature contends that bribes to circumvent bad government controls are like unofficial deregulation and can have positive effects, such as promoting enterprise development (Huntington 1968; Leff 1964; Liu 1985). This view—bribery as grease on the wheels of commerce—may hold conceptually only in a very narrow sense if bad regulations are fixed independently of the behavior of public officials. Yet in reality, officials often have discretion in the type and amount of harassment and regulations inflicted on individual firms. Tax inspectors can overreport taxable income (Hindriks, Keen, and Muthoo 1999), and fire inspectors can decide how many times to check a firm for safety "violations." Using data from two independent surveys on more than 6,000 firms in 75 countries, Kaufmann and Wei (1999) showed that firms that pay more administrative bribes waste more time with bureaucrats than those firms that do not pay bribes.

Thus, the empirical evidence suggests that a firm engaging in petty or administrative bribery (for example, for licenses or red tape) does not necessarily benefit from paying bribes; neither does the business community or society more generally. Research evidence on the costs of corruption for overall business development is growing. For example, Fisman and

Figure 6.4. Corruption Is Regressive: Results from Diagnostic Surveys

Bribery paid by enterprises in Ecuador, 1999

Ratio of firms' bribe costs in total revenues (percent)

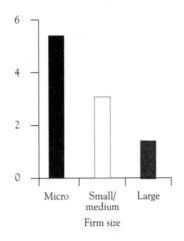

Firm size

Bribery paid by households in Ecuador, 1999

Bribe costs to household income ratio (percent)

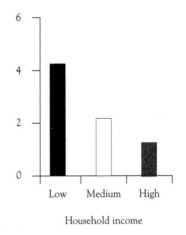

Household income

Note: Estimates subject to a margin of error.
Source: World Bank (2000e).

Svensson (1999) found that in Uganda, administrative corruption reduces a firm's propensity to invest and grow, and Hellman, Jones, and Kaufmann (2000a) found that in those economies in transition where "grand" corruption is more prevalent, the growth and investment rate of the enterprise sector is much smaller, while security of property rights is impaired.

Corruption not only hobbles dynamic enterprise development, but it affects smaller firms and new entrants in particular. Newer and smaller firms tend to bear the brunt of the bribery "tax," as evidenced by a recent analysis of 3,000 enterprises in transition economies.[4] Accordingly, smaller firms are prepared to pay significantly more taxes than their larger counterparts for their bribes to be reduced.

This research on transition economies also provides insights into the link between political influence, grand corruption (more specifically, state capture), and enterprise performance. In a number of countries in the former Soviet Union, the survey finds that firms (including many with FDI) that purchased parliamentary laws, presidential decrees, and influence in central banks do benefit in the short run (in terms of revenues and the firm's own investment). Yet as stated earlier, their actions inflict a large indirect cost on the development of the rest of the enterprise sector. These findings demonstrate that while individual firms engaging in state capture may benefit privately (in contrast with administrative corruption—figure

Figure 6.5. Corruption and Absence of Meritocracy in Public Agencies Impair Access to Services to the Poor: Results from Public Officials' Diagnostic Surveys

Corruption control in central agencies in Paraguay and access to services by the poor

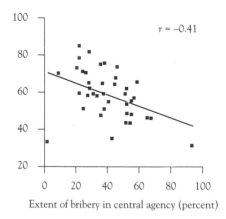

Civil service meritocracy in municipalities in Paraguay and access to services by the poor

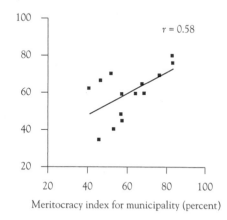

Corruption control in municipalities in Bolivia and access to public services by the poor

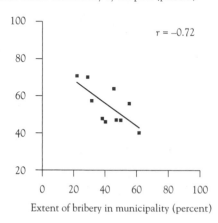

Civil service meritocracy in municipalities in Bolivia and poverty alleviation impact of public services

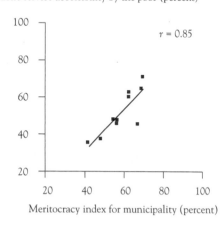

Notes: Each depicted observation (dot) represents a central agency or municipality in the pertinent country. Based on public officials survey on governance, "Poverty alleviation impact" represents the percentage of cases in which the public services delivered are helpful to reduce poverty and "Accessibility to the poor" represents the percentage of cases in which the public services delivered are accessible to the poor, as reported by public officials in the diagnostic survey.

Sources: World Bank (2000e).

6.6), such a form of grand corruption imposes a particularly pernicious social cost on enterprise development. (See annex 6 for details on the unbundling of the measurement of corruption into state capture, public procurement kickbacks, and administrative corruption).

Causes of Corruption

Empirical studies of the causes of corruption are fairly new. Yet, the emerging evidence suggests that some determinants are important. The available research supports the notion that corruption is a symptom of deep institutional weaknesses.

Absence of Political Rights and Civil Liberties

Political rights, which include democratic elections, a legislature, and opposition parties, and civil liberties, which include rights to free and independent media and freedom of assembly and speech, are negatively correlated

Figure 6.6. "Petty Bribery" versus State Capture: Does Engaging in Corruption Benefit the Firm?

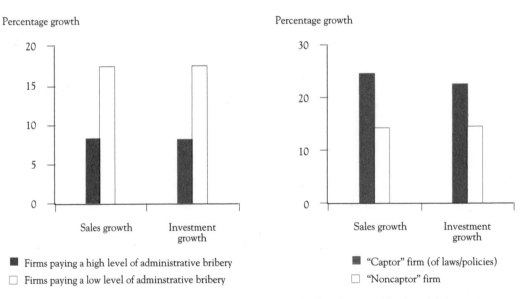

Administrative corruption does not benefit the firm (averages from all transition countries)

State capture through purchase of policies and laws benefits the captor firm

Firms paying a high level of administrative bribery
Firms paying a low level of administrative bribery
"Captor" firm (of laws/policies)
"Noncaptor" firm

Source: Hellman, Jones, and Kaufmann (2000a). Details in annex 6 and at http://www.worldbank.org/wbi/governance.

with corruption. Figure 6.7 shows the high correlation between civil liberties and freedom of the press with corruption. Increasing evidence points to the empowerment of civil society in effectively addressing corruption (figure 6.7). Furthermore, the enterprise survey evidence from transition economies suggests that the capture of state policies and laws by corporate interests is associated with the absence of full civil liberties (Hellman, Jones, and Kaufmann 2000a). The worldwide empirical evidence also suggests that the inclusion of women, whether measured in terms of parliamentary representation or social rights, does help achieve such empowerment (Kaufmann 1998). Devolution, such as fiscal decentralization (Collier 1999; Fisman and Gatti 2000), under the right circumstances may also help control corruption. In addition, evidence points to a significant correlation between corruption and the rule of law.

Public Finance and Regulation

Corruption is higher in countries with a high degree of state ownership in the economy, excessive business regulation and taxes, arbitrary application of regulations, and trade restrictions. Monopolized economies also tend to have more corruption.

Civil liberties and a free press can help control corruption

Figure 6.7. Corruption and Civil Rights

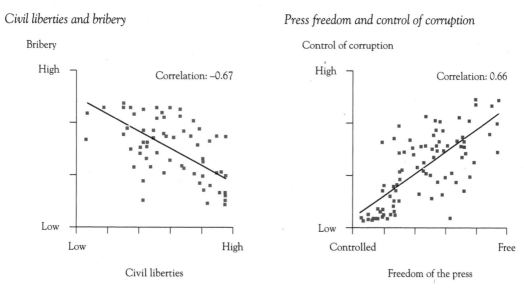

Source: Kaufmann (1998).

Civil Service

Civil service professionalism, which includes training, hiring, and promotion systems, is also associated with less corruption. Contrary to conventional wisdom, the evidence on civil service pay is often ambiguous. Better public sector salaries on their own may not explain a significant reduction in corruption. For example, Ecuadorian public sector agencies that offer better pay to employees do not have a lower incidence of corruption. In many settings, a few of the more senior politicians or government officials often cause the most damaging corruption. While in some countries raising salaries of selected key civil service personnel may be warranted, this is unlikely to bear fruit without complementary measures. Among these, meritocracy in hiring, promoting, and firing within an agency is associated with less corruption (figure 6.8). The contrasting results between the low impact of higher salaries, on the one hand, and the significant effect of meritocracy, on the other, exemplify the need to conduct in-depth, empirical diagnostics within countries intent on formulating serious anticorruption programs.[5]

A Multifaceted Anticorruption Strategy

Given what is known about the main determinants of good governance and corruption, what kinds of programs may have an impact?[6] Improving governance requires a system of checks and balances in society that restrains arbitrary action and bureaucratic harassment by politicians and bureaucrats, promotes voice and participation by the population, reduces incentives for the corporate elite to engage in state capture, and fosters the rule of law. Futhermore, the ongoing research on state capture highlights the need to place checks and balances on the "elite" corporate sector through promoting a competitive market economy and an active civil society. A meritocratic and service-oriented public administration is another salient feature of the strategy.

Key Reforms

Figure 6.9 synthesizes the strategy of key reforms for improving governance and combating corruption. However, how to combine and sequence these reforms to achieve the greatest impact on corruption is a particularly daunting challenge, as is the task of detailing and adapting a strategy to each country-specific reality. For instance, a country that has been subject to state capture by the corporate elite will require a different strategy than a country where the main source of misgovernance originates in political structures or in bureaucracy. Specific questions about governance reforms

Figure 6.8. Meritocracy Can Reduce Corruption: Evidence for each Agency from Surveys of Public Officials in Three Countries

Corruption in some agencies in Ecuador is associated with lack of meritocracy

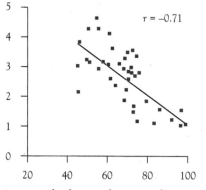

Corruption in some municipalities in Paraguay is associated with lack of meritocracy

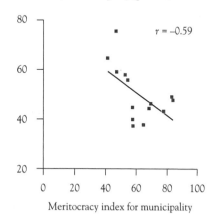

Corruption in some agengies in Bolivia is associated with lack of meritocracy

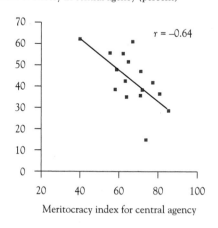

Corruption in some municipalities in Bolivia is associated with lack of meritocracy

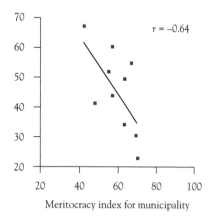

Note: Each depicted observation (dot) represents a central agency or municipality in the pertinent country. Extent of bribery is measured by the reported percentage of public services and contracts that are affected by bribery in a central agency or municipality. The meritocracy index (0–100) is constructed using the survey questions related to personnel management in a central agency or municipality, as reported by public officials.

Sources: World Bank (2000e); the contributions of Ed Buscaglia, Maria Gonzalez de Asis, Turgul Gurgur, Akiko Terada, Youngmei Zhou, and Pablo Zoido-Lobatón to this line of research on public officials are acknowledged.

Figure 6.9. Multipronged Strategies for Combating Corruption and Improving Governance: Recognizing the Political Economy

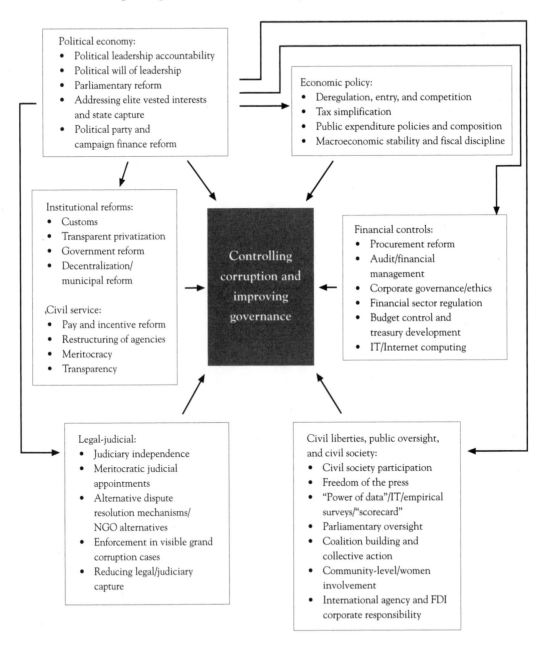

Political economy:
- Political leadership accountability
- Political will of leadership
- Parliamentary reform
- Addressing elite vested interests and state capture
- Political party and campaign finance reform

Economic policy:
- Deregulation, entry, and competition
- Tax simplification
- Public expenditure policies and composition
- Macroeconomic stability and fiscal discipline

Institutional reforms:
- Customs
- Transparent privatization
- Government reform
- Decentralization/ municipal reform

Civil service:
- Pay and incentive reform
- Restructuring of agencies
- Meritocracy
- Transparency

Controlling corruption and improving governance

Financial controls:
- Procurement reform
- Audit/financial management
- Corporate governance/ethics
- Financial sector regulation
- Budget control and treasury development
- IT/Internet computing

Legal-judicial:
- Judiciary independence
- Meritocratic judicial appointments
- Alternative dispute resolution mechanisms/ NGO alternatives
- Enforcement in visible grand corruption cases
- Reducing legal/judiciary capture

Civil liberties, public oversight, and civil society:
- Civil society participation
- Freedom of the press
- "Power of data"/IT/empirical surveys/"scorecard"
- Parliamentary oversight
- Coalition building and collective action
- Community-level/women involvement
- International agency and FDI corporate responsibility

IT Information technology.
Source: Author, in collaboration with the World Bank's Public Sector Group.

therefore include what types of changes are feasible under what political conditions and how reforms should be prioritized within the political, civil society, and corporate realities of each country setting.

Competition and Entry. In some transition and developing countries, a source of grand corruption is the concentration of economic power in monopolies that then wield political influence on the government for private benefits. The problem is particularly acute in countries rich in natural resources, where monopolies in oil, gas, and aluminum, for instance, wield considerable economic and political power that leads to different forms of corruption: nonpayment of taxes, nontransparent offshore accounts, purchasing licenses and permits, and purchasing votes and decrees that restrict entry and competition. Demonopolization, deregulation, facilitation of entry and exit (through liquidation of assets and effective bankruptcy procedures), and promotion of competition are vital.

Accountability of the Political Leadership. Measures are being implemented in various countries that provide checks and balances for the political leadership and senior officials in their commitment to good governance and anticorruption through public disclosure and transparency of their own actions, finances, income, and assets. In several countries this has entailed the following:

- Public disclosure of votes in parliament
- Repeal of unconditional parliamentary immunity
- Public disclosure of sources and amounts of political party financing
- Public disclosure of incomes and assets of senior public officials and their key dependents
- Regulations against conflicts of interest for public officials
- Protection of personal and employment security for public officials who reveal abuse of public office by others (whistleblower statutes).

Meritocratic and Service-Oriented Public Administration. Recruiting and promoting on merit, as opposed to political patronage or ideological affiliation, is positively associated with both government effectiveness and control of corruption. Reforms in this area have included creating independent, professional institutions with checks and balances (for example, a civil service recruitment commission) and introducing a comprehensive performance management system with pay and promotion linked to performance. In Malaysia and Thailand, this led to increased recruitment and retention of managerial and professional staff and to increased effectiveness in civil service performance. In addition, allowances and noncash benefits often need to be simplified, monetized, and made transparent. Care needs to be exercised in avoiding wholesale salary increases as a panacea.

Transparency and Accountability in Public Expenditure Management.[7] Basic systems of accountability in the allocation and use of public expenditures constitute a fundamental pillar for good governance. Accountability in public expenditure management requires the following: (a) a comprehensive budget and a consultative budget process, (b) transparency in the use of public expenditures, (c) competitive public procurement, and (d) an independent external audit.

The budget must first have comprehensive coverage of a government's activities. Many countries face problems of budgetary transparency, where major areas of budget expenditure do not pass through the treasury system, and there is substantial recourse to extrabudgetary funds and no effective system of controlling expenditure commitments. Several countries in transition, such as Hungary and Latvia, have made progress in addressing these problems with comprehensive treasury reform programs.

Second, disclosure matters. Many industrial countries (for instance, Australia and the United Kingdom) publish frameworks for public expenditure strategies, which are both a major tool for clarifying strategic choices and a means of enhancing the transparency of the policy objectives and the output targets underpinning annual budgets. More recently, South Africa has developed the Medium-Term Expenditure Framework, revised annually and published on the web, as a means of clarifying strategic choices and establishing publicly accountable objectives for public expenditure.

Third, transparent and competitive public procurement is key to clean government. Reducing corruption requires adhering to strict discipline in terms of transparent and competitive bidding of major contracts, maximizing the scope of public oversight and scrutiny. The information technology revolution is proving to be a catalyst. Indeed, to make the process of government procurement more efficient and curb corruption, three Latin American countries (Argentina, Chile, and Mexico) have recently adopted electronic government acquisition systems. All procurement notices and their results are placed on a publicly available web site. Other important innovations related to activist external monitoring are taking place as well. NGOs are increasingly playing a role in spearheading public audiences to have a greater voice in establishing rules of the game for large-scale procurement projects (such as in the subway system in Buenos Aires) and throughout the transparent bidding process itself (where NGOs such as

Transparency International have innovated). The World Bank has also taken an active role in aggressively pursuing firms engaged in misprocurement in projects; for instance, delisted firms that have been barred from bidding in Bank-funded projects for having engaged in corrupt procurement are publicly available on the Bank's web site.

Fourth, establishing independent external audits matters. Several transition and emerging economies, such as the Czech Republic and Poland, have established supreme audit institutions, which are genuinely independent and have a constructive impact on public financial management systems. In the Czech Republic, audit reports are published, presented to the legislature, and discussed in the cabinet, along with a proposed plan for corrective actions, in the presence of the supreme audit institution and relevant ministers.

Promoting the Rule of Law. According to the *New Palgrave Dictionary of Economics and the Law*, the rule of law is defined by opposing it to the rule of powerful men or women. This summarizes the challenge in many countries, where powerful politicians, leaders, elite interests, or oligarchs often influence the practical operations of the parliament, judiciary, and legal enforcement institutions such as the police. These countries often have an adequate set of laws on the books, yet the failure is in their effective application and enforcement. And in some countries such laws have been captured by elite interests. The evidence from a vast array of worldwide data (synthesized in figure 6.1) suggests that there is a rule of law crisis in many countries of the former Soviet Union and in Africa, as well as in some in Latin America. The institutional dysfunction in such countries stands in sharp contrast to others, where, however imperfectly, the capacity of legal and judiciary institutions is improving. Illustrating the performance of courts in different countries, figure 6.10 shows how honest, reliable, and fair courts are reported to be by the enterprise sector in Estonia and Hungary. By contrast, in countries like the Russian Federation and Ukraine, they are seen as corrupt, very partial and unfair, unreliable, and nonenforcing.

Misgovernance in the judiciary and legal institutions does not always originate solely in the public sector. In some countries elite corporate interests exert corrupt pressures as well, as also gleaned from the recent enterprise survey in transition countries and illustrated in figure 6.11, which suggests the extent of capture (by enterprises including FDI) of the legal and judiciary system in some countries.

Thus, even if the legal institutions are fully staffed by trained judges and personnel, they can be subject to capture by politicians or corrupt corporate interests. In this context, the public sector legal institutions are an integral

Figure 6.10. High Variation in the Quality of Courts in Selected Economies

(view of the corporate sector on four dimensions; a larger inner diamond means a better performing court)

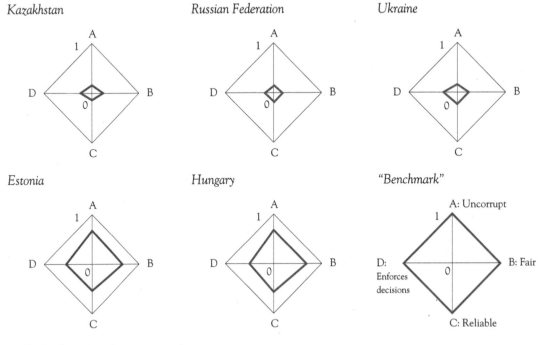

Quality dimensions of courts measured:
A Uncorrupt.
B Fair.
C Reliable.
D Enforces decisions.

Note: Four-pronged diamond on a scale of 0–1, where 1 indicates 100 percent of firm respondents giving highest rating in each relevant court quality dimension. The lower right corner panel is a hypothetical ideal benchmark, if 100 percent of firms would give perfect scores.

Source: Hellman and others (2000); see also annex 6. Based on a 1999 enterprise survey in transition economies.

part of the governance problem, and not part of the solution. This reduces the relevance of conventional advice on improving governance through the creation of institutions within the public sector (such as an ethics office and anticorruption department) passing anticorruption laws, providing technical assistance in the form of computers or other hardware, or sending sitting judges to training or "study tours." Instead, innovative mechanisms to improve governance are often needed, such as alternative dispute resolution mechanisms, providing for more systematic involvement by NGOs and other alternative institutional arrangements, dissemination strategies through the media, and exploiting more fully and transparently the power

Figure 6.11. Legal and Judicial Capture by the Corporate Sector in Selected Transition Economies

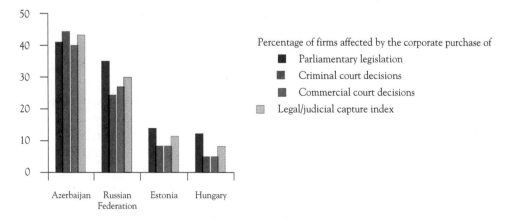

Proportion of enterprise sector affected by legal/judiciary corporate capture

Percentage of firms affected by the corporate purchase of
- ■ Parliamentary legislation
- ■ Criminal court decisions
- ■ Commercial court decisions
- ▨ Legal/judicial capture index

Note: The legal/judicial capture index is the simple average of the firms reporting the effect of corporate purchase of parliamentary legislation, of criminal court decisions, and of commercial court decisions. Estimates subject to margin of error.

Source: Hellman, Jones, and Kaufmann (2000a,b); see also for details columns 1, 4, and 5 in table A.6.1 in annex 6. Data from 1999.

of data and information within and outside the public sector. Equally important, the major challenge of addressing legislative capture in many countries would often require parliamentary and political reforms, such as public disclosure of all parliamentary votes, scaling back immunity laws for members of parliament, and political finance reform.

Survey Diagnostic Tools for In-Country Governance Assessment

The collection, analysis, and dissemination of country-specific data on corruption are altering the policy dialogue on corruption and empowering civil society through collective action. Yet important challenges remain, including the ongoing refinement of methods that transform survey evidence into reform priorities and how best to complement in-depth empirical diagnostic surveys with in-depth focus group methodologies—fully involving stakeholders on the key governance challenges within the country. A key challenge involves the development of an effective strategy for implementing the reform agenda. Once survey data and their analysis are available, countries where political will is present must begin the more difficult task of prioritizing measures according to the country reality and introducing reforms to root out the sources of corruption.

Sustaining the reform effort with broadly based participation involving all government branches, civil society, and the business community constitutes another challenge to the anticorruption and governance-improvement agenda (box 6.1). With cooperation from the private sector and NGOs, the government can leverage reform by allowing private competition alongside public provision of some services; for example, the adoption of private forms of alternative dispute resolution to compete with the judiciary or private provision of garbage collection at the municipal level. In-depth governance and anticorruption survey diagnostics (and their concomitant data analysis) need to be institutionalized, so that statistics on agency-specific corruption can be monitored and acted upon periodically. Broad dissemination of the vast amounts of statistics being generated through diagnostic surveys and studies of governance and capture can further empower stakeholders to strengthen and sustain institutional change.

The design and implementation of agency-specific, in-depth diagnostic surveys for public officials (figures 6.5 and 6.8), households or users (figure 6.4), and enterprises (figures 6.4 and 6.11) constitute an innovation that provides tangible inputs for countries committed to implementing capacity building and institutional change programs. New survey instruments can collect detailed information on behavior in even the most dysfunctional government agencies and on the delivery of specific services. For example, comparisons of the price of saline purchased by different hospitals, after accounting for transport and other idiosyncratic costs, can show whether corruption exists in public hospitals. Used with other empirical devices, such diagnostic surveys can focus the political dialogue on concrete areas for reform and rally civil society behind reform efforts.

Such country self-diagnostic data, used by a variety of in-country stakeholders and disseminated through participatory workshops, have mobilized broader support for consensus building and collective action for institutional reforms. Countries such as Albania,[8] Bolivia, Georgia, and Latvia have progressed from using diagnostics to taking concrete action. Bolivia is emphasizing civil service and procurement reforms. Latvia has given priority to tax and customs reforms. In Georgia, following the abysmal survey results regarding the state of the judiciary, President Shevardnadze decided that all judges had to be retested, which was broadcast live on television. Two-thirds of the judges failed the examination and were replaced.

In other countries, similar governance improvement efforts are taking place at the *municipal* level. For instance, in a number of Ukrainian cities specific actions to improve the effectiveness of local government in delivering public services are being carried out following diagnostic surveys. Pioneered in Bangalore, India, in the early 1990s, the now well-known

Box 6.1. Governance and Survey Diagnostic Tools: The Power of Empirics

The first set of in-depth governance and corruption diagnostic surveys of public officials, firms, and citizens was carried out in Albania, Georgia, and Latvia in 1998. More recently, implementation of refined and expanded versions of these diagnostic surveys has been carried out in other countries, focusing more broadly on the complex governance of key agencies in the country and assessing the main institutional determinants of misgovernance and corruption there. Challenging conventional wisdom, the new surveys of public officials, enterprises, and citizens find respondents willing to provide detailed information on misgovernance that they have observed and experienced (as opposed to merely indicating their vague perceptions about countrywide corruption, for instance).

Survey respondents report on embezzlement of public funds, theft of state property, bribery to shorten processing time, bribery to obtain monopoly power, and bribery in procurement. For instance, in 1998 in Georgia embezzlement of public funds and judiciary corruption, inter alia, was identified as a serious problem. At that time theft of state property was identified as a particular problem in Albania. Bribery in procurement and customs is a common challenge in most settings where these diagnostic surveys have been implemented. Weakness in the judiciary was identified as one of the primary causes of corruption in Albania, while regulatory failures are much less important there than in Georgia and Latvia, for instance. In these diagnostic surveys, detailed statistics are collected on the frequency and cost of bribes paid by enterprises to regulators in different agencies as well as the shortcomings of public service delivery and other performance and effectiveness indicators. A multiplicity of governance dimensions is included in these diagnostics, permitting an in-depth analysis of issues such as meritocracy, discretionality, budgetary transparency, and poverty alleviation focus and impact. The analysis of these statistics then serves as a vital input for prioritizing in the formulation of a governance improvement reform program.

A significant share of administrative bribes is paid to officials to avoid taxes, customs duties, and other liabilities to the state. Some bribes—such as kickback payments to public officials, for lawmaking and judicial decisions, or for public procurement—are found to be particulary costly. The survey results indicate that agencies and activities viewed by public officials as particularly corrupt command the highest price for securing jobs, suggesting that securing such public positions is viewed as a private investment with a significant expected private return.

When the data were presented in workshops to members of the business community, major civil society, and the executive and legislative branches, the policy debate abruptly changed from vague, unsubstantiated, and often personalized accusations to one focused on empirical evidence and systemic weaknesses that needed to be addressed. Action programs were formulated and implementation of institutional reforms began.

Source: Kaufmann, Pradhan, and Ryterman (1998). For a detailed governance and anticorruption diagnostic implementation guide see http://www.worldbank.org/wbi/governance.

citizen "scorecard" user surveys allow citizens to evaluate the quality of local government services (box 6.2). In Campo Elias, Venezuela, thanks to the leadership of the mayor, a courageous woman who believes in the power of governance data to inform and mobilize for action, the reported incidence of corruption has been halved (Gonzalez de Asis 2000).

Box 6.2. "Voice" as a Mechanism to Enforce Transparency and Accountability

Client and citizen surveys that incorporate feedback from citizens have helped to improve public sector performance in many countries. The scorecard method pioneered by Sam Paul in Bangalore, India, embodies this approach. It entails periodic citizen evaluations of local municipalities and their accounts of public services, bribery, and extortion. Evidence exists that public agencies in Bangalore have taken concrete steps to improve service delivery.

In Mendoza, Argentina, citizens have participated in crafting transparent rules related to public procurement. A number of localities throughout the world have embraced similar participatory processes. As part of its pioneering system of participatory budgeting, Porto Allegre, Brazil, holds citywide assemblies where expenditure priorities for education, health, transport development, taxation, city organization, and urban development are discussed. The assemblies then elect members to a citywide participatory budgeting council, which decides the city's investment plan. Preliminary evidence shows that more roads have been paved and the number of students enrolled in primary and secondary school has doubled.

Increasingly, voice- and transparency-enhancing reforms are being furthered via the Internet revolution, and not only in areas such as procurement, discussed previously. In Chile, just during the past year, the share of the tax paying population filing tax returns over the Internet increased from 5 to 30 percent. Furthermore, the combination of the latest statistical, computing, and Internet technology is also promoting greater accountability in political elections, as witnessed recently in the extremely efficient, accurate, and speedy counts in Argentina, Chile, and Mexico, in sharp contrast with elections in a number of other countries.

Thus, data are powerful in mobilizing support for reforms, but the obstacles presented by grand corruption and state capture by vested interests resisting such reforms are also powerful. Therefore, political leadership, civil society, private sector investors, and the donor community need to build on the insights and momentum generated by the diagnostics and utilize and disseminate statistics in conjunction with promoting civil liberties and media involvement, and resulting in higher accountability and actions against corruption.

Transparency through Voice and Participation

Corruption can yield to knowledge and an informed citizenry. Indeed, the empowerment of civil society with more rigorous and reliable information is a key pillar of reform. Transparency is an important component of public empowerment and voice. As a result, policymaking and large public projects should be predicated on incorporating the voice and participation of stakeholders in development (see box 6.2 for a discussion of transparency and governance). Indeed, World Bank research shows that the greater the participation of beneficiaries in project design and implementation, the better the project and service performance.

Civil Liberties Matter

In previous sections in this chapter, we presented the close association between civil liberties and freedom of the press on the one hand, and control of corruption and state capture on the other (figure 6.7). Yet the paramount importance of civil and political liberties transcends its worth in lowering corruption, or merely as an "input" to a developmental outcome: it is a basic good that enhances welfare per se. At the same time, assessing whether civil liberties do matter as an input in developmental and financial outcomes is of relevance within the debate in the aid community regarding fiduciary responsibilities to make aid effective.

Evidence from more than 1,500 World Bank–financed projects suggests that civil liberties and citizen participation are important factors for development outcomes. Researchers focused on measuring the impact of participatory and civil liberties variables on project performance and found consistent, statistically significant, and empirically large effects of civil liberties on project rates of return. Depending on the measure of civil liberties used, if a country were to improve its civil liberties from the worst to the best, the economic rate of return of projects could increase by as much as 22.5 percentage points (table 6.2). Because these civil liberty indexes use different scales, a more standard method of comparison is to calculate how much the economic rate of return would increase if each index category were improved by one standard deviation. As seen in the last column of table 6.2, this still gives significant results, suggesting an impact of citizen voice on government performance. Moreover, the report *Assessing Aid* (World Bank 1998a) found that while both civil liberties and electoral democracy have beneficial effects on government performance, the main channel of influence is likely to be the availability of civil liberties.

In Rajasthan, India, a people's organization called Mazdoor Kisan Shakti Sanghathan held a public hearing where it exposed misappropriation by local governments of development funds intended for local workers. This generated village demand for further investigation into the government. Local governments, being under public and press scrutiny, were compelled to oblige. Corruption was reduced. The government of Rajasthan recognized the people's right to official documents and enacted landmark legislation (Bhatia and Dréze 1998) (see box 6.3).

Governments and citizen groups can elicit voice through surveys and data collection in more systematic ways. Client surveys can cast light on citizens' experiences with government services and identify suggestions for performance improvement. Follow-up surveys can be used to ensure accountability and ensure that improvements are in the desired direction.

Table 6.2. Impact of Civil Liberties on Project Socioeconomic Rates of Return

Civil liberties variable	Specification on independent variables				Effect on economic rate of return of one standard deviation increase in civil liberties
	With exogenous control variables only	With regional dummies	With policy variables	With regional dummies and policy variables	
Freedom House Civil liberties					
(1978–87)[a]	1.81	1.16	1.71	1.07	1.57
(N = 649)	(0.0005)	(0.079)	(0.002)	(0.114)	
Humana					
(1982–85)	0.290	0.299	0.296	0.289	5.19
(N = 236)	(0.003)	(0.007)	(0.002)	(0.013)	.
Media pluralism					
(1983–87)	4.61	4.45	3.66	3.43	3.12
(N = 448)	(0.0001)	(0.002)	(0.001)	(0.026)	
Freedom to organize					
(1983–1987)	3.17	1.81	2.41	−0.26	2.70
(N = 448)	(0.0001)	(0.184)	(0.006)	(0.854)	

N = number of observations.

Note: Standard error is in parentheses. Average economic rate of return on projects is in the range of 12–16 percent.

Source: Isham, Kaufmann, and Pritchett (1997).

Generating data and disseminating them widely are potent instruments to mobilize civil society and apply pressure on political structures. For example, simple comparative charts illustrating findings on corruption can help mobilize and give voice to previously silent and disparate citizenry groups.

Toward a Social Contract: Facilitating Civil Society Oversight and Participation

Civil society oversight and participation over the decisionmaking and functioning of the public sector has been a crucial counterweight and instrument for combating corruption and improving governance. This involves making the state transparent to the public and empowering the citizenry to play an active role. While a few OECD countries have been in the forefront in transparency reforms, in many of the transition and emerging economies the public sector culture is still one of secrecy of decisionmaking. Often, parliamentary votes are not publicly disclosed, public access to government information is not assured, and judicial decisions are typically not available to the public. Moreover, despite a growing civil

Box 6.3. Millions of "Auditors" Improve Transparency and Governance in Budgetary Accounts and Beyond

Transparency means empowering the citizenry to become millions of auditors in society, providing voice and access to a free press. It enables the flow of timely and reliable economic, social, and political information about private investors' use of loans and the creditworthiness of borrowers, government service provision, monetary and fiscal policies, and the activities of international institutions. By contrast, a lack of transparency means that someone, such as a government minister, public institution, corporation, or bank, is deliberately withholding access to or misrepresenting information.

In general, a lack of transparency increases the scope for corruption by creating informational asymmetries between the regulators and the regulated entities. Corruption affects all major areas of public administration: revenue collection as a means of raising public funds and revenue allocation as a means of providing public goods. It affects public regulation as a means of mitigating information failures in markets, particularly capital markets. Recent empirical research of financial crisis episodes indicate that the likelihood of such crises was significantly larger where transparency was absent. In-depth governance diagnostics of public agencies discussed earlier within a country also suggest that agencies with transparent flows of information tend to exhibit lower corruption and better governance and performance overall.

society, the government typically does not involve NGOs in the monitoring of its decisionmaking processes or performances. Concentrated media ownership and recent restrictions on reporting have weakened the ability of the media to ensure accountability of the public sector.

Consequently, changing the culture to one of transparency involves a fundamental change in the way decisions in the public sector are made. The types of transparency reforms that have been demonstrated internationally to be effective include the following:

- Ensuring public access to government information (freedom of information)
- Requiring certain types of government meetings to be open to public observation
- Conducting public hearings and referenda on drafts, decrees, regulations, and laws
- Publishing judicial and legislative decisions and keeping a registry
- Ensuring freedom of the press by prohibiting censorship, discouraging use by public officials of libel and defamation laws as a means for intimidating journalists, and encouraging diversity of media ownership
- Involving civil society to monitor its performance in areas such as anticorruption and large-scale public procurements bidding

- Utilizing the new web-based tools on the Internet for transparency, disclosure, public participation, and dissemination.

Civil society's role ought to be seen as dynamic and providing an opportunity to political leaders intent on building the credibility of the state through its potential in coalition building and collective action. For instance, new activities in many countries where the World Bank provides assistance involve supporting the collective teamwork of civil society, the media, experts, the private sector, and the reformists in the executive and legislative branches in formulating governance and anticorruption reform programs. The process of involvement by the key stakeholders in civil society creates a momentum toward ownership and sustainability of the reforms and builds credibility, as is taking place in some countries in Eastern Europe, Africa, and Latin America, for instance.

Conclusions

Governance needs to be understood in a broader context than merely addressing corruption, which is a key symptom of more fundamental institutional weaknesses. Both governance and corruption need to be rigorously unbundled and understood analytically and empirically. Misgovernance distorts policymaking and the allocation of factors of production, which in turn slows income and welfare growth and increases poverty. The many failed capacity building approaches in the past did not pay enough attention to fostering good governance, to controlling corruption, to improving the bureaucracy and civil service, to promoting civil liberties and participatory approaches, to understanding the origins and consequences of state capture, or to furthering knowledge about the political economy of institution building. Governance needs to enter center stage in capacity building and institutional change strategies. Understanding of particular vested interests by different influential groups is needed—including the corporate sector (both domestic and FDI)—as is the recognition that *incentives, prevention, and systemic-change* challenges within institutions vitally affect governance, and are at least as important as traditional law enforcement aspects.

Governance, voice, and participation will be key for an improved approach to technical assistance and capacity building in the future. Improving governance should be seen as a process integrating three vital components: (a) knowledge, with rigorous data and empirical analysis, including in-country governance diagnostics and transparent dissemination, utilizing the latest information technology tools; (b) leadership in the political, civil society, and international arena; and (c) collective action via systematic participatory and consensus building approaches with key stakeholders in society (for which the technology revolution is also assisting). Collective responsibility also implies that transnational corporations, the domestic private sector, and international agencies need to collaborate with national governments and leadership intent on improving governance.

The evidence points to the need for a more integrated and comprehensive approach to provide a climate for successful development. Economic institutions and policy measures, such as the budget and the nature of public investment programs, are important, as are civil liberties and participation, with which they interact. This underpins the case for a more holistic approach to development that links economic, institutional, legal, and participatory variables.

Participation and voice are vital in increasing transparency, providing for the necessary checks and balances, and ameliorating state capture by the elite's vested interests. It is not enough to get basic economic policies right on paper; the political economy forces at play must also be recognized. These forces will vary from country to country. In some countries addressing legal, regulatory, and procurement reform will be necessary to improve governance and control corruption. In others, where state capture by the corporate elite and when there is weaker political will to reform, civil society oversight, enterprise competition, and working to improve property right protection could be key.

For an enhanced focus on poverty alleviation, a concerted approach that integrates rigorous empirical understanding of the governance challenges within a country, encourages active involvement by all key stakeholders, tailors it to the country's own realities, and is championed by the country's leadership is likely to bear fruit.

Notes

1. The plethora of indicators measuring various aspects of governance are ordinal; that is, they have a qualitative or subjective element. The data are nonetheless relevant. First, for some aspects of governance, these are the only kind of data available (and it is now possible to disentangle the "noise" from the "signal"). Almost by definition, hard data (numerical-cardinal) have until now been virtually impossible to obtain in a systematic format, and for those few governance dimensions where such cardinal data exist, they are accompanied by a large margin of error and/or methodological questions. Second, for many aspects of governance, survey results (even if they contain an element of perception) do matter at least as much as official data. For instance, if a

country's business sector regards the judicial system as an arm of the government and avoids using the courts, it will think twice about investment decisions. See annex 6 for details.

2. The asymmetry of the horizontal bars is explained by the differences in the variance inside each quartile. While differences in between countries are small in the first two quartiles, the differences are larger in the third and fourth.

3. The econometric methodology and its empirical application suggest that governance variables do affect different socioeconomic variables such as infant mortality, literacy, and income per capita in a *causal* way. However, having established that governance variables *jointly* do matter significantly for socioeconomic outcomes, care needs to be exercised in disentangling the independent causal impact on developmental variables of each single subcomponent of governance. Given the existence of multicolinearity among the various subcomponents of governance, it is possible that the observed impact of voice on infant mortality, for instance, is picking up by proxy other governance determinants such as corruption or rule of law. See also annex 6 for methodological details.

4. Hellman and others (see http://www.worldbank.org/wbi/governance).

5. Other factors in the empirical work on causes of corruption also appear to be important. As expected, income per capita and education are correlated with lower corruption when other factors are held constant. General developmental variables are often proxies for more specific determinants of corruption, such as the quality of public sector institutions or the rule of law (see Ades and Di Tella 1999 for a useful review).

6. Much of this section is owed to collaborative work with Sanjay Pradhan, Randi Ryterman, and the Public Sector Group. See also World Bank (2000h).

7. We owe much of this section on Public Expenditure Management to the work of Allistair Moon, Sanjay Pradhan, and Gary Reid.

8. In 1998 the head of government, cabinet members, and hundreds of civil society stakeholders participated in Albania's national governance workshop, which took place at the same time as the semifinals of soccer's World Cup in France. The workshop featured the main findings of in-depth diagnostic results and a debate on the priorities for action. It concluded with a commitment by the leadership to a progovernance program. Exemplifying the importance ascribed to it by the nation, on the next day the front pages of all the newspapers in Tirana featured charts showing the results of governance diagnostics, while the World Cup soccer results were relegated to the back pages. Albania is carrying out an anticorruption program, including judicial and customs reform, with support from the World Bank.

SEIZING THE OPPORTUNITIES FOR CHANGE

We must use time creatively, and forever realize that the time is always ripe to do right.

—Nelson Mandela, *Higher Than Hope: The Authorized Biography of Nelson Mandela*

This book has revisited the development experiences of recent decades, with a focus on the 1990s. The final decade of the 20th century saw striking progress in parts of the world, but also stagnation and reversals, even in countries that had previously enjoyed rapid growth. As prosperity spread and the quality of life improved for many in society, poverty is estimated to have persisted stubbornly or worsened for others. Greater population pressures, little access to education, and degraded natural resources made the poor increasingly vulnerable to the volatility of growth.

Between 2000 and 2010, the population of developing (including transition) economies is projected to grow from 5 billion people to 6 billion. If countries follow a business-as-usual scenario, the number of people in the developing world (excluding China) living below the poverty line could swell by some 130 million. This book addresses ways to improve future outcomes.

The Framework and Themes

Human, natural, and physical capital assets are a country's main resources for growth and welfare improvements. Their distribution, growth, and productivity largely determine people's income and welfare. The poor rely on human and natural capital in addition to physical capital, so the accumulation and productivity of these assets have a strong impact on poverty. Surveys show that "the poor rarely speak of income, but focus instead on managing assets—physical, human, social, and environmental—as a way to cope with their vulnerability" (Narayan and others 2000).

Growth based on relatively undistorted (or balanced) accumulation is likely to be less volatile and to be sustained over the long term. This theme is supported by the country evidence in chapter 2. First, a comparison of reformers and nonreformers showed that reforms helped to accelerate growth in the 1990s; however, this growth (in many instances) was based on a sharp rise in physical capital accumulation, while investments in human and natural capital lagged behind. Second, an econometric analysis of 20 mostly middle-income countries showed that the *rate* of economic growth declines as the stock of physical capital increases for given levels of human and natural capital, but the accumulation of human capital assets, by increasing access to education and health care, can arrest this decline. Third, an econometric analysis of 70 developing countries confirmed the previous findings about capital accumulation and showed that when natural capital is also considered as a factor of production, human capital can substitute for natural capital to some extent and reduce dependence on it as a source of growth.

Improving the Distribution of Opportunities

For growth to reduce poverty effectively, the assets of the poor need to be augmented. Their main asset is their human capital. Yet, inequality in education is staggering. If capabilities are normally distributed across the population—regardless of whether people are rich or poor—the inequality in accessing basic education and jobs would represent one of the greatest welfare losses to society. When the quality of schooling is low and the inequality in schooling is high, the poor are hurt most by inadequate education. The underinvestment in the human capital of the poor is attributable to wealth gaps, gender gaps, market failures, and policy distortions.

In addition, many countries have not adequately focused public investment in basic education. A reallocation toward basic education is needed to improve the efficacy of public spending. Education at all levels, including higher education, needs to benefit from private investments and public-private partnerships. Decentralized decisionmaking and community-managed schools hold great promise for improving education outcomes. However, to make education more productive for the poor, they need to be empowered with land, equity capital, training, and job opportunities in open and competitive markets (chapter 3).

Sustaining Natural Capital

Several indicators of the quality of natural capital, with the notable exception of access to clean water and sanitation, have tended to deteriorate in both slow- and fast-growth economies. For the developing world as a whole, depletion of natural capital (forest, energy, and minerals) and damage from carbon dioxide emissions is estimated at 5.8 percent of GDP. This deterioration of natural capital imposes significant current costs and diminishes prospects for future growth. Faster growth has the potential to make more resources available to invest in natural capital accumulation, but actions are needed to ensure the quality of the growth process. Thus, the grow-now-clean-up-later approach needs to give way to an environmental policy that is integrated with growth policies.

The book documents successful initiatives that simultaneously incorporated actions to stimulate growth and protect natural capital. These measures often involve selective state interventions and focus on collaborative approaches with local communities and the private sector. Global and national problems can be simultaneously addressed through international cooperation, including transfer mechanisms for payments to compensate for global externalities. As a consequence, the pursuit of high-quality growth is possible, and desirable, without extensive degradation of the atmosphere, forests, and rivers, or any other aspects of natural capital (chapter 4).

Dealing with Global Financial Risks

Integration with the global financial system has undeniable technological and economic benefits for countries, but it also exposes them to shocks and to great volatility in currency values, interest rates, and capital flows. The shocks can bring about important output and job losses, corporate and banking distress, and increased poverty. Thus, countries need suitable mechanisms to balance the benefits of globalization with its risks. They must reduce the risks of panic and crises, while maintaining their commitment to market openness.

A sound macroeconomic policy environment is essential to sustained growth, but recent experience shows that macroeconomic stability cannot do it alone. It must be complemented by actions to remove the explicit or implicit government guarantees that provide incentives for short-term capital inflows, to strengthen domestic regulation and supervision of banks and other intermediaries, to rebuild the information infrastructure of financial markets, and to improve corporate governance and transparency. Countries must also maintain public support for open capital markets. In democratic countries this entails providing insurance to citizens—either through the marketplace or through redistributive public expenditures on education, health, and transfer payments (chapter 5).

Improving Governance and Fighting Corruption

Government has a key role in delivering the public goods essential for achieving balanced and sustained growth and for reducing poverty. It also needs to have effective and streamlined regulatory regimes to address externalities and market failure. Misgovernance and corruption distort policy-making and the allocation of key production factors, consequences that slow income and welfare growth and increase poverty. Many development projects and investments have failed because too little attention was paid to fostering good governance and civil liberties, controlling corruption, improving the bureaucracy, and building institutional capacity.

Participation by beneficiaries, attention to the voices of people and competitive enterprises, and accountability and transparency in governments are vital to controlling corruption and improving governance. New approaches to coalition building and the integration of the latest methods of governance and corruption surveys with new technologies for timely analysis and dissemination are producing encouraging results in some countries. Collective action from such a participatory consensus-building process, coupled with the power of information, disclosure, transparency, and knowledge and capacity building, can nurture the political will and technical ability to address misgovernance and sustain institution building (chapter 6).

Actions to Ensure Quality

The emerging themes help clarify four dimensions that shape the quality of the growth process: distribution of opportunities, sustainability of the environment, management of global risks, and governance (box 7.1). These elements directly contribute to development. They have a two-way relationship with growth, they add to the impact of growth on welfare, they help make growth more sustained, and they address the conflicts that growth might pose to sustainability.

The book provides evidence from a range of areas and sources showing that a focus on quantity will not in itself ensure quality. So public spending levels alone cannot give an adequate indication of impact. In a WHO study that ranks 191 countries on the quality (including fairness and broad coverage) of their health systems, the United States is 1st in health expenditure per capita but 37th in overall health system performance. France—4th in

Box 7.1. Actions for Quality

What might be the policy implications for ensuring quality growth? The book has presented several, which can be organized under three principles.

Policies for Undistorted Growth of Physical, Human, and Natural Capital

- Avoid direct or indirect subsidies to capital, such as tax breaks, allocation of monopoly powers and subsidies, special privileges that feed corruption, and implicit guarantees on rates of return.
- Invest efficiently in human capital and ensure access for the poor through incentives and allocation of public investments in education.
- Sustain natural capital by clarifying property rights, avoiding unrealistically low levels of royalties for natural resources, and enforcing environmental taxes.

Attend to the Stability and Distributive Aspects of Growth

- Ensure that the poor can access education, technology, and health services, as well as land, credit, skills training, and job opportunities in open markets.
- Ensure effective regulatory frameworks and anticorruption measures to accompany financial openness and privatization.
- Align reforms and restructuring to mechanisms for mitigating the costs of crises, which will likely be borne disproportionately by the poor.

Build the Governance Framework for Development

- Involve all stakeholders—the private sector, including transnational firms and the domestic private sector, NGOs, civil society, and the government—in implementing a commonly shared development agenda.
- Empower people through voice, participation, and greater civil and political liberties.
- Support economic liberalization by promoting institutional development and better governance.

---

per capita expenditure—is 1st in performance, Colombia is 22nd, Chile 33rd, Costa Rica 36th, and Cuba 39th (WHO 2000).

The book also shows the effects of market failures. On the ability of the poor to build human capital. On the undervaluation and subsequent overexploitation of natural capital. And on undue instability in financial markets. A focus on quality highlights the role of regulatory policies and public expenditures in dealing with these market failures.

The answer is not necessarily to increase the regulatory burden of the economy or to increase public expenditures. Instead, it is to reallocate public expenditure following new priorities and to change the nature of regulation—eliminating regulations that are counterproductive and improving those that address market failures. What should be the new public expenditure priorities? Do more to promote the buildup of human capital, especially among the poor. Invest more to prevent further degradation of

173

natural capital and reduce regressive subsidies benefiting physical capital. Target regulations at failures in financial markets and in markets that affect the use of environmental resources.

Where Have the Policies for Quality Worked—or Not?

There is no single setting in which the attributes of quality have been emphasized with uniform success. However, the following four country experiences illustrate the pursuit of quality aspects of growth, with varying degrees of effectiveness.

Investing Efficiently in Basic Education: The Republic of Korea

Starting with a war-torn economy and a poor natural resource base, Korea had an average annual GDP per capita of just over US$500, based on 1980 PPP dollars, in the late 1950s. GDP per capita then doubled in each of the next three decades, driven by relatively broadly based, export-oriented growth. The growth was accompanied by rapid poverty reduction and relatively equitable income distribution (Leipziger 1997).

Korea spent an average of 3.4 percent of GNP on public education in the 1980s, which was in line with the regional average. However, unlike other developing countries, Korea spent two-thirds of its education budget on compulsory basic education in the 1960s and early 1970s. In the 1990s, public subsidies to primary school students were two to three times those to college students. Tertiary education was financed mainly by private spending. Korea was able to expand basic education rapidly and reduce educational inequality, as measured by a drop in the education Gini coefficient from 0.55 in 1960 to 0.22 in 1990.

The Korean government supported favored industries through directed lending, subsidies, and guarantees. In liberalized but inadequately regulated environments, these measures led to excessive foreign borrowing and wasteful investment by the corporate sector and intensified financial fragility. Both positive and cautionary lessons can be drawn from the Korean experience.

Broad-Based Growth within an Incomplete Agenda: Kerala, India

On such dimensions of social development as education, health, the gender gap, civil and political liberties, poverty reduction, and inequality, the development performance of Kerala, India, is comparable to that of much richer economies. A baby born in Kerala can expect to live longer than one born in Washington, D.C. However, Kerala's measured economic growth has, until recently, been lower than average among Indian states.

Kerala attended to the qualitative aspects of development while neglecting first-generation, growth-oriented policies. For balanced asset growth, market-friendly economic policies need to complement social initiatives. The lack of progress in implementing an open and competitive environment for economic activities has hindered economic growth in Kerala. Once these first-generation policy reforms are implemented, the high level of social development should provide a basis for sustained high-quality growth.

Ravallion and Datt (1999) found that the poverty-reducing impact of growth varies with initial literacy, farm productivity, and standard of living in rural areas relative to that in urban areas. In states with high literacy rates and equitably distributed basic education every additional percentage point of growth has a stronger impact on poverty reduction than is the case in other states. The elasticity of poverty reduction to nonfarm growth in Kerala was the highest of all states in India. If all Indian states had Kerala's elasticity of poverty reduction, the share of their people in poverty would have fallen nearly three times as fast —at 3.5 percent a year, not 1.3 percent.

Balancing Economic Growth and Sustainable Natural Capital: Costa Rica

Costa Rica has a high literacy rate, economic and political stability, and no military budget. Income distribution and social indicators are among the best in Latin America. Yet the country needed to address several environmental problems, from urban pollution, excessive agrochemical use, and overexploitation of fisheries to biodiversity loss and a deforestation rate in the 1980s estimated at 3 percent a year.

Costa Rica responded with an innovative and comprehensive system of forest protection. A system of compensation through markets for carbon sequestration, watershed conservation, and biodiversity protection has helped protect forests. The system generates its own resources through a dedicated fuel tax on domestic consumers, contracts with hydropower utilities, and payments by international parties for carbon emissions offsets.

The Ministry of Environment and Energy has supported research-based policy reforms for environmental protection and environmental education programs for schoolchildren. Environmental impact assessments are mandatory for most projects, including commercial and residential construction and mining. The law sets strict guidelines on protection of water resources, wetlands, natural monuments, protected natural areas, and marine and coastal resources. It also sets strict guidelines on all types of pollution and on abuse of land and improper waste disposal. The plan now is to increase the effectiveness of the laws, to strengthen the capacity of institutions responsible for enforcement, and to enter into partnerships with the private sector and civil society (Thomas 1998).

Balancing Openness, Risk Management, and Social Protection: Chile

After a decade of rapid opening of markets and volatile growth in the 1980s, Chile took measures for risk management in the 1990s. First, Chile implemented a highly targeted system of social assistance through health, education, and housing programs and income transfers. The government's social investments increased by 75 percent between 1987 and 1994, which, complementing robust economic growth, made solid contributions to poverty reduction. Second, as capital flows became more volatile, the independent central bank implemented selective capital controls on short-term capital inflows between 1991 and 1998. Arguably, they have helped to increase the wedge between domestic and foreign interest rates and change the composition of capital inflows toward longer maturities (Gallego, Hernandez, and Schmidt-Hebbel 1999).

These and other policies have contributed to rapid economic growth with a significant decline in poverty. The incidence of poverty fell from 41 percent of the population in 1987 to 23 percent in 1994, while the incidence of severe poverty (based on a lower poverty/indigence line) fell from 13 to 5 percent. Income inequality seems to have stabilized since 1987, after rising during most of the 1960–85 period (Ferreira and Litchfield 1999). However, natural resources have been underprotected and overexploited. In addition, the distribution of education has become less equitable, as reflected by a widening gap in years of schooling between the rich and poor (World Bank 1997b).

Political Economy of Quantity versus Quality

The varied experiences of economies suggest that an emphasis on quality is essential on three counts. First, quality directly promotes well-being by influencing a more even distribution of education and health care and an improved environment. Growth and quality aspects—linked to each other in a two-way relationship—need joint attention.

Second, the pace of growth is less volatile and more sustainable when quality aspects are considered. Where growth rates are highly variable over time, the negative impacts are especially pronounced for the poor.

Third, economies that focus on quality can deal better with difficult tradeoffs. One tradeoff mentioned in this book is the temptation to subsidize physical capital or overexploit natural capital in an effort to promote growth. In this and similar cases, a focus on the qualitative aspects of growth helps to manage the tradeoffs.

Most countries—and much policy advice—have stressed macroeconomic stabilization and liberalization first. Meanwhile, actions on the qualitative aspects, such as the distribution of education and the sustainable use of natural capital, are postponed. The evidence presented here shows the fundamental limitations of this approach and the benefits of joint action.

Reformers have sometimes found it necessary to take advantage of windows of opportunity for liberalization, when vested interests and opposition to liberalization have been muted. Whether the qualitative dimensions also receive priority may depend on other conditions, including the spread of democratic institutions. In an increasingly mature and participatory setting, a country would not want to postpone the important qualitative aspects of growth to a time when the costs of addressing them will have multiplied.

Sometimes, political difficulties can impede progress, even when the importance of the qualitative aspects is clear. Interest groups may drive a wedge between policy design and implementation. Collusion between politicians and the elite may distort the allocation of public resources to reward the owners of physical capital. For example, tax holidays, implicit guarantees on infrastructure, monopoly powers, and easy access to natural resources often benefit the rich, but hurt the poor.

The political economy of reforms, less explored than other aspects of growth, is an area difficult to evaluate. Yet some initiatives seem unambiguously to be worthwhile. Fostering beneficiary participation, encouraging country ownership of reform programs, and promoting political representation of the poor are a good beginning.

Going Forward

How can countries accord greater priority to the quality dimensions of growth? And how can they finance and support such objectives in practice? Several observations drawn from the discussion in this book can guide efforts in that direction:

- Explicit attention to ensuring transparency and reducing corruption and rent-seeking will not only raise national saving and investment and promote sustained growth, but will also help to distribute its fruits more equitably.
- Some quality dimensions lend themselves to full-cost pricing or taxation, both of which generate public resources.
- Other measures to ensure quality require a reallocation of public expenditures—reducing subsidies and distortions in some areas and increasing public investment in others.
- Attending to quality does not have to mean more government intervention, but rather may mean more involvement of the private sector, nongovernmental organizations, and civil society in implementing shared goals.
- Broader civil outreach can nurture civil liberties and participatory processes that can help to sustain policy changes.
- All this in turn would call for a much greater focus on skills, technological development, and capacity building and the effectiveness with which this is done.

The evidence in this book provides strong motivation for focusing on the quality aspects marking the ability of people to shape their lives—for example, the equality of opportunities for human development, sustainability of the environment, management of global risk, and the manner of governing—along with the traditional facets of growth. Governments do not have to assume the entire burden of giving greater priority to the quality dimensions—nor should they.

Rather than calling for more government intervention, the evidence in this book calls for greater voice and participation by the private sector, NGOs, and civil society. A broader involvement by all can move the emphasis of development beyond measured GDP growth to include social and environmental progress, greater empowerment and voice, and better governance. This reallocation of priorities will refine the contribution of the qualitative aspects of the growth process and focus the spotlight on what development truly means.

BROAD OBJECTIVES AND INSTRUMENTS

C ontinuous assessment of development progress and policies requires a broader than usual framework even if all elements are not quantifiable. Here we look at development goals and policy instruments and formulate some hypotheses about the links between them. A formal model and discussion of the empirical results are in chapter 2 and annex 2.

People value at least three dimensions of life in current and future time periods. They gain direct satisfaction from education and other aspects of human capital, such as life expectancy or literacy; from clean air and water and other stocks of natural capital; and from flows of consumption goods, such as food and shelter. They also care about the welfare of future generations and their enjoyment of all these aspects of life (at some discount rate). A society will try to get the most from human, natural, and physical capital, subject to the total resource constraint. Together, increases in these dimensions signify quality growth.

The simple associations among the goals and policies, in the form of correlations and scatter charts, are presented here. Annex 2 presents an econometric analysis, which complements a vast literature in this area.

Goals and Policy Measures

We constructed composite indexes for human development and environmental sustainability, enabling us to focus on three measures of quality of growth rather than a large number: human development, economic growth, and environmental sustainability. The policy instruments include those emphasized in the *World Development Report 1991* (World Bank 1991) along with several others. The correlations between policies and goals are shown in table A1.1. These correspond to the summary figures 1.2 and 1.5 in chapter 1. The associations between policies and component indicators forming the indexes are not shown. Scatter plots for selected combinations of goals and policies are shown in figure A1.1, after controlling for the effects of initial period income.

The goals and the proximate variables used are

- *Human development indicators.* We constructed a human development index from data on reductions in infant mortality, reductions in the illiteracy rate, and increases in life expectancy. The period over which changes were computed was from the early 1980s to the

Table A1.1. Relationships between Development Objectives and Policy Instruments, 1981–98

	Goals								
	Human development			*GDP growth*			*Sustainable development*		
Instruments	*Correlation coefficient*	*Significance level*	*Number of countries*	*Correlation coefficient*	*Significance level*	*Number of countries*	*Correlation coefficient*	*Significance level*	*Number of countries*
Educational spending/ GDP	0.04	0.72	87	–0.02	0.84	88	0.17	0.21	56
Health spending/GDP (1990–98)	–0.01	0.95	70	*–0.28*	0.02	71	0.18	0.23	49
Budget surplus	0.12	0.40	55	*0.27*	0.05	55	0.01	0.97	39
Trade/GDP ratio	0.07	0.50	89	0.07	0.50	90	–0.05	0.69	56
Change in mean tariff	0.05	0.82	26	–0.09	0.65	26	–0.10	0.65	25
Capital account openness index (1988)	0.21	0.22	36	0.00	0.99	36	–0.22	0.23	31
Financial repression index (1996)	–0.16	0.50	21	0.26	0.26	21	–0.35	0.12	21
M2/GDP	*0.36*	0.00	89	*0.29*	0.01	90	–0.08	0.58	56
Domestic environmental action (dummy variable)	–0.16	0.15	80	*0.24*	0.03	81	–0.10	0.47	56
International environmental action (dummy variable)	0.11	0.35	80	0.08	0.49	81	*–0.24*	0.08	56
Rule of law index (1997–98)	*0.34*	0.00	86	*0.41*	0.00	87	0.18	0.19	55
Government effectiveness index (1997–98)	*0.35*	0.00	81	*0.27*	0.00	82	0.05	0.73	55

Notes: Improvement in human development is defined as the Borda index of reduction in infant mortality, reduction in illiteracy, and increase in life expectancy between the 1980s and 1990s. Improvement in sustainable development is defined as the Borda index of decreases in carbon dioxide emissions, deforestation, and water pollution between the 1980s and 1990s. Correlations that are significant at least at the 10 percent level are shown in bold italics.

Source: World Bank (2000c); authors' computations.

Relationships between objectives and instruments

Figure A1.1. Development Objectives and Policy Instruments

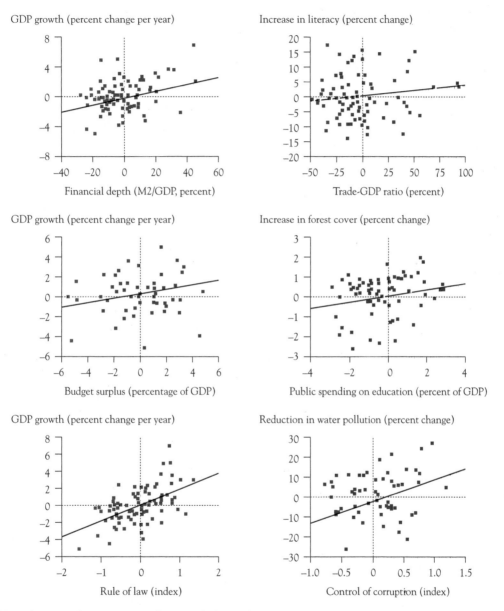

Note: The scatter plots are constructed using residuals from the regressions of the respective variables—pertaining to both the axes—against GDP per capita in 1981.

Source: World Bank (2000c); authors' computations.

late 1990s. We wanted to incorporate in the index variables reflecting income distribution, reduction in the incidence of poverty and the gender gap in educational attainment, but did not because data were unavailable for many countries.

- *Sustainable development indicators.* We constructed a composite index of the negative annual rate of deforestation, reductions in carbon dioxide emissions per capita, and reductions in water pollution per capita. The period used was again from the early 1980s to the late 1990s. We wanted to include in the index a measure of air pollution in the major cities in developing countries, but comparable data were available only for recent years.
- *Income growth.* We used growth rates between 1981 and 1998 of GDP and intermediate indicators such as capital stock and TFP growth, as used in many empirical studies, such as those employed by Barro (1990), Easterly (1999a), Easterly and others (1993), Nehru and Dhareshwar (1993), Pritchett (1998), World Bank (1991), and Young (1992).

Policy instruments were represented by the following:

- *Social spending on education and health.* They were expressed as percentages of GDP, averaged over available values for the period: 1981–97 for education spending and 1990–98 for health spending. Due to data limitations, we could not include allocation of spending on basic education and preventive health services (Filmer, Hammer, and Pritchett forthcoming; López, Thomas, and Wang 1998).
- *Environmental commitment.* We used two dummy variables to represent environmental commitment: one for domestic action, based on environmental strategy formulation and profiling, and another for international action, based on the signing of the Global Treaty on Climate Change. Unfortunately, more refined indicators of government policies toward sustainable development are not yet available.
- *Macroeconomic policy.* We used budget surplus as a percentage of GDP (Barro 1990; Fischer 1993).
- *Openness.* We used the trade-to-GDP ratio, parallel-market premium, change in mean tariff, and a measure of capital controls based on Quinn (1997) and Quinn and Toyoda (1997) (a higher value of the index represents a greater degree of openness to capital inflows; see annex 5).
- *Financial depth, prudence, and risk management.* We used financial depth as measured by the ratio of M2 to GDP and an index of financial

repression (based on Williamson and Mahar 1998; a lower value of the index represents a more liberal financial system).

- *Governance indicators.* Six governance indicators—rule of law, government effectiveness, control of corruption, voice and accountability, regulatory burden, and political instability and violence—have been examined in this book. Of this list, the first three have been used in this annex. For further details and analysis see chapter 6 and annex 6.

Composite Indexes of Human and Sustainable Development

We used the Borda ranking technique to construct a single index for human development and one for sustainable development. The indicators for the index of human development are

- Reduction in infant mortality between the 1980s and 1990s
- Reduction in adult illiteracy between the 1980s and 1990s
- Increase in life expectancy between the 1980s and 1990s.

The indicators for the index of sustainable development are

- Decline in emissions of carbon dioxide per capita between the 1980s and 1990s
- Decreases in emission of organic water pollutants (kilograms per day per worker) between the 1980s and 1990s
- The negative of annual average rate of deforestation measured over 1980–95.

The Borda ranking procedure involves assigning each country a point equal to its rank in each component criterion. Each country's points over all the components are averaged, and the averages are used to re-rank the countries. The procedure allows the aggregation of indicators with different units of measurement and different periods and country coverages; that is, it allows comparisons among countries across categories even when the number of countries studied varies by category. For more details regarding the Borda ranking techniques see Fine and Fine (1974a,b), Goodman and Markowitz (1952), Smith (1973), and Thomas and Wang (1996).

We also tried an alternative method of aggregation that transformed each component variable into a standardized score, with a mean of 0 and a standard deviation of 1, and then averaged them. In the significance of correlation coefficients, the results were substantially similar.

FRAMEWORK AND EVIDENCE

This annex provides a framework and empirical evidence for chapter 2.

A Welfare Function

Define an additive and separable welfare function, U, for a society that consists of N individuals

$$(A2.1) \quad U = \sum_{i=1}^{N} u(c_i) + \sum_{i=1}^{N} v(h_i; R),$$

where c_i is the consumption of individual i, h_i is the human capital of individual i, and R is the (aggregate) level of environmental assets. R is assumed to be a pure public good, and hence its distribution among the population is irrelevant. Also, $u(\cdot)$ and $v(\cdot)$ are increasing and strictly concave in their arguments. A second-order approximation of U evaluated at the mean or average values of c and h yields

$$(A2.2) \quad U \approx Nu(\bar{c}) + \sum_{i=1}^{N} u'(\bar{c})(c_i - \bar{c}) + \frac{1}{2} \sum_{i=1}^{N} u''(\bar{c})(c_i - \bar{c})^2$$

$$+ Nv(\bar{h}; R) + \sum_{i=1}^{N} v'(\bar{h}; R)(h_i - \bar{h}) + \frac{1}{2} \sum_{i=1}^{N} v''(\bar{h}; R)(h_i - \bar{h})^2,$$

where $\bar{c}$ is average or per capita consumption, $\bar{h}$ is average or per capita human capital, $u'(\bar{c})$, $v'(\bar{h}; R)$ are first derivatives with respect to c and h, respectively, evaluated at mean values $\bar{c}$ and $\bar{h}$ and $u''(\bar{c})$, and $v''(\bar{h}; R)$ are second derivatives. Taking expectations we obtain the average welfare per individual i,

(A2.3) $E(U) \approx u(\bar{c}) + \dfrac{1}{2} u''(\bar{c})\sigma_c^2 + v(\bar{h}; R) + \dfrac{1}{2} v''(\bar{h}; R)\sigma_h^2 ,$

where σ_c^2 is the variance of consumption across the population and σ_h^2 is the variance of the distribution of human capital across the population. By strict concavity of $u(\cdot)$ and $v(\cdot)$, we have that $u'' < 0$ and $v''(\cdot) < 0$. Thus, aggregate or expected welfare is increasing in $\bar{c}$ and $\bar{h}$ and decreasing in σ_c^2 and σ_h^2. Moreover, because $v(\cdot)$ is increasing in R, $\partial v''/\partial R \approx 0$ is sufficient to obtain that $E(U)$ is also increasing in R.

From the definition in the text, sustained growth requires that the expansion of physical capital through time be accompanied by positive growth of human capital without worsening its distribution. Also, sustained growth is likely to diminish poverty and is not consistent with a worsening of income distribution. Sustained growth increases $\bar{c}$ and $\bar{h}$ and reduces, or at least does not increase, σ_c^2 and σ_h^2. Thus, sustained growth is likely to increase welfare, $E(U)$ in equation (A2.3), as long as R does not fall or falls at a sufficiently slow pace.

Private Sector Optimization

As indicated in the text, human capital (h) and natural capital (R) are subject to two possible externalities associated with consumption and production. Consumption externalities stem from the fact that the positive direct effects of h and R on the welfare function may be only partially considered by the private sector in its resource allocation decisions. Production externalities arise because much of the positive technological spillovers associated with h may not be considered by the private sector. In addition, part of the value of R as a productive resource may also be ignored by the private sector, particularly in cases where natural capital property rights are not well defined.

Here we make an extreme assumption: that all the direct consumption values of h and R on the welfare function (as well as the distributional effects represented by σ_c^2 and σ_h^2) are ignored by the private sector's production decisions. Moreover, we assume that production externalities establish a wedge between the private marginal products of h and R and the true marginal products of these resources. That is, the private sector only considers a fraction of the contribution of h and R to production. In addition, we assume that a minimum subsistence consumption level, c_s, exists. The representative household needs a consumption level of c_s to survive and will not allow consumption to reach levels below c_s. That is, we impose a subsistence constraint, $c - c_s \geq 0$.

Under these assumptions, the relevant problem is maximization of the discounted present value of $u(\bar{c})$—as opposed to that of $E(U)$—subject to the following constraints:

(A2.4) (i) $\dot{k} = G(k, h; R; A(k, h); p) - c - I_h^g - I_h^p - I_R^g$

   (ii) $c - c_s \geq 0$

   (iii) $\dot{h} = I_h^g + I_h^p$

   (iv) $\dot{R} = \phi(R) + \beta I_R^g - \psi[G(\cdot)],$

   (v) $k(0) = k_0;$ $h(0) = h_0;$ $R(0) = R_0$

where k is per capita physical capital, $G(\cdot)$ is the economy's per capita GDP function, $A(\cdot)$ is a productivity index, p stands for policy variables and exogenous factors, I_h^g is government investment in human capital, I_h^p is private investment in human capital, β is a parameter, I_R^g is government investment in natural capital, $\phi(R)$ is a growth function of the renewable resources through time, and $\psi(\cdot)$ is an increasing function of GDP that reflects the possibly negative direct impact of increased economic activity on natural capital. We assume that population, N, is fixed, so that by using appropriate units it can be normalized to 1. Hence, the distinction between total and per capita variables in equation (A2.4) becomes irrelevant. Also, for algebraic simplicity we assume a zero rate of depreciation of k and h. Assuming a constant logarithmic depreciation rate for these assets, as is usually done, does not affect any of the results.

Several comments about equation (A2.4) are in order:

- It is assumed that I_h^g and I_R^g are policy variables.
- We assume that the effect of GDP on natural capital is not at all internalized by the private sector, and that, as a consequence, the private sector will not invest in natural capital. Thus, equation (A2.4) (iv) is only used as an accounting identity and is not directly (and ex ante) taken into consideration in decisions by the private sector, even though the evolution of R will affect its future decisions.
- The effect of h on $G(\cdot)$ is only partially incorporated into the decisions of the private sector. The government may fill a part or the full extent of the possible human capital underinvestment gap left by the private sector.
- We allow k and h to affect knowledge represented by the productivity function $A(\cdot)$. It is assumed that knowledge is a public good that any firm can access at zero cost. In line with the "learning by doing" hypothesis, we follow Arrow (1962) and Romer (1986) and assume that learning by doing works through each firm's investment in k. However, we specify that learning by doing requires

human capital, or that human capital facilitates and increases the effectiveness of this process. Thus, the function $A(\cdot)$ is assumed to be increasing in its arguments and the marginal effect of k on A increases with h, that is, $\partial^2 A/\partial k \partial h > 0$.

- Equation (A2.4) (i) implies that public investment in human capital is financed out of total savings via lump sum taxes. An alternative approach is to assume that public investments are financed via an income tax proportional to GDP, as in Barro (1993).

- Production of human capital is assumed to be generated through the same productive process as physical capital and consumer goods. This assumption has often been used in the literature (see, for example, Barro and Sala-I-Martin 1995). Alternatively, one may postulate a separate production function of h as in Lucas (1988) or Rebelo (1991). Although the latter is a more realistic approach, the assumption of a common production function for consumer and all investment goods considerably reduces the algebra and does not alter the basic conclusions.

The Case of a Middle-Income Economy with Initial Consumption far above Subsistence

First we assume that constraint (A2.4) (ii) is not binding; the economy is sufficiently rich to allow $c > c_s$ at all times. We will analyze the role of the subsistence constraint in the case of the poor economy.

It can be shown that the private sector in this model invests only in k if the marginal product of physical capital, $G_k(\cdot)$, is higher than the marginal product of human capital as perceived by the private sector, $G_h^p(\cdot)$.[1] It will invest in both k and h if $G_h^p = G_k$ and will only invest in h if $G_h^p > G_k$. Thus, assuming that k is initially relatively low, $I_h^p = I_R^p = 0$ and $\dot{k} > 0$. Of course, the main reason why the private sector only invests in one factor is our assumption that all factors are produced out of a common production function. If we allow for a different production function for h, the private sector may be shown to invest in both k and h even outside the long-run equilibrium. However, the essential point is that the private sector tends to underinvest in human and natural capital relative to physical capital. That is, the private sector tends to have too narrow an investment portfolio as long as the positive external effects associated with h and R are larger than those associated with k regardless of whether h or R have separate production functions. In a sense, the extreme specification (apart from simplifying the algebra) helps to highlight the fact that the market economy tends to overspecialize its investment choice.

From the first-order conditions of the above problem one can derive the growth rate of the economy in the usual way if $G_k > G_h^p$. Economic growth is an increasing function of the gap between the marginal return to capital and its marginal cost, $b(\cdot)$. Under the usual assumption of constant risk aversion—for example, that $-u''(c) \cdot c/u'(c) \equiv \theta > 0$, is a constant—and where $u(c)$ is defined in equation (A2.3), the rate of economic growth is

$$(A2.5) \quad \dot{c}/c = \frac{1}{\theta} [G_k(k, h; R, A; p) - b(r; p)],$$

where $\dot{c}/c$ is the rate of growth of consumption per capita (we have suppressed the bar over c) $G_k(\cdot)$ is a function reflecting the marginal product of physical capital for a given level of A, and r is the discount rate.[2]

There are four possible cases:

i. *Sustained growth requires absolute balanced asset growth.* This case occurs if the aggregate production function $G(\cdot)$ is subject to constant returns to scale (CRS); for example, the spillover effects of k and h on $A(\cdot)$ are negligible. Therefore, G_k is a function only of factor ratios. Assume that h and R remain constant as $\dot{c}/c > 0$ and $\dot{k}/k > 0$. In this case the private sector does not invest in R and h. Thus, growth will be unbalanced relying exclusively on the accumulation of k. Because of CRS, $G_k(\cdot)$ declines as k increases. As a result, the expression in square brackets in (A2.5) declines and the "Solow curse" applies. A positive rate of growth cannot be sustained unless the government invests in h and/or R. (The growth decline is, of course, more rapid if R falls as a consequence of growth). So in this case, sustained growth can only be achieved by the government investing in h and R, so that $\dot{k}/k = \dot{h}/h = \dot{R}/R$. Absolute balanced growth of the three assets is required to sustain a positive growth rate.

ii. *Sustained growth can be achieved with unbalanced asset growth.* This case may occur if large technological spillovers associated with capital accumulation exist. In this case it is possible that the marginal product of k does not decline because A is increasing in k. Now even if h and R do not increase or if they decline at a sufficiently low rate, the growth rate can still be sustained. So in this case we can have sustained yet unbalanced growth based purely on physical capital growth and technological spillovers.

iii. *Sustained growth can be achieved with semibalanced asset expansion.* This could happen if there is a high degree of substitution between h and R in the G_k function. Substitution between h and R allows for two possible subcases as $h > h^c$, where h^c is a critical level of human capital:

a. Under CRS with no spillover effects growth can be sustained if h and k grow at identical rates, that is, the k/h ratio remains constant. *Absolute semibalanced asset growth* is necessary to produce this scenario.

b. Spillover effects that effectively imply that the production function exhibits increasing returns to scale in k and h, but that the net marginal product of k is decreasing in k. In this case, h may grow at a pace slower than k, that is, *relative semibalanced asset growth* is needed.

In this case $\partial G_k/\partial R$ decreases as h increases and $\partial G_k/\partial R \approx 0$ as $h \geq h^c$, where h^c is at a certain critical level. That is, as h increases over h^c, economic growth becomes independent of R, although R still has a positive marginal product. Note that the relevant substitution is for the marginal product of k function, not for the production function, as is usually assumed. This implies that the relevant substitution between h and R relates to third-order effects and not to second-order effects as the usual Hicksian or Allen elasticities of substitution imply.

iv. *Sustained growth can be achieved with relative asset growth balance.* This case may occur if technological spillovers are dependent on both k and h, with a strong complementary relationship in the A function and $h < h^c$. We argue in the text that the technological spillovers associated with physical capital are not likely to be large in developing countries that do not have a sufficiently high and increasing level of general education. That is, the elasticity of substitution between h and k in the $A(\cdot)$ function is small. If h is too low, the effect of k on A will be small. In this case, sustained growth can be achieved only if h and R increase so that $G_k(\cdot)$ does not fall as k increases. This implies that sustained growth can be achieved with relative, rather than absolute, balanced asset growth. An economy can sustain a positive rate of growth when the public sector invests in h and R at a rate generally lower than the rate of physical capital accumulation.

The empirical results presented in the text allow us to rule out the first and second cases. That is, although complete or absolute asset balance is not necessary for sustained growth, growth based only on physical capital accumulation is not sustainable either. According to the empirical findings, the last two cases are empirically the most relevant. Poor countries that do not have large levels of human capital require that human and natural capital grow at a certain rate, which is generally lower than that of physical capital, to sustain growth. That is, the last case reflects best the situation for poor economies that have not yet developed a solid human capital base. The third case, especially subcase (iii)b, is the most relevant to middle-income countries that already have a significant level of human capital.

Figure A2.1 illustrates balanced and unbalanced growth processes under the assumption that there are no economies of scale or technological spillovers associated with capital accumulation and that $h > h^c$, which implies that changes in R play no role on economic growth. The marginal product $G_k(G_h)$ is decreasing (increasing) in the physical capital to human capital ratio. In the figure, G_h is the true marginal product of human capital, x is the marginal contribution of human capital to welfare as a consumer good, and therefore $G_h + x$ is the total and true marginal social contribution of human capital. G_h^p is the marginal contribution of human capital as perceived by the private sector.

For an economy that grows from a low k/h ratio, the marginal product of k falls along the G_k schedule as k/h increases. In the absence of intervention, a laissez faire economy will continue accumulating physical capital until it reaches point B, at which juncture no further growth occurs; k/h does not increase. At this point, $G_k = b$ where b is the marginal cost and, hence, growth stops. In the lower quadrant of figure A2.1 we relate growth of consumption, $\dot{c}/c$, to the level of k/h. In the absence of intervention, $\dot{c}/c$ continuously declines until it reaches point L at $(k/h)^0$ where $\dot{c}/c = 0$. (This case represents growth pattern 1 discussed in chapter 2.)

If the public sector invests in human capital, however, long-run growth is possible. An optimal intervention would entail a public sector investment in human capital once the economy reaches $(k/h)^*$ or point D, where the marginal product, G_k, of physical capital is equal to the social marginal product of human capital $G_h + x$. At this point, $G_k = G_h + x > b$, so the economy is still growing. However, as growth is now balanced with $\dot{k}/k = \dot{h}/h$, k/h remains constant at $(k/h)^*$. In the lower quadrant, the optimal intervention implies that the k/h stops growing at $(k/h)^*$ at point d. Here we have a positive and sustainable growth rate of consumption equal to $(\dot{c}/c)^*$. (This situation reflects growth pattern 3 in chapter 2.)

Alternatively, the government may choose to subsidize investors in physical capital by reducing b or increasing G_k over time (see equation A2.5). However, these subsidies must be financed. Assuming that they are financed through lump sum taxes, the budget constraint, equation A2.4 (i), implies that the government must reduce I_h^g and/or I_R^g. However, this means that the economy becomes even more dependent on subsidies as a means to sustain growth. In figure A2.1 this pattern of growth can be shown by a shift to the right of the G_k schedule due to the capital subsidies (or by a fall of b). But the budget constraint implies that the government has less resources to

Figure A2.1. Constant Returns to Scale and No Technological Spillovers

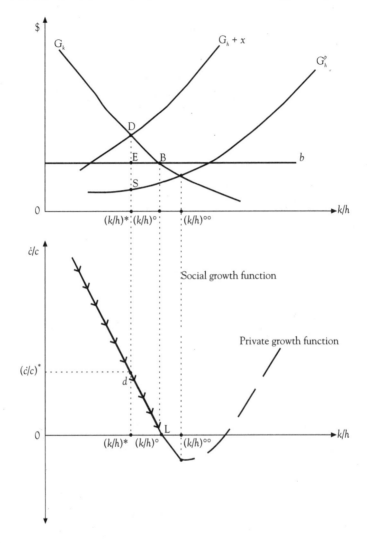

Source: Author.

invest in human capital. Thus to preserve growth (to maintain a positive gap between G_k and b) subsidies must be continuously increased over time. That is, schedule G_k should be constantly shifting to the right by permanent and increasing subsidies. Economic growth becomes dependent on ever increasing subsidies to capital owners with the consequent negative impact on income distribution and human and natural capital. (This is growth pattern 2 discussed in chapter 2.)

The Case of a Poor Economy

Here we consider a poor economy where the initial level of consumption is only slightly above subsistence and is in the process of growing toward a steady-state level of growth. We call this a semisubsistence economy. The idea is that the poor constitute by themselves a subeconomy where most of the growth arises from their own efforts to save and invest. The semisubsistence economy does have contacts with the modern sectors because the poor sell some of their products to the modern sectors and because some of the poor are able to migrate into the modern sectors. For the sake of brevity and simplicity we do not explicitly model either of these processes. We simply postulate that the GDP function of the poor is dependent on shocks arising from the rich sectors through the variable p in the $G(\cdot)$ function. For example, a recession in the modern economy is translated into a fall in p, which in turn causes both the $G(\cdot)$ and the $G_k(\cdot)$ functions to be displaced downward. Another possible shock arises from the degradation of R caused by an expansion of the modern sector into areas where the poor live.[3] We assume that the economy is initially growing by investing primarily in k. The growth of h depends 100 percent on government expenditures in human capital.

We define two limiting cases. The first is where income minus depreciation of the asset stocks is exactly sufficient to cover the level of subsistence consumption:

$$(A2.6) \quad c^s = h_0 \left\{ G\left[\left(\frac{k}{h}\right)^s, 1; \frac{R_0}{h_0}, A; p \right] - \delta_k \left(\frac{k}{h}\right)^s - \delta_h \right\},$$

where h_0 is the initial level of human capital and R_0 is the initial level of natural capital, and we now assume a postive depreciation rate for k and h (δ_k and δ_h).

That is, for a given level of R_0, h_0 and exogenous policy variables p, there is a unique level $(k/h)^s$ that permits the economy to exactly satisfy its minimum subsistence consumption. If $k/h > (k/h)^s$, the economy is above subsistence with potential for positive net savings and growth. If $k/h < (k/h)^s$, the economy is not able to cover the depreciation of its stocks of capital, and therefore, with actual consumption equal to c^s, stocks are being reduced. That is, the economy is running down its capital. This causes negative growth as k/h falls.

The other limiting case is when the economy is barely able to satisfy its subsistence consumption only if it uses its total output without allowing any replacement of stocks:

$$(A2.7) \quad c^s = h_0 G\left[\left(\frac{k}{h}\right)^{ss}, 1; \frac{R_0}{h_0}, A; p \right].$$

Once $k/h = (k/h)^{ss}$, households need to use all their output for consumption. At $(k/h)^{ss}$ the economy becomes infeasible.

Note that both $(k/h)^s$ and $(k/h)^{ss}$ are dependent on the levels of h_0, R_0, A, and p. It can easily be seen that $(k/h)^s$ and $(k/h)^{ss}$ are both decreasing in h_0, R_0, A, and p (assuming that $G(\cdot)$ is increasing in p, that is, p represents positive exogenous factors). Thus, a negative shock due, for example, to a recession in the modern economy that reduces the terms of trade of the poor or the level of R due to intrusion of commercial interests on the natural resources owned by the poor (which ironically is more likely to happen during boom times in the modern sector), will increase $(k/h)^s$.

Suppose that the economy is initially at $(k/h)_0$ greater than $(k/h)^s$. That is, it is growing toward $(k/h)^*$ (see figure A2.2). Suppose now that a recession occurs in the modern sector reducing p. This will cause $(k/h)^s$ to increase. If the new $(k/h)^s$ is now greater or equal to $(k/h)_0$, then the semisubsistence economy is thrown into a subsistence trap that could lead to negative growth driving k/h toward $(k/h)^{ss}$.

Consider the case where the initial shock occurs at time t and is eventually reversed and p is brought back to its original level at time $t + \tau$. Here there are two possibilities:

- The fall of k/h between times t and $t + \tau$ is not too large and $(k/h)^s_t > (k/h)_{t+\tau} > (k/h)^s_{t+\tau}$. That is, at $t + \tau$, when the policy is returned to its original level, the critical $(k/h)^s_{t+\tau}$ (which is equal to the original level $(k/h)^s_0$) is still below the level of $(k/h)_{t+\tau}$ (which is lower than the initial level $(k/h)_0$). In this case, the shock had only a temporary negative effect on growth. But once p is returned to its original level, the semisubsistence economy retakes its growth path.
- The fall of k/h between t and $t + \tau$ is large so that $(k/h)^s_t > (k/h)^s_{t+\tau} > (k/h)_{t+\tau}$. That is, as p returns to its original level at time $t + \tau$, the level of $(k/h)_{t+\tau}$ has fallen so low that it is now lower than the original critical level. In this case we have what is referred to as "hysterisis": the temporary shock has a permanent effect on the economy, and even if the shock disappears, the economy does not return to its original level. The effect of the shock causes an irreversible retrocess of the poor economy. The economy falls in a poverty cycle leading k/h to continuously fall towards $(k/h)^{ss}$, at which point it ceases to exist as a viable economy.

Figure A2.2 may help clarifying these points. The figure shows possible paths for the poor economy. If initially the k/h ratio is above the critical $(k/h)^s$, the economy is in a path of accumulation following the FJ line in the middle panel in figure A2.2 toward $(k/h)^*$. Throughout this path per capita

Figure A2.2.   Subsistence, Growth, and Poverty Traps among the Poor: The Case of Constant Returns to Scale and No Spillovers

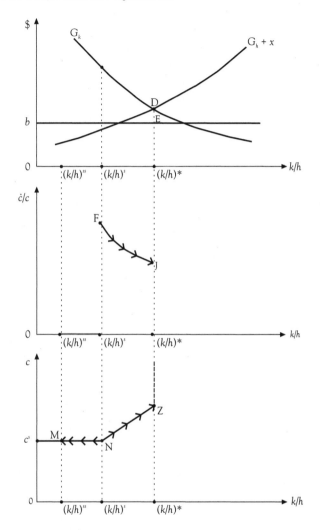

Source: Author.

consumption is continuously growing, although at a decreasing rate. Eventually, the economy reaches $(k/h)^*$, at which point it grows at a constant rate indefinitely. The lower panel shows the evolution of the consumption level, which increases permanently. Suppose now that a negative shock takes place while the economy is along the FJ path. This causes both the schedules G_k and $G_h + x$ to shift downward with a new intersection at a point lower than

D, which implies a lower rate of long-run growth. But the most important consequence is that $(k/h)^s$ will move to the right as it increases because of the reduced level of G implied by a negative shock. The key issue is whether the initial (k/h) ratio is now below or above the new critical $(k/h)^s$ after the shock. If (k/h) is below the new $(k/h)^s$, the path of the economy reverses along a stagnation path such as the path NM in the lower panel of the figure. That is, the economy, which was originally growing, becomes stagnant and eventually, as it reaches point M, becomes infeasible.

Suppose the initial k/h is sufficiently low so that the economy enters a stagnation phase, with a declining k/h ratio, but that after a period of time the level of p is reestablished at its original level. The question is whether or not the new $(k/h)^s$ is above the current k/h ratio. If it is above, then the economy does not retake its original growth path. It continues into a downward spiral, further reducing its wealth. That is, the reversal of the growth process becomes permanent and a purely temporary shock has had a permanent, irreversible effect, triggering a vicious cycle of poverty and asset disaccumulation.

Econometric Specification Used to Estimate Growth Functions

A basic behavioral equation arising from both neoclassical and endogenous growth models is the following:

(A2.8) $g = \phi[F_K(K, H, R; A, p) - C_K(r, \delta, p)],$

where g is the rate of GDP growth per capita; K, H, and R are per capita physical, human and natural capital, respectively; p is a vector of policy variables and prices; A is a productivity factor; F_K is the marginal return to K; C_K is the marginal cost of capital that typically depends on the discount rate (r), depreciation rate (δ), and presumably on policy variable p (such as subsidies to investment); and $\phi(\cdot)$ is a monotonic and increasing function.

Equation (A2.8) indicates that growth is dependent on the gap between the marginal returns to capital and its marginal cost. If such a gap is positive, growth is also positive, and growth comes to a halt if such a gap disappears. Moreover, under certain commonly assumed conditions, growth is directly proportional to this gap.

Thus, this basic behavioral expression relates economic growth to the level of asset stocks, total factor productivity, discount rates, and policy variables. Most empirical growth studies, however, do not use this behavioral approach and instead rely on various forms of growth accounting identities that relate growth to *changes* in asset stocks instead of their levels as a growth theoretic model suggests.

Our empirical analysis is based on equation (A2.8). If one includes time in a discrete form, it is natural to postulate that growth in one period depends on asset stocks at the end of the previous period. Thus a more operational expression for equation (A2.8) is,

$$(A2.9) \quad g_{it} = \phi[F_K(K_{it-1}, H_{it-1}, R_{it-1}; A_{it}, p_{it}, \alpha_{it}) - C_K(r^i, \delta_i, p_{it}; \alpha_i)],$$

where i stands for country and t is time. We assume that r^i and α_i are country fixed characteristics that influence technology and costs. That is, countries differ in terms of their discount rates, r^i, and technological or institutional characteristics, α_i (for example, property rights and rule of law).

We note that in equation (A2.9) growth at time t is dependent on *lagged asset stock levels* instead of *current flow of asset changes* as assumed in many empirical studies. That is, this growth theoretic equation provides for natural "instrumental" variables by postulating growth as a function of last period stock levels. This goes some way in decreasing biases arising from contemporaneous correlation between explanatory variables and the error term due to endogeneity of such variables. Lagged stock *levels* are much less likely to be endogenous to growth rates than contemporaneous stock *changes*.

Since we are relating current growth to lagged stocks of assets, we have that $K_{it-1} = (1 - \delta)K_{it-2} + I_{it-1}$, where I_{it-1} is investment per capita in period $t - 1$. So replacing this in equation (A2.9), we find that using lagged stock levels in the growth regression is equivalent to regressing growth on twice lagged stocks and lagged investment. If we repeat this process by substituting K_{it-2}, using a similar expression we can go back to the first year asset stock. So estimating equation (A2.9) is equivalent to estimating growth on the per capita lagged investment levels of each asset and the "initial" level of each asset. Hence, this specification implicitly uses the initial level of income (given that the initial income level is a function of all initial assets) as an explanatory factor. That is, we could, in principle, relate the estimated coefficients of assets to analyses of convergence of growth rates across countries.

We also assume that the unobserved total factor productivity is related to assets stocks and other country characteristics, for example, $A_{it}(K_{it-1}, H_{it-1}, R_{it-1}, \alpha_i)$. That is, even if F_K is declining in K_{it-1}, the growth rate can be increasing or nondecreasing in K_{it-1} if the technological and scale spillovers are powerful enough. That is, if the partial effect of K_{it-1} on A_{it} is positive and of sufficient magnitude so that $dF_K/dK_{it-1} = \partial F_K/\partial K_{it-1} + (\partial F_K/\partial A_{it})(\partial A_{it}/\partial K_{it-1}) > 0$. Thus, we estimate a reduced form of equation (A2.9) allowing for fixed country effects,

$$(A2.10) \quad g_{it} = \psi[K_{it-1}, H_{it-1}, R_{it-1}, p_{it}] + \beta_i + f_t + \mu_{it},$$

where $\psi(\cdot)$ is a general well-defined function, β_i is a coefficient capturing the country fixed effect related to the effects of α_i and r^i in equation (A2.9), and μ_{it} is a random disturbance. The coefficient f_t corresponds to time effects. The empirical estimation uses various functional forms for $\psi(\cdot)$, including a logarithmic one and a translog form to allow for interasset and policy interactions.

The use of country fixed effects deals with biases arising from omitted variables corresponding to possibly large numbers of country-specific variables that are not observed. Thus, the specification in equation (A2.10) helps to reduce biases due to both endogeneity of explanatory variables by using lagged asset stock variables as instruments, and omitted variables by using fixed effects.

Evidence from Developing Countries

Table A2.1 presents the empirical evidence for the section "Econometric Evidence: 20 Middle-Income Countries."

Tables A2.2 and A2.3 show empirical results for the section "Econometric Evidence: 70 Developing Countries."

Table A2.4 shows some empirical studies on the impact and size of capital subsidies.

Notes

1. Consistent with the discussion above, $G_{bh} < G_h$, where G_h is the true marginal product of human capital.

2. The marginal cost function, b, is equal to $r + \delta$, where δ is the depreciation rate of capital. Here we allow for policies, p, to affect the marginal cost of capital.

3. This is consistent with one stylized fact that is valid for several tropical countries, especially in Latin America and Asia: though the poor are most dependent on natural resources, most destruction of these resources is caused by large commercial interests that intrude into resources owned by the poor (see the ample empirical evidence on these issues provided by Kates and Haarmann 1992).

Table A2.1. The Growth Equation under Various Specifications

(dependent variable: GDP growth per capita)

Variables	Fixed effects		Random effects	
	Equation 1	Equation 2	Equation 3	Equation 4
Average schooling	0.005	0.004	–0.012	–0.013
	(0.025)	(0.020)	(0.009)	(0.009)
Schooling × reform dummy variable	0.084**	0.084**	0.049**	0.049**
	(0.024)	(0.024)	(0.018)	(0.018)
Per capita capital stock	–0.021*	–0.021**	–0.012**	–0.009**
	(0.012)	(0.010)	(0.005)	(0.004)
Capital × reform dummy variable	–0.016**	–0.016**	–0.008**	–0.008**
	(0.005)	(0.005)	(0.004)	(0.004)
Dummy 1982–85	–0.019**	–0.019**	–0.017**	–0.018**
	(0.005)	(0.005)	(0.005)	(0.005)
Labor force	–0.001	n.a.	–0.006	n.a.
	(0.067)	n.a.	(0.006)	n.a.
Standard deviation of log of schooling	–0.018	–0.018	–0.034**	–0.033**
	(0.019)	(0.016)	(0.012)	(0.012)
Homoscedasticity (Breusch-Pagan test)	Rejected at 5 percent	Rejected at 5 percent	Not rejected at 5 percent	Not rejected at 5 percent
White test of specification	Rejected at 5 percent	Rejected at 5 percent	n.a.	n.a.
Hausman test: Fixed vs. random effects	n.a.	n.a.	Not rejected at 5 percent	Not rejected at 5 percent

n.a. Not applicable.

* Significant at the 10 percent level.

** Significant at the 5 percent level.

Note: All variables are in log form. All explanatory variables are lagged by one period. Standard errors of the coefficients are in parentheses. Data from 20 countries are presented. White's heteroscedasticity consistent standard errors are reported under fixed effects.

Source: López, Thomas, and Wang (1998).

Table A2.2. GDP Growth Rates Regressed on Stocks Per Worker, Using All Countries with Available Data from 1965 to 1990

Variables	No cross-products: fixed effects (with country dummies)	No cross-products: fixed effects (with country and time dummies)	Translog: fixed effects (with country and time dummies)
Observations	335	335	335
Countries	67	67	67
Log likelihood	−631.70	−606.30	−605.80
ln (capital/labor)	10.34	11.36	13.21
	(4.79)	(5.67)	(3.19)
ln (forest area/labor)	−1.31	−0.54	8.86
	(−0.68)	(−0.31)	(2.15)
ln (education)	−19.56	−21.41	−12.32
	(−5.68)	(−6.60)	(−2.42)
$[\ln (\text{capital/labor})]^2$	−0.74	−0.95	−1.11
	(−6.34)	(−6.93)	(−4.88)
$[\ln (\text{forest area/labor})]^2$	0.31	0.36	0.09
	(2.74)	(3.25)	(0.62)
$[\ln (\text{education})]^2$	1.36	1.44	0.84
	(5.52)	(6.20)	(1.64)
ln (capital/labor) × ln (forest area/labor)	n.a.	n.a.	0.108
	n.a.	n.a.	(−0.54)
ln (capital/labor) × ln (education)	n.a.	n.a.	0.467
	n.a.	n.a.	(0.78)
ln (forest area/labor) × ln (education)	n.a.	n.a.	−0.596
	n.a.	n.a.	(−2.03)

n.a. Not applicable.

Notes:

1. t-statistics are in parentheses.

2. The dependent variable is annual per capita GDP growth computed over a five-year interval using annual data. The regression is $\ln(\text{GDP}) = a + bt + e$, where e is the residual. Growth rate equals $100^{*}[\exp(b)\text{-}1]$.

3. Parameters were computed by iterated feasible generalized least squares (FGLS), and therefore should be equivalent to maximum likelihood estimation.

4. The correction for AR(1) selected a single parameter for all countries together.

5. The correction for groupwise heteroscedasticity was done by computing a group variance for each country.

6. Measures of per capita GDP and labor were taken from Summers' and Heston's Penn World Tables Mark 5.6. Measures of education were taken from Barro and Lee (1997). They represent average years of education for people 25 years and older. Measures of per capita capital were taken from King and Levine (1993). Measures of forest area (resource stock) were taken from World Resources 1996–97 Data Disk, and is originally from FAOSTAT. The Penn World Tables may be downloaded from http://www.nuff.ox.ac.uk/Economics/Growth/. The Barro-Lee and King-Levine datasets may be downloaded from the World Bank's Web page at http://www.worldbank.org/html/prdmg/grthweb/ddkile93.htm. The forest data may be downloaded from the Food and Agriculture Organization of the United Nations web page at http://apps.fao.org/.

Source: López, Thomas, and Wang (1998).

Table A2.3. Elasticities for Stocks Per Worker on GDP per Capita Growth Rates

Variables	Minimum value	Maximum value	Average
		Elasticity	
No cross-products allowed			
Capital/labor	0.038	–0.081	–0.040
	(0.019)	(0.022)	(0.009)
Forest area/labor	0.007	0.071	0.047
	(0.046)	(0.027)	(0.022)
Education (average schooling of labor force)	–0.056	0.056	0.018
	(0.011)	(0.020)	(0.011)
Translog function			
Capital/labor	0.046	–0.093	–0.045
	(0.022)	(0.026)	(0.012)
Forest area/labor	0.034	0.050	0.044
	(0.049)	(0.029)	(0.023)
Education	–0.031	0.035	0.012
	(0.028)	(0.022)	(0.013)

Notes:

1. Elasticities are computed by converting the percentage growth rate to the log of the growth rate by dividing the percentage by 100.

2. Marginal effects are computed using the fixed effects regression with country and time dummies, corrected for groupwise heteroscedasticity for all countries, and a common AR(1) term for autocorrelation. Data are for all countries, 1965–90.

3. Marginal values (dy/dx) computed for the unlogged x's are simply the exponential of their respective logged values. This means that x bar is not the true mean.

4. Marginal values for the translog formulation utilize the mean values of the log of the crossed term.

5. Standard errors are in parentheses. They are based on variability in the parameter estimates only (including covariances between parameters) and not on any variability in the minimum or maximum variable mean.

6. The elasticity of labor is computed as the negative of the sum of the elasticities for capital/labor and resources/labor.

Source: López, Thomas, and Wang (1998).

Table A2.4. Selected Empirical Studies on the Impact and Size of Capital Subsidies

Authors	Methods	Major findings
Studies on the impact of subsidies		
Bergström (1998). "Capital Subsidies and the Performance of Firms."	The study examines the effects on TFP of public capital subsidies to firms in Sweden between 1987 and 1993. Panel data were used.	"In many countries, governments grant different capital subsidies to the business sector in order to promote growth… The results suggest that subsidization can influence growth (in a short run), but there seems to be little evidence that the subsidies have affected productivity" (p. 1).
Bregman, Fuss, and Regev (1999). "Effect of Capital Subsidization on Productivity in Israeli Industry."	It uses a time-series cross-section microdata set for 620 firms for Israel.	"An industrial policy of subsidizing physical capital investment has been utilized in many countries…. We estimated that for the years 1990-94, this policy has resulted in production inefficiencies ranging from 5 to 15 percent for subsidized firms" (p. 77).
Harris (1991). "The Employment Creation Effects of Factor Subsidies."	Uses CES (constant elasticity of substitution) production function and a simulation model for the Northern Ireland manufacturing industry, 1955–83.	"The results indicate that, since manufacturing industry in the province tends to operate with a labor-intensive technology and, its price elasticity of demand for output is very low, the employment-creating effects of capital subsidies are strongly negative" (p. 49).
Lee (1996). "Government Interventions and Productivity Growth."	Uses four-period panel data for the years 1963–83.	"Industrial policies, such as tax incentives and subsidized credit, were not correlated with total factor productivity growth in the promoted sectors" (p. 391).
Lim (1992). "Capturing the Effects of Capital Subsidies."	Uses firm-level data from 3,900–4,900 firms in Malaysia, from 1976 to 1979.	"Most developing countries provide fiscal incentives to encourage domestic and foreign investment. This study shows that these schemes subsidize significantly the use of capital and produce greater capital intensity in Malaysian manufacturing" (p. 705).
Oman (2000). "Policy Competition for Foreign Direct Investment," OECD Development Centre.	The study addresses three sets of questions: (a) to what extent do governments compete for FDI, (b) the effect of competition, and (c) implications for policymakers.	"Incentive-based competition for FDI is a global phenomenon: governments at all levels in both OECD and non-OECD countries engage in it worldwide… The distortionary effect of incentives…can be significant… It can be counterproductive for governments to offer costly investment incentives" (p. 7–9). Investment incentives in the automobile industry are shown in a table on page 73.
Studies on the size of subsidies		
Gandhi, Gray, and McMorran (1997).	Estimated subsidies that damaged the environment.	"Estimated subsidies to energy, roads, water, and agriculture in developing and transition economies total over $240 billion per year in the 1990s. Cutting these subsidies in half would free over $100 billions of finance for sustainable development" (p. 10).
Moore (1999). "Corporate Subsidies in the Federal Budget."	A testimony before the Budget Committee, U.S. House of Representatives.	"Corporate welfare is a large and growing component of the federal budget" (p. 1). In 1997, the Fortune 500 corporations are estimated to have received nearly US$75 billion in government subsidies.

(table continues on following page)

Table A2.4 continued

Authors	Methods	Major findings
de Moor and Calamai (1997). *Subsidizing Unsustainable Development: Undermining the Earth with Public Funds.*	A report to the Earth Council, which estimated public subsidies in four sectors.	"In OECD countries, total annual subsidies in four sectors, energy, road transport, water and agriculture, amounted to $490 –$615 billion, and in non-OECD countries, $217–$272 billion. Total subsidies in all four sectors are estimated at $710–$890 billion worldwide" (p. 93).
Gulati and Narayanan (2000). "Demystifying Fertilizer and Power Subsidies in India."	This paper estimates the amount of subsidies and examines the real beneficiaries.	"Broadly half of the huge agricultural subsidy on fertilizers and power... comprising 2 percent of GDP, is either going to industry in the case of fertilizers or is being stolen by non-agricultural consumers in the case of power" (p. 784).

Note: A more detailed table is available on request from the authors.
Source: Authors.

DISTRIBUTION OF EDUCATION, OPENNESS, AND GROWTH

Economic theories suggest a strong causal link from education to growth, but the empirical evidence has not been unanimous and conclusive. López, Thomas, and Wang (1998) focus on two factors that explain why the empirical studies have not overwhelmingly supported the theories. First, the distribution of education affects economic growth. Second, the economic policy environment greatly affects the impact of education on growth by determining what people can do with their education. Reforms of trade, investment, and labor policies can increase the returns from education. Using panel data from 20 developing countries for 1970–94, we investigated the relationship between education, policy reforms, and economic growth and made the following observations:

- *The distribution of education matters.* An overly skewed distribution of education tends to have a negative impact on per capita income in most countries. Controlling for education distribution and using the appropriate functional form leads to positive and significant effects of average education on per capita income, while failure to do so leads to insignificant or negative effects of average education.
- *The policy environment matters greatly.* Results indicate that economic policies that suppress market forces tend to reduce the impact of education on economic growth. Moreover, the stock of physical capital is negatively related to economic growth for economies in the sample, implying a declining marginal productivity of capital.

The Extended Production Function with Distribution of Education

We used a model in which physical capital is fully tradable, but human capital is not. The level, as well as the distribution, of human capital enters the aggregate production function. If education matches the dispersion of ability, the marginal effect of education distribution on income vanishes. If the dispersion of education is greater than the dispersion of ability, the per capita income can be increased by reducing the dispersion of education. If the dispersion of education is less skewed than ability, then governments should concentrate investment on a few people with greater ability to learn.

The education Gini coefficient is calculated in two steps. First, an education Lorenz curve is constructed based on the proportions of population with various levels of schooling and the length of each level of schooling, which shows the cumulative years of schooling with respect to the proportion of population. Then the education Gini coefficient is calculated as the ratio of the area between the Lorenz curve and the 45 degree line (perfect equality) to the total area of the triangle. An alternative definition of the education Gini coefficient is the ratio to the mean schooling of half the summation of the absolute differences of school attainment between all possible pairs of individuals in a country (Deaton 1997).[1] Table A3.1 presents education Gini coefficients for 20 countries, and preliminary data estimated for 85 countries are available from Thomas, Wang, and Fan (2000).

Using quinquennial data from 20 mostly middle-income countries, aggregate production functions were estimated. Table A3.2 reports four estimates of the aggregate per capita production function for 1970–94. The first column presents the traditional fixed effect log-linear model that ignores both of the above explanatory factors: education distribution and the policy environment. As the first column shows, human capital has a negative and significant effect on production; this is where the "education puzzle" lies.

The second column shows the fixed effect model in log-linear form, but the estimation allowed the distribution of education to play a role in the function. Column two allows no country-specific effect from education distribution and shows positive associations between human capital stock, its distribution, and level of income. In this case, the coefficient of average education becomes positive and statistically significant at 5 percent. The effect of education distribution on the production function was statistically different across countries. This cross-country diversity of the effect of education dispersion is consistent with the idea that the *effect of education dispersion is likely to vary and change sign according to whether it is below or above its optimal level.*

The third column presents the results obtained by allowing for country-specific effects of education distribution. The coefficients of the variability

Table A3.1. Gini Coefficients of Education for Selected Countries, Selected Years

Country	1970	1975	1980	1985	1990
Algeria	0.8181	0.7683	0.7080	0.6525	0.6001
Argentina	0.3111	0.3257	0.2946	0.3182	0.2724
Brazil	0.5091	0.4290	0.4463	0.4451	0.3929
Chile	0.3296	0.3327	0.3151	0.3120	0.3135
China	0.5985	0.5541	0.5094	0.4937	0.4226
Colombia	0.5095	0.4594	0.4726	0.4752	0.4864
Costa Rica	0.4106	0.3916	0.4059	0.4165	0.4261
India	0.7641	0.7429	0.7517	0.7238	0.6861
Indonesia	0.5873	0.5817	0.5051	0.4388	0.4080
Ireland	0.2488	0.2454	0.2364	0.2377	0.2498
Korea, Republic of	0.5140	0.3942	0.3383	0.2877	0.2175
Malaysia	0.5474	0.5150	0.4719	0.4459	0.4204
Mexico	0.5114	0.4990	0.4978	0.4695	0.3839
Pakistan	0.8549	0.8450	0.8170	0.8065	0.6448
Peru	0.5048	0.5028	0.4258	0.4371	0.4311
Philippines	0.4327	0.3578	0.3404	0.3360	0.3285
Portugal	0.4985	0.5142	0.4255	0.4350	0.4315
Thailand	0.4185	0.4257	0.3591	0.3891	0.3915
Tunisia	0.8178	0.7589	0.6935	0.6710	0.6168
Venezuela, RB	0.5789	0.5585	0.3919	0.3970	0.4209

Source: López, Thomas, and Wang (1998). For data on additional countries, see Thomas, Wang, and Fan (2000).

of education for the various countries are jointly significant at 1 percent. However, 7 of the 20 country-specific coefficients are not statistically different from zero.

The last column uses the standard deviation in logs as another measure of dispersion of education. This measure of dispersion exerts a much greater effect on per capita income. Most of these country-specific coefficients are negative, and 8 out of 20 coefficients are highly significant.

Table A3.3 presents the results obtained by using the nonlinear specification suggested by the theoretical model. That is, this specification deals with both the omitted variable and the functional form specification problems. In all three specifications, the coefficients of average education are positive and statistically significant at the 5 percent level. In this functional form, the distribution of education is positively associated with the level of income, which is still consistent with the model that states that a certain level of education dispersion is important for production, especially in considering technological progress and innovation.

Table A3.2. Production Function: Linear Estimation
(dependent variable: log of per capita GDP)

Variables	Fixed effects, excluding effect of education distribution	Fixed effects, log-linear allowing for education distribution effect using coefficient of variability of education	Fixed effects, log-linear allowing for education distribution effect using coefficient of variability of education	Fixed effects, allowing for education distribution effects using standard deviation of the log of education
Human capital	−0.275**	0.491**	0.004	−0.380**
	(0.085)	(0.106)	(0.112)	(0.131)
Physical capital	1.108**	0.981**	1.066**	1.083**
	(0.033)	(0.012)	(0.022)	(0.071)
Dummy 1982–85	−0.063**	−0.077**	−0.063**	−0.033**
	(0.012)	(0.012)	(0.011)	(0.009)
Education distribution effects		1.187**		
		(0.133)		
Brazil			2.828**	−0.423**
			(0.350)	(0.196)
Chile			−0.020	−0.320
			(0.309)	(0.279)
China			0.354**	−1.197**
			(0.139)	(0.225)
Colombia			0.765	−0.300
			(0.916)	(0.269)
India			0.012	0.015
			(0.278)	(0.299)
Korea, Republic of			1.146**	0.012
			(0.089)	(0.148)
Mexico			0.843**	−0.475
			(0.264)	(0.306)
Malaysia			2.494**	−0.690**
			(0.196)	(0.304)
Peru			0.574	−0.409
			(0.559)	(0.344)
Philippines			−2.138	−0.861**
			(2.627)	(0.275)
Thailand			−2.478**	−0.541**
			(0.618)	(0.175)
Venezuela, RB			1.032**	−0.109
			(0.142)	(0.330)
Algeria			−0.685*	0.818*
			(0.378)	(0.471)
Argentina			1.307**	−0.367
			(0.316)	(0.269)
Costa Rica			−3.849**	−0.666**
			(0.579)	(0.222)

(table continues on following page)

Table A3.2 continued

Variables	Fixed effects, excluding effect of education distribution	Fixed effects, log-linear allowing for education distribution effect using coefficient of variability of education	Fixed effects, log-linear allowing for education distribution effect using coefficient of variability of education	Fixed effects, allowing for education distribution effects using standard deviation of the log of education
Indonesia			2.081**	−1.004**
			(0.298)	(0.157)
Ireland			1.287**	0.251
			(0.161)	(0.284)
Pakistan			−0.024	−0.292
			(0.165)	(0.321)
Portugal			−0.001	0.027
			(0.483)	(0.238)
Tunisia			0.654**	−0.065
			(0.188)	(0.484)

* Significant at the 10 percent level.

** Significant at the 5 percent level.

Note: A first-order autoregressive coefficient was estimated by maximum likelihood for each country separately. This information was used to correct the data. Standard errors (in parentheses) reported are White's heteroscedastic consistent. All variables are in log forms, except for dummies.

Source: López, Thomas, and Wang (1998).

Empirical Analysis on Education and Investment Returns

Based on the World Bank's lending experience during the past 20 years, Thomas and Wang (1997) examined whether education and openness can improve the developmental impact of investment projects. The model is a country's production function separated into export production and production for domestic markets. The reduced forms are as follows:

$$P(Sat = 1)_i = \alpha \cdot \dot{E}_i + \beta \cdot \dot{X}_i + \gamma \cdot G_i + \varphi \cdot R_i + \varepsilon_i$$

$$ERR_i = \alpha \cdot \dot{E}_i + \beta \cdot \dot{X}_i + \gamma \cdot G_i + \varphi \cdot R_i + \varepsilon_i$$

where $P(sat = 1)_i$ is the probability of a project i being rated as satisfactory, ERR_i is the economic rate of return for project i, $\dot{E}_i$ is the change in average level of schooling of the labor force for the country where the project is located and the period when the project is implemented, $\dot{X}_i$ is the vector of variables indicating export growth or openness, G is the vector of variables indicating governance and institutional capability, and R includes exogenous variables and regional dummies. The first

Table A3.3. Production Function: Nonlinear Estimation
(dependent variable: log of per capita GDP)

Variables	Nonlinear, allowing for one distribution effect	Nonlinear, allowing for distribution effects to vary across continents	Nonlinear, allowing for distribution effects to vary across countries with different levels of education variability
Human capital	0.369**	0.272**	0.159**
	(0.049)	(0.051)	(0.056)
Physical capital	0.842**	0.863**	0.897**
	(0.018)	(0.019)	(0.017)
Dummy 1982–85	–0.066**	–0.065**	–0.061**
	(0.012)	(0.12)	(0.011)
Education distribution *effects ($\rho\sigma_a$)*			
Overall	7.532**		
	(0.831)		
Latin America		13.040**	
		(2.407)	
Asia		9.541**	
		(1.611)	
Africa		3.720**	
		(0.656)	
Europe		8.140**	
		(2.362)	
Low variability			11.416**
			(3.624)
Medium variability			32.595**
			(10.195)
High variability			3.145**
			(0.533)

* Significant at the 10 percent level.
** Significant at the 5 percent level.
Note: A first-order autoregressive coefficient was estimated by maximum likelihood for each country separately. This information was used to correct the data. All variables are in log form except for dummies. Data from 20 countries were used in the analysis. Standard errors are in parentheses.
Source: López, Thomas, and Wang (1998).

equation is estimated using Probit analysis because the dependent variable is a discrete (0/1) variable, and the second equation using Tobit procedure because ERRs are truncated at 5 percent.

Project Data

After each World Bank project is completed, a project completion report is written and two performance measures are calculated. Operations

Evaluation Department staff evaluate the project and assign an overall performance rating of satisfactory or unsatisfactory in achieving the project's development objectives. An ex post economic rate of return (ERR) is also calculated for projects in eight sectors—infrastructure, agriculture, industry, energy, water, urban, transport, and tourism—where the stream of project benefits can be quantified. The ERR is the discounted stream of project costs and benefits over the life of the project, evaluated at economic prices. The ex post ERRs are calculated approximately two to three years after project completion, at which time the evaluators know the actual investment costs and the actual operating costs and demand, but they still need to estimate the future stream of benefits.

Explanatory Variables

No attempt is made to build a complete model of determinants of project success, which would require sector- and project-level information as well as country-level information. Four groups of explanatory variables were used:

- Education, which can be measured by three variables. They include changes in the average years of schooling of the labor force between project approval and evaluation years; interaction of education and openness, measured by deviations in trade shares; and initial level of education, which was based on Nehru, Swanson, and Dubey (1995) and updated by Patel.
- Indicators of openness, including the foreign exchange black market premium and deviations in trade shares, defined by actual trade share minus predicted trade share that were estimated by a simple gravity model.
- Governance and institutional capability, which can be reflected indirectly by an index for corruption in government (*International Country Risk Guide* 1982–95), by shares of government consumption in GDP, and shares of budget surplus/deficit in GDP. The second and third measures can reflect the government's ability to control its finances and implement strict fiscal prudence and discipline.

Regression results are presented in table A3.4. The findings suggest the importance of trade openness and education for improving investment project performance and the potential gains from outward-oriented learning. Good governance and strict fiscal discipline are also found to be conducive to higher project returns (see Thomas and Wang 1997).

Table A3.4. Education, Openness, and Lending Project Performance

Independent variables	Dependent variable = economic rate of return		Dependent variable = satisfactory or not	
	Tobit coefficient	Prob > Chi	Probit coefficient	Prob > Chi
Education variables				
Change in education levels between the approval and evaluation years	3.33	0.01	0.34	0.00
Education x trade openness (measured by deviations from predicted trade shares)	0.00	0.04	0.00	0.45
Lack of openness				
Log of foreign exchange black market premium (3-year moving average)	–3.14	0.04	–0.23	0.01
Institution and governance				
Share of budget surplus/deficit in GDP (3-year moving average)	0.26	0.05		
Corruption in government (1 = more, 6 = less)			0.06	0.04
Other controlling variables and dummies				
Initial level of GDP per capita in the project approval year	0.00	0.95	–0.06	0.02
Dummy for project complexity	–4.27	0.00	–0.45	0.00
Sub-Saharan Africa	5.31	0.41	1.56	0.00
East Asia	9.13	0.15	2.56	0.00
South Asia	10.47	0.09	2.13	0.00
Latin America and the Caribbean	7.77	0.24	1.92	0.00
Europe, Middle East, and North Africa	10.80	0.09	2.20	0.00
Log likelihood	–3,209.00		–1,032.00	
Number of observations	830.00		1,826.00	

Note: Prob = 0.05 means rejection of coefficient = 0 at 95 percent confidence. The regressions cover projects evaluated in 1974–92.
Source: Thomas and Wang (1997).

Selected Literature on Asset Distribution and Growth

Table A3.5 includes a selected set of empirical studies on asset distribution and economic growth, which provided some of the evidence used in chapter 3.

Notes

1. The education Gini coefficient can be calculated using the formula below:

$$\gamma = \frac{1}{\mu N(N-1)} \sum_{i>j} \sum_{j} \mid x_i - x_j \mid .$$

where γ is the Gini index, μ is the mean of the difference in school grade attained, and N is the total number of observations (see Deaton 1997).

Table A3.5.   Selective Empirical Studies on Asset Distribution, Growth, and Poverty

Authors	*Methodology*	*Major findings*
Maas and Criel (1982)	Calculated education Gini coefficients based on enrollment data for 16 East African countries.	Inequality in the distribution of education opportunities varies enormously across countries.
Ram (1990)	Calculated standard deviations of education for about 100 countries.	As the average level of schooling rises, educational inequality first increases, and after reaching a peak, starts to decline. The turning point is about seven years of education.
O'Neill (1995)	1. Assumed that the stock of human capital is the accumulation of the past education, not sensitive to current income level. 2. Used the variance of income and that of human and physical capitals in analysis. 3. Used both quantities and prices of human and physical capital.	Among the developed countries, convergence in education levels has resulted in a reduction in income dispersion. However, worldwide, incomes have diverged despite substantial convergence in education levels.
Ravallion and Sen (1994)	Presented a country case study on assessment of effectiveness of poverty reduction policy.	Land-contingent poverty alleviation schemes in Bangladesh made an impact on poverty reduction, "though the maximum gains turn out to be small" (p. 823).
Deininger and Squire (1996)	Land Gini coefficient Average GDP growth (1960–90)	Countries with more equitable land distribution tend to grow faster.
Ravallion (1997)	Income Gini coefficient Growth rate	At any positive rate of growth, the higher the initial inequality, the lower the rate at which income-poverty falls.
Birdsall and Londoño (1998)	A cross-country analysis using a traditional growth model, after controlling for capital accumulation, initial income and education levels, and natural resources.	Initial levels of educational inequality and land Gini coefficient have strong negative impacts on economic growth and income growth of the poorest.
Deininger and Squire (1998)	Provided cross-country data on income and asset (land) distribution	"There is a strong negative relationship between initial inequality in the asset distribution and long-term growth; inequality reduces income growth for the poor, but not for the rich; and available longitudinal data provides little support for the Kuznets hypothesis."
Li, Squire, and Zou (1998)	Land Gini coefficient Income Gini coefficient	Income Gini coefficient is positively related to log of land Gini coefficient
IDB (1998)	Regression using data from 19 countries, land Gini, income Gini, education, standard deviation of education	Income inequality (Gini) is negatively related to land Gini, and positively related to standard deviation of education.

(table continues on following page)

213

Table A3.5 continued

Authors	Methodology	Major findings
López, Thomas, and Wang (1998)	A production function with nontradable education is estimated using quinquennial data for 20 countries, after controlling for physical capital, labor, and so forth. Education Gini coefficients were estimated by attainment data.	1. The distribution of education matters for income levels as well as for growth. 2. Trade openness and reforms improved the productivity of human capital in growth models.
Ravallion and Datt (1999)	Used 20 household surveys for India's 15 major states in 1960–94 to study the issue of "when is growth pro-poor." Elasticities of poverty to nonfarm output were estimated.	The growth process was more pro-poor in states with higher initial literacy, higher farm productivity, and higher rural living standards relative to urban residents. Kerala has the highest elasticity of poverty to nonfarm output.

Source: Compiled by authors.

MEASURING NATURAL CAPITAL

Systematic quantitative analysis of the links between the state of the environment and economic growth has been hampered by a lack of reliable data on natural capital. Because of the increasing need for rigorous research on the subject, a number of initiatives have been directed at collecting more reliable and systematic data worldwide: data on deforestation compiled by the Food and Agriculture Organization of the United Nations; urban air pollution measurements compiled by the WHO; statistics on access to sanitation, clean water, and many other environmental aspects compiled by the UNDP; and the Global Environmental Monitoring System.

The *World Development Indicators* (WDI) is an annual publication of the World Bank and includes a large body of environmental data taken from the sources mentioned above and many others as well. By bringing together useful data from diverse sources in a user-friendly format, the WDI has rapidly become a one-stop shop for accessing environmental data. Most environmental data used in chapter 4 and elsewhere in this report have been drawn from WDI tables.

In addition to being a rich source of data, the WDI is also a useful reference on how to access other sources of data. The publication and its data tables may be accessed on the web at: www.worldbank.org/data/wdi.

Two indexes for natural capital have been constructed on the basis of data available in the WDI, namely:

- *The sustainable development index to measure environmental outcomes.* This is a change index constructed by giving equal weights to annual rates of deforestation between 1980 and 1995, decrease in water pollution proxied by the emissions of organic water pollutants in kilograms per day per worker between the 1980s and 1990s, and decline in carbon dioxide emissions in per capita metric tons between the 1980s and 1990s.

- *The environmental policy index as a measure of government commitment to protecting natural capital.* This includes two dummy variables: one for domestic action based on the formulation of a national environmental strategy and environmental profiles and the other for international action based on signing the Convention on Climate Change.

Both indexes are preliminary and work is ongoing to develop more comprehensive and reliable indicators. The following web site gives an idea of World Bank efforts in this direction: http://www-esd.worldbank.org/eei/.

FINANCIAL OPENNESS

Our broad measure of financial openness incorporates controls and/or restrictions on both current and capital account transactions. It is constructed as the simple arithmetic average of quantitative measures of degree of controls or restrictions on 27 individual transactions related to import payments, export proceeds, invisible transactions, and capital account transactions as shown in table A5.1. This classification is based on the International Monetary Fund's annual report on *Exchange Arrangements and Exchange Restrictions*.

The scoring draws on the methodology developed by Quinn and Inclan (1997). It is based on a five-tiered scale that ranges from 0 to 2 for each item, indicating the degree of openness (0 highly controlled, 2 highly liberal) defined as follows:[1]

0.0 Laws and/or regulations that impose quantitative or other regulatory restrictions on a particular transaction, such as licenses or reserve requirements, that completely forbid such economic transactions.

0.5 Laws and/or regulations that impose quantitative or other regulatory restrictions on a particular transaction, such as licenses or reserve requirements that partially forbid such economic transactions.

1.0 Laws and/or regulations requiring the particular transaction to be approved by the authorities or subjecting it to heavy taxes when applicable, whether in the form of multiple currency practices or other taxes.

1.5 Laws and/or regulations requiring the particular transaction to be registered, but not necessarily approved, by the authorities and also taxed when applicable.

2.0 No regulations requiring the particular transaction to be approved or registered with authorities and free of taxation when applicable.

Table A5.1. International Transactions

Category	*Type of transaction*
Imports and import payments	Foreign exchange budget
	Financing requirements for imports
	Documentation requirements for release of foreign exchange for imports
	Import licenses and other nontariff measures
	Import taxes and/or tariffs
	State import monopoly
Exports and export proceeds	Repatriation requirements
	Financing requirements
	Documentation requirements
	Export licenses
	Export taxes
Payments for invisible transactions and current transfers	Controls on these payments
Proceeds from invisible transactions and current transfers	Repatriation requirements
	Restrictions on use of funds
Capital account transactions	Capital market securities
	Money market instruments
	Collective investment securities
	Derivatives and other instruments
	Commercial credits
	Financial credits
	Guarantees, sureties, and financial backup facilities
	Direct investment
	Liquidation of direct investment
	Real estate transactions
	Personal capital movements
	Commercial banks and other credit institutions
	Institutional investors

Source: IMF (1998).

Applying this coding methodology, the estimated financial openness index ranges from 1.93 for Ireland and Luxembourg to 1.12 for Ethiopia (see table A5.2).

A more narrowly defined index, which captures the degree of openness to capital account transactions, can be arrived at in a similar manner. The narrow index uses only the 13 transactions listed in the capital account transactions category in table A5.1.

Table A5.2. Financial Openness Index, Selected Countries, 1997

Open		Largely open		Partially closed		Largely closed	
Country	Index	Country	Index	Country	Index	Country	Index
Argentina	1.78	Croatia	1.54	Bahamas, The	1.36	Bangladesh	1.21
Australia	1.77	Ecuador	1.54	Belize	1.44	Barbados	1.28
Austria	1.92	Honduras	1.56	Benin	1.48	Bhutan	1.19
Bahrain	1.73	Israel	1.59	Botswana	1.48	Brazil	1.19
Belgium	1.88	Mongolia	1.56	Bulgaria	1.46	Ethiopia	1.12
Bolivia	1.79	Philippines	1.59	Burkina Faso	1.49	India	1.20
Canada	1.92	Poland	1.54	Burundi	1.39	Malawi	1.26
Denmark	1.92	Slovak Republic	1.58	Cameroon	1.41	Malaysia	1.34
Egypt, Arab Rep. of	1.81	Slovenia	1.50	Cape Verde	1.39	Morocco	1.27
El Salvador	1.91	Turkey	1.52	Chile	1.43	Pakistan	1.31
Estonia	1.88			China	1.37	Syrian Arab Rep.	1.20
Finland	1.83			Colombia	1.38		
France	1.73			Congo, Dem. Rep. of	1.42		
Germany	1.84			Costa Rica	1.48		
Greece	1.91			Czech Republic	1.48		
Guatemala	1.73			Dominican Republic	1.49		
Guyana	1.72			Ghana	1.43		
Iceland	1.74			Hungary	1.49		
Ireland	1.93			Indonesia	1.46		
Italy	1.84			Korea, Rep. of	1.42		
Jamaica	1.76			Lesotho	1.41		
Japan	1.73			Mali	1.49		
Kuwait	1.77			Malta	1.40		
Latvia	1.88			Moldova	1.46		
Lithuania	1.85			Mozambique	1.41		
Luxembourg	1.93			Namibia	1.33		
Mauritius	1.82			Papua New Guinea	1.36		
Mexico	1.69			Romania	1.48		
Netherlands	1.87			Russian Federation	1.43		
New Zealand	1.90			South Africa	1.44		
Nicaragua	1.82			Sri Lanka	1.43		
Norway	1.83			Thailand	1.46		
Panama	1.90			Tunisia	1.39		
Paraguay	1.81			Ukraine	1.36		
Peru	1.90						
Portugal	1.84						
Singapore	1.78						
Spain	1.82						
Sweden	1.86						
Switzerland	1.88						
Trinidad and Tobago	1.67						

(table continues on following page)

Table A5.2 continued

Open		Largely open		Partially closed		Largely closed	
Country	Index	Country	Index	Country	Index	Country	Index
United Kingdom	1.86						
United States	1.85						
Uruguay	1.77						
Venezuela, RB	1.84						
Zambia	1.79						

Note: Open: none or minimal regulation for outward and inward transactions and a generally nondiscriminatory environment. Largely open: some regulations are exercised on outward or inward transactions with the need for documentary support but without the need for government approval. Partially closed: regulation and government approval is required for outward and inward transactions and usually granted. Largely closed: substantial restrictions and government approval is required and seldom granted for outward and inward transactions.

Source: Author estimate.

Note on Country Vulnerability and Volatility Measures

The vulnerability classification is based on our estimates of volatility in private capital flows, based on the following forecasting equation:

$$(A5.1) \quad KF_{it} = \alpha_i + \beta_i KF_{i(t-1)} + u_{it}$$

where KF_{it} denotes total net private capital flows for country i in year t and u_{it} denotes the error term.

Volatility in country i is defined as

$$(A5.2) \quad V_i = \frac{S(u_{it})}{GDP_{i, 1996}}$$

where $S(u_{it})$ is the ordinary least squares estimate of the standard error of the residuals in equation (A5.1) using time series data from 1975 to 1996. See table A5.3 for the index.

Note on Gross Domestic Product Gaps

The present values of the difference between the potential GDP, extrapolated on the basis of historical growth rates of the real economy (1980–96) and the actual or estimated GDP from 1997 through 1999, is calculated as the economic cost due to the financial crisis. The present value was calculated to 1996 values using a real discount rate of 3 percent per year. Expressed as a percentage of the stock of debt in 1996, the estimated costs of the crises were 81 percent for Malaysia, 97 percent for Indonesia, 128 percent for Thailand, and 291 percent for Korea. A similar computation for Brazil yields an estimate of 21 percent. Note that for Korea, the debt stock figure used is for 1997.

Table A5.3. Developing Countries Classified by Degree of Volatility to Private Foreign Capital Flows

Highly volatile		Volatile		Moderately volatile		Least volatile	
Country	Index	Country	Index	Country	Index	Country	Index
Jamaica	3.23	Mexico	1.54	Colombia	0.99	Uganda	0.63
Gabon	2.93	Ecuador	1.50	Tunisia	0.98	Brazil	0.60
Nigeria	2.07	Kenya	1.49	Indonesia	0.95	Paraguay	0.58
Venezuela, RB	2.04	Nicaragua	1.48	Turkey	0.93	China	0.54
Malaysia	1.97	Bolivia	1.44	Argentina	0.91	Sri Lanka	0.46
Jordan	1.82	Chile	1.38	Costa Rica	0.85	Pakistan	0.44
Panama	1.79	Ethiopia	1.31	Uruguay	0.83	Guatemala	0.43
Cameroon	1.60	Philippines	1.27	Egypt, Arab Rep. of	0.74	Dominican Republic	0.39
Zambia	1.59	Honduras	1.04	Tanzania	0.72	India	0.38
Zimbabwe	1.59	Thailand	1.01	Morocco	0.64	El Salvador	0.32
						Nepal	0.29
						Bangladesh	0.10

Sources: World Bank (1999c); authors' computations.

Note on the Binomial Logit Model

The binomial *logit* model is used to estimate the impact of the independent variables on the likelihood that a country would fall in the high democracy-high financial openness category. In this model, the dependent variable is defined by a dichotomous random variable y, which takes the value of 1 if country i belongs to the high democracy-high financial openness category, and 0 if it does not. This is given by

$$y_i = p_i + e_i,$$

where p is the probability that a given country belongs in the high democracy-high financial openness category, and specified as $p = F(a'x)$, where x is a vector of independent variables, a is the corresponding vector of coefficients, $F(a'x)$ is the cumulative distribution function, and e_i is an error term assumed to follow the Bernoulli distribution.

Expressing the probability for the i-th observation via the *logit* model, we will obtain

$$F(a'x_i) = \frac{\exp(a'x_i)}{1 + \exp(a'x_i)}.$$

Subsequently, the *logit* transformation would yield:

$$\log \frac{p_i}{1 - p_i} = a'x_i.$$

In this chapter we focus on the explanatory variables defined as

- Log of total social expenses as a percentage of GDP (average 1990–96) (x_1)
- Log of GDP per capita, current U.S. dollars (average 1990–96) (x_2).

This binomial model was estimated by the maximum likelihood method using cross-country data for a sample of 67 countries for which consistent data on the two explanatory variables were available. Computationally, we obtained the maximum likelihood using the Newton-Raphson algorithm, which utilized the STATA *logit* procedure. The results were generated after five iterations. The estimated results are reported in the text in table 5.3. The results indicate that both per capita income and the ratio of social expenditures to GDP have a statistically significant impact in explaining the likelihood that a country falls into the high-high category. The model also performs well in predicting the percentage of countries that are correctly classified as belonging to the high-democracy high-financial openness group, that is, out of 27 countries in the high-high group, 19 were correctly predicted to be in that group (based on the threshold probability of 0.5), thus producing a 70.37 percent correct classification rate.

Summary Statistics for Variables Used in Chapter 5

Several statistical analyses were performed during the course of this chapter. Table A5.4 provides summary statistics of the main variables and their sources. Relationships between these variables are explored in figure A5.1 and table A5.5.

Notes

1. For some countries where data on certain transactions were unavailable, average values of 1 were assigned.

Table A5.4. Summary Statistics for Selected Industrial and Developing Countries

Variables	Mean	Standard deviation	Minimum	Maximum	Number of countries
Political rights	3.42	2.18	1.00	7.00	123
Civil liberties	3.09	1.73	1.00	7.00	138
Capital account openness	15.39	3.62	8.50	22.00	97
Financial openness	38.21	6.48	21.50	48.50	99
Transfer payments	3.09	3.09	0.001	13.84	68
Social expenditure	17.82	11.77	3.35	49.11	51
Trade openness	70.60	45.90	15.21	378.67	141
Income per capita	5,803.00	8,645.00	91.59	37,198.00	68

Note: Political rights, from *Freedom in the World*, 1998, published by the Freedom House; a country grants its citizens *political rights* when it permits them to form political parties that represent a significant range of voter choice and whose leaders can openly compete for and be elected to positions of power in government.

Civil liberties, from *Freedom in the World*, 1998, published by the Freedom House; a country upholds its citizens' *civil liberties* when it respects and protects their religious, ethnic, economic, linguistic, and other rights, including gender and family rights, personal freedoms, and freedoms of the press, belief, and association.

Capital account openness is a measure of the degree of controls and/or restrictions applying to only capital account transactions (13 transactions as classified by the IMF AREAER) and are defined in table A5.1.

Financial openness is a broader measure incorporating controls and/or restrictions on both current and capital account transactions (see table A5.1).

Transfer payments, Government Financial Statistics: Average of central, state, and local expenditure as percentage of GDP. Transfers to other levels of national government, 1991–97; countries with the minimum for this variable are: Chile, Costa Rica, Dominican Republic, Greece, Ireland, Lesotho, Panama, Sri Lanka, and Thailand. Demark has the maximum value for this variable.

Social expenditure, Government Financial Statistics and UNESCO: Average of central, state, and local expenditure as percentage of GDP, 1991–97; Pakistan has the minimum for this variable. Denmark has the maximum value for this variable.

Trade openness, World Development Indicators: Average trade as percentage of GDP, 1980s.

Income per capita, average income per capita, 1990–97; in the sample of countries the minimum is US$91.60 for Mozambique and the maximum of US$37,199 for Switzerland.

Sources: Freedom House (1998); IMF (1999, various issues); UNESCO (1998); World Bank (1999f).

Figure A 5.1. Correlations of Financial Openness with Political Rights and Civil Liberties

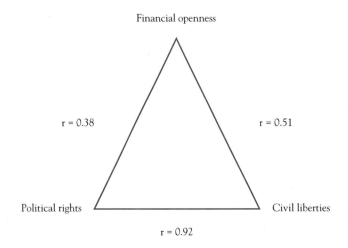

Note: The estimated correlation coefficients are statistically significant at 1 percent (based on the z-test).
Source: Author's computations.

Table A5.5. The Relationship among Financial Openness, Democracy, and Social Expenditure

Variables	Financial openness	Capital openness	Political rights	Civil liberties	Trade openness	Social expenditure	Transfer payments	Income per capita
Financial openness	1.00							
Capital account openness	0.91	1.00						
Political rights	−0.32*	0.22*	1.00					
Civil liberties	−0.55*	0.46**	0.91*	1.00				
Trade openness	0.18	0.21*	−0.06	−0.14	1.00			
Social expenditure	0.52*	0.42**	−0.72*	−0.74*	0.28**	1.00		
Transfer payments	0.23	0.17	−0.19	−0.21	−0.14	0.31**	1.00	
Income per capita	0.52*	0.44**	−0.54*	−0.68*	0.29*	0.67*	0.26	1.00

* Significant at the 0.01 level of confidence.
** Significant at the 0.05 level of confidence.
Sources: Based on data from Freedom House (1998); IMF (1999, various years); UNESCO (1998); World Bank (1999f); see table A5.4 for variable explanation.

GOVERNANCE AND CORRUPTION INDEXES

AGGREGATION METHODS, NEW EMPIRICAL
MEASURES, AND ECONOMETRIC CHALLENGES

Recent interest in the consequences of political economy factors, formal and informal institutions, rule of law, legal and judiciary capture, and corruption has been accompanied by a proliferation of data purporting to measure various aspects related to what may be broadly called governance. In this annex we summarize some recent research relating to methodological and empirical results on governance and corruption presented in the text of chapter 6. The first part of the annex summarizes the empirical challenges on governance indicators, while the second part summarizes the research project unbundling the measurement of corruption into administrative bribery, state capture (which includes legal and judiciary capture), and public procurement kickbacks.

Defining and Unbundling Governance

Inter alia, this report unbundles the concept of governance into six aggregate component indicators that were constructed by Kaufmann, Kraay, and Zoido-Lobatón (KKZ) (1999a,b). Details about these aggregates and the notion of governance underlying them are given in the chapter text.

The aggregate indicators are based on more than 300 measures produced by 13 different organizations. The sources include published and unpublished data from a number of private forecasting and business risk organizations, think tanks, and other NGOs, and the results of surveys carried out by multilateral and other organizations. The database covers 170 countries. Currently, the data are for only one period: 1997–98. The data and further details on the econometric methodology are available at http://www.worldbank.org/wbi/governance.

Governance, or the manner of governing, encompasses the process of selecting, monitoring, and replacing governments, and refers to the government's capacity to formulate and implement sound policies and the respect of citizens and the state for its institutions. In chapter 6, we presented the following six component indexes of governance are measured: (a) voice and accountability, (b) political stability, (c) government effectiveness, (d) regulatory burden, (e) rule of law, and (f) control of corruption. For each of the six aspects of governance, a large number of individual indexes from different sources were identified as relevant and aggregated to form one of the six composite measures. The aggregation uses an unobserved components model. Advantages that derive from the method include

- A large number of single, and rather noisy, indicators is transformed into a smaller number of more reliable aggregate indicators. These aggregates reflect the statistical consensus of many different sources in a rigorous aggregation method that separates signal from noise. As a result, these aggregate indicators are more precise than more conventional indicators.
- This method computes statistically sound margins of error around the estimates of governance for individual countries; that is, one can be relatively confident about the degree of uncertainty associated with country-specific estimates of governance.

The methodology used emphasizes a limitation of current governance indicators: they are unable to produce precise measures. In view of the margins of error surrounding the estimated measures of governance, small differences in the estimates will not be statistically or practically significant. It would be misleading to offer very precise rankings of countries according to their level of governance. Instead, broad country groupings, along the lines of a traffic light approach, is statistically defensible and is presented in the chapter text.

The above summarizes some of the methodological issues addressed in "Aggregating Governance Indicators" (KKZ 1999a) and in their interpretation. Furthermore, in this paper KKZ organize the data so that within each one of the six governance clusters, each individual indicator measures a similar underlying basic concept of governance. There are considerable benefits from combining these related indicators into an aggregate governance indicator for each cluster, because (a) aggregate indicators span a much larger set of countries than any individual source, (b) aggregate indicators can provide more precise measures of governance than individual indicators, and (c) it is possible to construct quantitative measures of the precision of both the aggregate governance estimates for each country, as well as their components. This allows formal testing of hypotheses regarding cross-country differences in governance.

For each of these clusters, KKZ combine the component indicators into an aggregate governance indicator using an unobserved components model. This model expresses the observed data in each cluster as a linear function of the unobserved common component of governance, plus a disturbance term capturing perception errors and/or sampling variation in each indicator. Estimates are then generated of each of the six governance measures for each country, as well as measures of their precision. The choice of units for governance ensures that the estimates of governance have a mean of zero, a standard deviation of 1, and range from around –2.5 to around 2.5. Higher values correspond to better outcomes. Since the distribution of governance conditional on the observed data is assumed to be independent across countries, it is possible to make probabilistic statements comparing governance in pairs of countries.

It is found that the underlying governance concepts in each cluster are not very precisely estimated, as depicted in figures 6.1 and 6.2 in chapter 6. The rather large size of these confidence intervals has important implications for the use of these aggregate governance indicators. Small differences in point estimates of governance across countries are not statistically significant. As a result, users of this data should focus on the *range* of possible governance for each country as summarized in the 90 percent confidence intervals shown in figure 6.1 in chapter 6. For two countries at opposite ends of the scale of governance, whose 90 percent confidence intervals do not overlap, it is reasonable to conclude that there are significant differences in governance. For pairs of countries that are closer together and whose 90 percent confidence intervals overlap, circumspection is in order and seemingly precise comparisons ought to be avoided.

Despite the imprecision of these aggregate indicators, they are very useful, for several reasons. First, since each of these aggregate indicators spans a much larger set of countries than any individual indicator, it is possible to make comparisons—however imprecise—across a much larger set of countries than would be possible with any single indicator. Second, each *aggregate* indicator provides a more precise signal of its corresponding broader governance concept than do any of its *individual* component indicators, as well as a consistent *summary* of the available evidence. Third, the measures of *precision* for each country are useful as well, because they enable formal statistical tests of cross-country differences in governance—instead of arbitrary comparisons. Fourth, it is possible to use information in the estimates of the precision of each aggregate to quantify the effect of measurement error in regression analyses that use governance indicators as right-hand-side (independent) variables.

In the companion paper ("Governance Matters," KKZ 1999b), the authors detail all external data sources, describe each individual variable, and analyze the relationship between the governance components and developmental variables. The cross-country data indicate a significant simple correlation between governance and socioeconomic outcomes (literacy, infant mortality, longevity, income per capita).

To explore the effect of governance or socioeconomic variables, controlling for other factors, specific econometric tests were done, based on a two-stage least squares regression of a particular socioeconomic dependent variable on a constant and on the governance component, using indicators of colonial heritage as instruments and following the approach of Hall and Jones (1999). The model is well-specified in the sense that (a) the instruments have strong predictive power for governance, and (b) the null hypotheses the these instruments affect incomes only through their effects on governance is not rejected. Concerns about measurement error and omitted variables are also addressed in detail in KKZ (1999b).

Measuring and Unbundling Corruption

Particular coverage to the challenge of addressing corruption was given in the text of chapter 6, given its importance within governance and the emergence of new empirical findings. Until recently, the measurement of corruption, where done, followed a unidimensional and generalized approach to this complex problem. Recent empirical advances in the study of corruption through improved survey techniques and approaches permit a more in-depth and multifaceted unbundling of corruption. In the chapter's text we reported on the interface between corporate strategies and national governance, and also showed that while on balance administrative bribery does not "pay" for business, "grander" forms of corruption such as state capture (figure 6.11) elicit significant private benefits to the captor firm (figure 6.6 in chapter 6), while resulting in large social costs. We detail below how such unbundling was carried out.

The Business Environment and Enterprise Performance Survey: Unbundling Corruption

The ability to distinguish between these various manifestations, causes, and consequences of different types of corruption stems from the concerted effort to conceptually and empirically unbundle the problem of corruption initiated within a large-scale survey of transition economies. The Business Environment and Enterprise Performance Survey (BEEPS) was conducted on the basis of face-to-face interviews with firm managers or owners in site visits during June through August 1999 in 22 countries and covered about 3,000 enterprises.

In each country, between 125 and 150 firms were interviewed with the exception of three countries where larger samples were used: Poland (250), the Russian Federation (550), and Ukraine (250). The survey questions examine corruption from a number of different angles providing consistency checks on each firm's responses. Moreover, tests were conducted to detect any systematic positive or negative bias among the firms' responses in any given country.

In designing the survey, corruption was approached as a multifaceted phenomenon requiring rigorous unbundling, and on such a basis a typology of corruption to distiguish between the different country patterns and consequences was arrived at. Particular emphasis was given to three dimensions of corruption: administrative corruption, public procurement corruption, and state capture (Hellman, Jones, and Kaufmann 2000a ["Seize the State, Seize the Day"]; Hellman and others 2000 ["Measuring Governance, Corruption, and State Capture"])—recognizing that different dimensions of corruption might have unique origins and consequences.

Typology of Corruption: Definitions

Administrative corruption refers to the distorted or arbitrary application and implementation of existing laws, rules, and regulations for illicit private gain by a public office holder, and is subject to a variety of quantitative measures in BEEPS (such as the percentage of administrative bribes paid by the firm as a share of their total revenues). *Public procurement corruption*, an important dimension of corrupt allocation of public finances and public resources, is measured through the percentage bribe fee paid to secure contracts. *State capture* refers to the actions of economic agents or firms both in the public and private sectors to influence the formation and formulation of laws, regulations, decrees, and other government policies (that is, the basic rules of the game) to their own advantage—as a result of illegal payments from private agents to public officials. For instance, an influential oligarch at the head of a powerful financial-industrial group may purchase the votes of legislators to erect barriers to entry in the energy sector.

Unbundling State Capture and Calculating an Overall Capture Index

Within BEEPS, firms were asked about their propensity to purchase legislative capture influence, and they were asked in some detail to report on the impact on the firm of different dimensions of state capture in the economy. For a selected group of transition economies (for full details and data, including measurement of margins of error, see Hellman, Jones, and Kaufmann 2000a; Hellman and others 2000), Table A6.1 presents the various dimensions of state capture that were measured, as well as the overall state capture index derived through the simple average of all subcomponents in the previous columns measuring the effects of the state capture component. In turn, the overall state capture index was used in the second panel of figure 6.6, while the measure of administrative corruption was used in the first panel of that figure. On the basis of the unbundled components of state capture, it is also possible to construct other subindexes of relevance. From table A6.1 a judiciary capture index can be calculated, for instance, based on the proportion of firms affected by the purchase of criminal and commercial court decisions (columns 4 and 5). The analysis of the causes (including absence of civil liberties and economic reforms) and consequences (on output and investment growth and property rights protection) of state capture is carried out through multivariate econometric analysis (including logit and ordinary least squares specifications). The in-depth analysis of the FDI links with state capture, public procurement kick-backs, and other forms of influence (including legal ones) is also based on the data from BEEPS and presented in detail in Hellman, Jones, and Kaufmann (2000b).

From Cross-Country Surveys to In-Depth Country Specific Diagnostics

For detailed action programming in a country, even much improved cross-country surveys cannot substitute for the need to carry out in-depth country diagnostics on governance and corruption within a particular setting. Such country-specific governance diagnostic tools are discussed in the text of the chapter, where further website references are also provided.

Table A6.1. Percentage of Firms Affected by Different Forms of State Capture, and Overall State Capture Index, Selected Countries, 1999

Country	Corporate purchase of						Overall state capture index[b]
	Parliamentary legislation (1)	Presidential decrees (2)	Central bank influence (3)	Criminal courts decisions (4)	Commercial courts decisions (5)	Political party finance (6)	(1 + ... + 6)
Azerbaijan	41	48	39	44	40	35	41
Bulgaria	28	26	28	28	19	42	28
Croatia	18	24	30	29	29	30	27
Estonia[a]	14	7	8	8	8	17	10
Georgia	29	24	32	18	20	21	24
Hungary[a]	12	7	8	5	5	4	7
Latvia	40	49	8	21	26	35	30
Moldova	43	30	40	33	34	42	37
Poland[a]	13	10	6	12	18	10	12
Romania	22	20	26	14	17	27	21
Russian Federation	35	32	47	24	27	24	32
Slovenia[a]	8	5	4	6	6	11	7
Ukraine	44	37	37	21	26	29	32

a. The state capture classification is *medium* for these countries. For all other countries listed the state capture classification is *high*.

b. The state capture index is the simple average of the measured subcomponents in columns 1 through 6. Subgrouping of such components also permits calculations of a judiciary or legal capture index (columns 1, 4, and 5, which under an extended interpretation could also encompass the purchase of presidential decrees in column 2), a stand-alone judiciary capture index (columns 4 and 5), or a legal capture index (columns 1 and 2).

Note: Individual estimates subject to margin of error. Such margins of error are significant, thus care ought to be exercised in the use of each individual estimate. Nonetheless, we have tested for country-specific respondent perception bias and did not find it to be significant (see Hellman and others 2000).

Sources: Hellman, Jones, and Kaufmann 2000a; see also http://www.worldbank.org/wbi/governance.

BIBLIOGRAPHY AND REFERENCES

The word "processed" describes informally reproduced works that may not be commonly available through libraries.

ADB (Asian Development Bank). 1997. *Emerging Asia: Changes and Challenges*. Manila.

Aldeman, Irma. 1975. "Growth, Income Distribution, and Equity-Oriented Development Strategies." *World Development* 3(2 and 3): 67–76.

Adelman, Irma, and Cynthia Taft-Morris. 1967. *Society, Politics and Economic Development: A Quantitative Approach*. Baltimore, Maryland: The Johns Hopkins University Press.

Ades, Alberto, and Rafael Di Tella. 1997. "National Champions and Corruption: Some Unpleasant Interventionist Arithmetic." *The Economic Journal* 107: 1023–42.

_____. 1999. "Rents, Competition, and Corruption." *American Economic Review* 80(4): 982–93.

Ahluwalia, Montek S. 1976. "Income Distribution and Development: Some Stylized Facts." *American Economic Review* 66(2): 128–35.

Akiyama, Takamasa. 1995. "Has Africa Turned the Corner?" World Bank, International Economics Commodities and Policy Unit, Washington, D.C. Processed.

Alba, Pedro, Amar Bhattacharya, Stijn Claessens, Swati Ghosh, and Leonardo Hernandez. 1998. "The Role of Macroeconomic and Financial Sector Linkages in East Asia's Financial Crisis." Paper presented in the Centre for Economic Policy Research/World Bank conference on Financial Crises: Contagion and Market Volatility, May, London.

Alesina, Alberto, and Dani Rodrik. 1994. "Distributive Politics and Economic Growth." *Quarterly Journal of Economics* 108: 465–90.

Alesina, Alberto, and Roberto Peortti. 1994. "The Political Economy of Growth: A Critical Survey of the Recent Literature." *World Bank Economic Review* 8(3): 351–71.

Alesina, Alberto, Vittorio Grilli, and Gian Maria Milesi-Ferretti. 1994. "The Political Economy of Capital Controls." In Leonardo Leiderman and Assaf Razin, eds., *Capital Mobility: The*

Impact on Consumption, Investment, and Growth. Cambridge, U.K.: Cambridge University Press.

Amin, Sajeda, and Anne R. Pebley. 1994. "Gender Inequality within Households: The Impact of a Women's Development Programme in Thirty-Six Bangladesh Villages." *Bangladesh Development Studies* 22(2–3): 121–54.

Ariyoshi, Akira, Kal Habermeier, Bernard Laurens, Inci Otker-Robe, Jorge Ivan Canales-Kiljenko, and Andrei Krilenko. 1999. *Country Experiences with the Use and Liberalization of Capital Controls.* Washington, D.C.: International Monetary Fund, Monetary Exchange Affairs Department.

Arneson, Richard. 1989. "Equity and Equality of Opportunity for Welfare." *Philosophical Study* 56: 77–93.

Arrow, K. 1962. "The Economic Implications of Learning by Doing." *Review of Economic Studies* 29(June): 155–73.

Åslund, Anders. 1999. "Why Has Russia's Economic Transformation Been So Arduous?" Paper presented at the Annual Bank Conference on Development Economics, April 28–30, Washington, D.C.

Aviation Week and Space Technology 151(6), August 9, 1999.

Banerjee, Abhijit. 1999. "Land Reforms: Prospects and Strategies." Paper presented at the Annual Bank Conference on Development Economics, April 28–30, World Bank, Washington, D.C.

Barro, Robert J. 1990. "Government Spending in a Simple Model of Endogenous Growth." *Journal of Political Economy* 98: s103–125.

_____. 1993. "Economic Growth, Convergence, and Government Policies." In Benjamin Zycher

and Lewis C. Solomon, eds., *Economic Policy, Financial Markets, and Economic Growth.* Boulder, Colorado; and Oxford, U.K.: Westview Press, in cooperation with the Milken Institute for Job and Capital Formation.

Barro, Robert, and J. W. Lee. 1994. "Losers and Winners in Economic Growth." In *Proceedings of the World Bank Annual Conference on Development Economics 1993.* Washington, D.C.: World Bank.

_____. 1997. "International Measures of Schooling Years and Schooling Quality." *American Economic Review, Papers and Proceedings* 86(2): 218–23.

Barro, Robert, and X. Sala-I-Martin. 1995. *Economic Growth.* New York: McGraw-Hill.

_____. 1996. *"Convergence," Economic Growth: Theory and Evidence,* vol. 1. International Library of Critical Writings in Economics no. 68. Cheltenham, U.K.: Elgar Reference Collection.

Baster, Nancy, ed. 1972. *Measuring Development: The Role and Adequacy of Development Indicators.* London: F. Cass (reprint). *Journal of Development Studies* 8(3) (original).

Basu, Kaushik, Garance Genicot, and Joseph E. Stiglitz. 1999. "Household Labor Supply, Unemployment, and Minimum Wage Legislation." Policy Research Working Paper no. WPS 2049. Development Economics, World Bank, Washington, D.C.

Beason, R., and D. E. Weinstein. 1996. "Growth, Economies of Scale, and Targeting in Japan (1955-1990)." *Review of Economics and Statistics* 78(2): 286–95.

Becker, Gary S. 1964. *Human Capital.* New York: Columbia University Press.

Behrman, Jere, and Nancy Birdsall. 1983. "The Quality of Schooling, Quantity Alone Is Misleading." *American Economic Review* 73(5): 928–46.

Behrman, Jere, and Anil B. Deolalikar. 1988. "Health and Nutrition." In Hollis Chenery and T. N. Srinivasan, eds., *Handbook of Development Economics,* vol. 1. Amsterdam: North-Holland.

Behrman, Jere, and James C. Knowles. 1999. "Household Income and Child Schooling in Vietnam." *World Bank Economic Review* 13(2): 211–56.

Behrman, Jere, Suzanne Duryea, and Miguel Szekely. 1999. "Schooling Investments and Aggregate Conditions: A Household-Survey-Based Approach for Latin America and the Caribbean." Global Research Project Paper. Global Development Network. Processed.

Benhabib, Jess, and Mark Spiegel. 1994. "The Role of Human Capital in Economic Development." In Mario Paganetto Baldassarri and Edmond S. Luigi Phelps, eds., *International Differences in Growth Rates: Market Globalization and Economic Areas.* Central Issues in Contemporary Economic Theory and Practice Series. New York and London: St. Martin's Press and Macmillan Press.

Bergström, Frederik. 1998. "Capital Subsidies and the Performance of Firms." Working Paper Series in Economics and Finance no. 285. Stockholm School of Economics, Stockholm, Sweden.

Berry, R. A., and W. R. Cline. 1979. *Agrarian Structure and Productivity in Developing Countries.* Baltimore, Maryland: The Johns Hopkins University Press.

Besley, Timothy. 1995. "Property Rights and Investment Incentives: Theory and Evidence from Ghana." *Journal of Political Economy* 103(5): 903–937.

Besley, Timothy, and Anne Case. 1994. "Unnatural Experiments? Estimating the Incidence of Endogenous Policies." Working Paper no. 4956. National Bureau of Economic Research, Cambridge, Massachusetts.

Bhagwati, Jagdish. 1973. "Education, Class Structure, and Income Equality." *World Development* 1(5): 21–36.

_____. 1982. "Directly Unproductive Profit-Seeking Activities." *Journal of Political Economy* 90(5): 998–1002.

Bhalla, Surjit S. 2000. "Growth and Poverty in India— Myth and Reality." Oxus Research and Investment. Processed. Available at http://www.oxusresearch.com.

Bhatia, Bela, and Jean Dréze. 1998. "For Development and Democracy." *Frontline.* Chennai, India, March 6. An abridged version is available at http://www.transparency.de/documents/workpapers/bhatia-dreze.html.

Binswanger, Hans P. 1991. "Brazilian Policies That Encourage Deforestation in the Amazon." *World Development* 19(7): 821–29.

Binswanger, Hans P., and Klaus Deininger. 1997. "Explaining Agricultural and Agrarian Policies in Developing Countries." *Journal of Economic Literature* XXXV(December): 1958–2005.

Binswanger, Hans P., Klaus Deininger, and Gershon Feder. 1995. "Power, Distortions, Revolt, and Reform in Agricultural Land Relations." In Jere Behrman and T. N. Srinivasan, eds., *Handbook of Development Economics,* vol. IIIb. Amsterdam: Elsevier Science.

Birdsall, Nancy. 1994. "Government, Population, and Poverty: A Win-Win Tale." In K. L. Kiessling and H. Landberg, eds., *Population, Economic*

Development, and the Environment. Oxford, U.K.: Oxford University Press.

Birdsall, Nancy, and Juan Luis Londoño. 1997. "Asset Inequality Matters: An Assessment of the World Bank's Approach to Poverty Reduction." *American Economic Review* 87(2): 32–37.

_____. 1998. "No Tradeoff: Efficient Growth via More Equal Human Capital Accumulation." In Carol Graham, Nancy Birdsall, and Richard Sabot, eds., *Beyond Tradeoffs: Market Reform and Equitable Growth in Latin America.* Washington D.C.: Brookings Institution Press in association with the Inter-American Development Bank.

BIS (Bank for International Settlements). 1997, 1998, various years. *Annual Report.* Basel, Switzerland.

Bloom, David E., and Adi Brender. 1993. "Labor and the Emerging World Economy." Working Paper no. 4266. National Bureau of Economic Research, Cambridge, Massachusetts.

Bloom, David E., and Richard B. Freeman. 1988. "Economic Development and the Timing and Components of Population Growth." *Journal of Policy Modeling* 10(1): 57–81.

Bloom, David E., and Jeffrey G. Williamson. 1998. "Demographic Transitions and Economic Miracles in Emerging Asia." *World Bank Economic Review* 12(3): 419–55.

Bojo, Jan. 1996. "The Costs of Land Degradation in Sub-Saharan Africa." *Ecological Economics* 16(2): 161–73.

Bojo, Jan, and Lisa Segnestam 1999. "Towards a Common Goal: The Experience of NEAPs and Their Relationship to NSDSs." Paper submitted to the Regional Consultative Meeting on Sustainable Development in Africa, September 7–9, Abidjan.

Bonilla-Chacin, Maria, and Jeffrey S. Hammer. 1999. "Life and Death among the Poorest." Paper presented at the World Bank Economist Forum, May 3–4, Washington, D.C.

Borensztein, E., J. De Gregorio, and J. W. Lee. 1998. "How Does Foreign Direct Investment Affect Economic Growth?" *Journal of International Economics* 45(1): 115–35.

Borensztein, Eduardo, Mohsin S. Khan, Carmen M. Reinhart, and Peter Wickham. 1994. "The Behavior of Non-Oil Commodity Prices." Occasional Paper no. 112. International Monetary Fund, Washington, D.C.

Bouis, Howarth E., Marilou Palabrice-Costello, Orville Solon, Daniel Westbrook, and Azucena B. Limbo. 1998. "Gender Equality and Investments in Adolescents in the Rural Philippines." Research Report no. 108. International Food Policy Research Institute, Washington, D.C.

Bourguignon, François. 1999. "Crime, Violence, and Inequitable Development." Paper presented at the Annual Bank Conference on Development Economics, April 28–30, World Bank, Washington, D.C.

Bregman, Arie, Melvyn Fuss, and Haim Regev. 1999. "Effects of Capital Subsidization on Productivity in Israeli Industry." *Bank of Israel Economic Review* 72: 77-101.

Brewer, Dominic J., Cathy Krop, Brian P. Gill, and Robert Reichardt. 1999. "Estimating the Cost of National Class Size Reductions under Different Policy Alternatives." *Education Evaluation and Policy Analysis* 21(2): 179–92.

Brown, Lester R., Christopher Flavin, and Hilary French. 1998. "State of the World 1998." In A *Worldwatch Institute Report on Progress Toward a Sustainable Society.* New York: W. W. Norton.

Brunetti, Aymo. 1997a. "Political Variables in Cross-Country Growth Analysis." *Journal of Economic Surveys* 11(2): 163–90.

_____. 1997b. *Politics and Economic Growth: A Cross-Country Data Perspective*. Paris: Organisation for Economic Co-operation and Development, Development Center Studies.

Brunetti, Aymo, Gregory Kisunko, and Beatrice Weder. 1997. "Credibility of Rules and Economic Growth." Policy Research Working Paper no. 1760. World Bank, Policy Research Department, Washington, D.C.

Bryant, Ralph C., and Edith Hodgkinson. 1989. "Problems of International Cooperation." In *Can Nations Agree? Issues in International Economic Cooperation*. Washington, D.C.: The Brookings Institution.

Buckley, Robert. 1999. "1998 Annual Review of Development Effectiveness." World Bank, Operations Evaluation Department, Washington, D.C.

Burgess, Robin. 2000. "Land Distribution and Welfare in Rural China." Paper presented at the Annual Bank Conference on Development Economics, April 20, World Bank, Washington, D.C.

Calvo, Guillermo A. 1999. "Contagion in Emerging Markets: When *Wall Street* Is a Carrier." University of Maryland, College Park. Processed.

Calvo, Guillermo A., and Enrique G. Mendoza. 1996. "Petty Crime and Cruel Punishment: Lessons from the Mexican Debacle." *American Economic Review, Papers and Proceedings* 86(2): 170–75.

Calvo, Guillermo A., Leonardo Leiderman, and Carmen M. Reinhart. 1994. "Capital Inflows to Latin America: The 1970s and 1990s." In Edmar L. Bacha, ed., *Economics in a Changing World: Proceedings of the Tenth World Congress of the International Economic Association*, vol. 4, *Development, Trade, and the Environment*. New York and London: St. Martin's Press and Macmillan Press in association with the International Economic Association.

Caprio, Gerard, and Patrick Honohan. 1999. "Restoring Banking Stability: Beyond Supervised Capital Requirements." *Journal of Economic Perspectives* 13(4): 43–64.

Card, David, and Alan B. Krueger. 1992. "School Quality and Black-White Relative Earnings: A Direct Assessment." *Quarterly Journal of Economics* 107(1): 151–200.

Castaneda, Beatriz. 1997. " An Index of Sustainable Economic Welfare for Chile." Masters Thesis. University of Maryland, College Park, Maryland.

Castro, R., F. Tattenbach, N. Olson, and Luis Gámez. 1997. "The Costa Rican Experience with Market Instruments to Mitigate Climate Change and Conserve Biodiversity." Paper presented at the Global Conference on Knowledge for Development in the Information Age, June 24, World Bank, Toronto.

Chenery, Hollis, Montek S. Ahluwalia, Clive Bell, John H. Duloy, and Richard Jolly. 1974. *Redistribution with Growth*. New York: Oxford University Press.

Chong, Albert, and Cesar Calderón. 1997a. "Empirical Tests on Causality and Feedback between Institutional Measures and Economic Growth." World Bank, Washington, D.C. Processed.

_____. 1997b. "Institutional Change and Poverty, or Why Is it Worth it to Reform the State?" World Bank, Washington, D.C. Processed.

_____. 1998. "Institutional Efficiency and Income Inequality: Cross-Country Empirical Evidence." World Bank, Washington, D.C.

Chomitz, Kenneth M., and David A. Gray. 1996. "Roads, Land Use, and Deforestation: A Spatial

Model Applied to Belize." Working Paper no. 3. Research Project on Social and Environmental Consequences of Growth-Oriented Policies. World Bank, Policy Research Department, Washington, D.C.

Chomitz, Kenneth M., Luis Constantino, and Esteban Brenes. 1998. "Financing Environmental Services: The Costa Rican Experience and its Implications." World Bank, Development Economics Research Group, Washington D.C. Processed.

Claessens, Stijn, Simeon Djankov, and Daniela Klingebiel. 1999. "Financial Restructuring in East Asia: Halfway There?" Financial Sector Discussion Paper 3. World Bank, Washington, D.C.

Cleaver, Kevin, and Gotz Schreiber. 1994. *Reversing the Spiral: The Population, Environment, and Agriculture Nexus in Sub-Saharan Africa*. Directions in Development. World Bank, Washington, D.C.

COCHILCO. 2000. *Annual Report of COCHILCO*. Report from the Senate of Chile.

Cohen, G. A. 1989. "On the Currency of Egalitarian Justice." *Ethics* 99: 906–944.

Collier, Paul. 1999. "On the Economic Consequences of Civil War." *Oxford Economic Papers* 51(January): 168–83.

Collier, Paul, and Anke Hoeffler. 1998. "On the Economic Causes of Civil Wars." *Oxford Economic Papers* 50(October): 563–73.

Collier, Paul, David Dollar, and Nicholas Stern. 2000. "Fifty Years of Development." World Bank. Washington, D.C. Processed.

Collins, Chuck. 1996. "Aid to Dependent Corporations." In Marc Breslow, Miller Reed, and Betsy Reed, eds., *Decoding the Contract: Progressive Perspectives on Current Economic Policy Debates*. Somerville, Massachusetts: Economic Affairs Bureau.

Collins, Susan M., and Barry P. Bosworth. 1996. "Economic Growth in East Asia: Accumulation Versus Assimilation." *Brookings Papers on Economic Activity* 2: 135–91.

Commander, Simon, Mark Dutz, and Nicholas Stern. 1999. "Restructuring in Transition Economies: Ownership, Competition, and Regulation." Paper presented at the Annual Bank Conference on Development Economics, April 28–30, Washington, D.C.

Cooper, Richard. 1998. "Should Capital-Account Convertibility Be a World Objective?" In *Essays in International Finance Series* 207. Princeton, New Jersey: Princeton University, Department of Economics, International Finance Section.

Corbo, Vittorio, Stanley Fischer, and Steven B. Webb. 1992. *Adjustment Lending Revisited: Policies to Restore Growth*. Washington, D.C.: World Bank.

Cornia, Giovanni A. 1999. "Rising Income Inequality and Poverty Reduction: Are They Compatible?" UNU/WIDER Research Project. Available at http://www.wider.unu.edu/wiid/wiid.htm.

Corsetti, Giancarlo, Paolo Pesenti, and Nouriel Roubini. 1998. "What Caused the Asian Currency and Financial Crisis?" New York University, New York. Processed.

Cropper, Maureen, and Charles Griffiths. 1994. The Interaction of Population Growth and Environmental Quality. *American Economic Review* 84: 250–54.

Cropper, Maureen, Charles Griffiths, and Muthukumara Mani. 1997. "Roads, Population Pressures, and Deforestation in Thailand, 1976–1989." Policy Research Working Paper no. 1726. World Bank, Policy Research Department, Washington, D.C.

Dailami, Mansoor. 1998. "Euphoria and Panic: Developing Countries' Relationship to Private Finance." *EDI Forum* 3(2): 1–3, 6.

_____. 2000. "Financial Openness, Democracy, and Redistributive Policy." Policy Research Working Paper no. 2372. World Bank, Washington, D.C.

Dailami, Mansoor, and Nadeem ul Haque. 1998. "What Macroeconomic Policies Are 'Sound?'" Policy Research Working Paper no. 1995. World Bank, Washington, D.C.

Daly, H. E. 1997. "Georgescu-Roegen Versus Solow/Stiglitz." *Ecological Economics* 22(3): 261–66.

Dasgupta, Partha. 1990a. "Well-Being and the Extent of Its Realization in Developing Countries." *Economic Journal* 100(4, supplement): 1–32.

_____. 1990b. "Well-Being in Poor Countries." *Economic and Political Weekly* (India) 25: 1713–20.

_____. 1993. *An Inquiry into Well-Being and Destitution.* New York: Oxford University Press.

_____. 1995. "Population, Poverty, and the Local Environment." *Scientific American* (February): 40–45.

Dasgupta, Partha, and Karl-Göran Mäler. 1994. "Poverty, Institutions, and the Environmental Resource Base." Environment Paper no. 9. World Bank, Environment Department, Washington, D.C.

Dasgupta, Partha, and Ismail Serageldin. 1999. *Social Capital: A Multifaceted Perspective.* Washington, D.C.: World Bank.

Dasgupta, Susmita, Ashoka Mody, Subhendu Roy, and David Wheeler. 1995. "Environmental Regulation and Development: A Cross-Country Empirical Analysis." Policy Research Working Paper no. 1488. World Bank, Policy Research Department, Washington, D.C.

De Gregorio, José. 1992. "Growth in Latin America." *Journal of Development Economics* 31(1): 59–84.

De Long, J. Bradford, and Lawrence Summers. 1991. "Equipment Investment and Economic Growth." *Quarterly Journal of Economics* 106(2): 445–502.

de Moor, André, P. G., and Peter Calamai. 1997. *Subsidizing Unsustainable Development: Undermining the Earth with Public Funds.* San Jóse, Costa Rica: Institute for Research on Public Expenditure and The Earth Council.

Deaton, Angus, 1997. *The Analysis of Household Surveys: A Microeconometric Approach to Development Policy.* Baltimore, Maryland: The Johns Hopkins University Press in association with the World Bank.

Deininger, Klaus. 1999. "Making Negotiated Land Reform Work: Initial Experience from Colombia, Brazil, and South Africa." Policy Research Working Paper no. 2040. World Bank, Policy Research Department, Washington, D.C.

Deininger, Klaus, and Bart Minten. 1996. "Determinants of Forest Cover and the Economics of Protection: An Application to Mexico." Working Paper no. 10. Research Project on Social and Environmental Consequences of Growth-Oriented Policies. World Bank, Policy Research Department, Washington, D.C.

Deininger, Klaus, and P. Olinto. 1999. "Asset Distribution Inequality and Growth." World Bank, Development Research Group, Washington, D.C. Processed.

Deininger, Klaus, and Lyn Squire. 1996. "A New Dataset Measuring Income Inequality." *World Bank Economic Review* 10(3): 565–91.

_____. 1998. "New Ways of Looking at Old Issues: Inequality and Growth." *Journal of Development Economics* 57(2): 259–87.

Demirgüç-Kunt, Asli, and Enrica Detragiache. 1998. "Financial Liberalization and Financial Fragility." Policy Research Working Paper no. 1917. World Bank, Development Research Group; and International Monetary Fund, Research Department, Washington, D.C.

Denison, E. F. 1962. *Sources of Economic Growth in the United States and the Alternative before Us*. New York: Committee for Economic Development.

_____. 1967. *Why Growth Rates Differ: Post-War Experience in Nine Western Countries*. Washington, D.C.: The Brookings Institution.

Devarajan, Shantayanan, and Jeffrey S. Hammer. 1998. "Risk Reduction and Public Spending." Policy Research Working Paper no. 1869. World Bank, Public Economics, Development Research Group, Washington, D.C.

Diewert, Walter Erwin. 1986. *The Measurement of the Economic Benefits of Infrastructure Services*. Berlin and New York: Springer-Verlag.

Dikhanov, Yuri, and Michael P. Ward. 2000. "Towards a Better Understanding of the Global Distribution of Income." World Bank, Development Economics Data Group, Washington, D.C. Processed.

Diwan, Ishac. 1999. "Labor Shares and Financial Crises." Working Paper. World Bank Institute, Washington, D.C.

Dixon, John A., and Paul Sherman. 1990. *Economics of Protected Areas: A New Look at Benefits and Costs*. Washington, D.C.: Island Press.

Dollar, David, and Aart Kraay. 2000. "Growth Is Good for the Poor." Working paper. World Bank, Policy Research Department, Washington, D.C.

Dooley, Michael. 1996. "A Survey of Literature on Controls over International Capital Transactions." *IMF Staff Papers* 43(December): 639–87.

Drage, John, and Fiona Mann. 1999. "Improving the Stability of the International Financial System." In *Financial Stability Review*, issue 6. Bank of England.

Drewnowski, Jan F., and Wolf Scott. 1966. "The Level of Living Index." Report no. 4. United Nations Research Institute for Social Development, Geneva.

Dréze, Jean, and Amartya Sen. 1995. *Hunger and Public Action*. WIDER Studies in Development Economics. Oxford, U.K.: Clarendon Press.

Dubey, Ashutosh, and Elizabeth M. King. 1996. "A New Cross-Country Education Stock Series Differentiated by Age and Sex." *Journal of Educational Planning and Administration* 11(1): 5–24.

Duraisamy, P., Estelle James, Julia Lane, and Jee-Peng Tan. 1998. "Is There a Quantity-Quality Tradeoff as Enrollments Increase? Evidence from Tamil Nadu, India." Policy Research Working Paper no. 1768. World Bank, Washington, D.C.

Dworkin, Ronald. 1981. "What Is Equity: Part 2. Equality of Resources." *Philosophy & Public Affairs* 10: 283–345.

Easterly, William. 1998. "The Joys and Sorrows of Openness: A Review Essay." Paper prepared for the Seminar on Economic Growth and Its Determinants, March 23–24, Ministry for Development Cooperation, The Hague, The Netherlands.

_____. 1999a. "Life during Growth." *Journal of Economic Growth* 4(3): 239–79.

_____. 1999b. "The Lost Decades: Explaining Developing Countries' Stagnation 1980–1998." Development Economics Research Group, World Bank, Washington, D.C.

_____. 1999c. "The Ghost of Financing Gap: Testing the Growth Model Used in the International

Financial Institutions." *Journal of Development Economics* 60(2): 423–38.

Easterly, William, and Aart Kraay. 1999. "Small States, Small Problems?" Policy Research Working Paper no. 2139. World Bank, Development Research Group, Macroeconomics and Growth, Washington, D.C.

Easterly, William, and Ross Levine. 2000. "It's Not Factor Accumulation: Stylized Facts and Growth Models." Working Paper. World Bank, Washington, D.C. Available at http://www.worldbank.org/html/prdmg/grthweb/pdfiles/fact3.pdf.

Easterly, William, and Hairong Yu. 2000. "Global Development Network Growth Database." Available at http://www.worldbank.org/research/growth/GDNdata.htm.

Easterly, William, Roumeen Islam, and Joseph E. Stiglitz. 1999. "Shaken and Stirred: Volatility and Macroeconomic Paradigms for Rich and Poor Countries." Michael Bruno Memorial Lecture, XIIth World Congress of the International Economics Association, August 27, Buenos Aires.

Easterly, William, Michael Kremer, Lant Pritchett, and Larry Summers. 1993. "Good Policy or Good Luck? Country Growth Performance and Temporary Shocks." *Journal of Monetary Economics* 32: 459–83.

Eastwood, Robert, and Michael Lipton. 1999. "The Impact of Changes in Human Fertility on Poverty." *Journal of Development Studies* 36(1): 1–30.

Edwards, Sebastian. 1999. "How Effective Are Capital Controls?" *Journal of Economic Perspectives* 13(4): 65–84.

EEPSEA (Economy and Environment Program for South East Asia). 1998. "Interim Results of a Study on the Economic Value of Haze Dam-ages in SE Asia." Economy and Environment Program for Southeast Asia, Singapore.

Eichengreen, Barry. 1996. *Globalizing Capital: A History of the International Monetary System.* Princeton, New Jersey: Princeton University Press.

Eichengreen, Barry, and Michael Mussa, eds. 1998. "Capital Account Liberalization: Theoretical and Practical Aspects." Occasional paper 172. International Monetary Fund, Washington, D.C.

Ehrlich, Paul R. 1968. *The Population Bomb.* New York: Ballantine.

Ekbom, Anders, and Jan Bojo. 1999. "Poverty and Environment: Evidence of Links and Integration into the Country Assistance Strategy Process." Discussion Paper no. 4. World Bank, Africa Region, Environment Group, Washington, D.C.

Esrey, Steven A., James Potash, Leslie Roberts, and Clive Shiff. 1990. "Health Benefits from Improvements in Water Supply and Sanitation: Survey and Analysis of the Literature on Selected Diseases." WASH Technical Report no. 66. U.S. Agency for International Development, Washington, D.C.

European Bank for Reconstruction and Development. 1999. Transition Report: Ten Years of Transition. London.

Evans, P., ed. 1996. "Government Action, Social Capital, and Development across the Public-Private Divide." *World Development* 24(6, special section): 1033–1132.

Fakin, Barbara. 1995. "Investment Subsidies during Transition." *Eastern European Economics* 33(5): 62–75.

Fedderke, Johannes, and Robert Klitgaard. 1998. "Economic Growth and Social Indicators: An Exploratory Analysis." *Economic Development and Cultural Change* 46(April): 455–89.

Feder, Gershon. 1987. "Land Ownership Security and Farm Productivity: Evidence from Rural Thailand." *Journal of Development Studies* 24(1): 16–30.

_____. 1993. "The Economics of Land and Titling in Thailand." In Karla Hoff, Avishay Braverman, and Joseph Stiglitz, eds., *The Economics of Rural Organizations: Theory, Practice, and Policy.* New York: Oxford University Press.

Ferreira, Francisco H. G., and Julie A. Litchfield. 1999. "Calm after the Storms: Income Distribution and Welfare in Chile, 1987–94." *World Bank Economic Review* 13(3): 509–38.

Ffrench-Davis, Ricardo, Patricio Leiva, and Roberto Madrid. 1992. "Liberalizacion Comercial y Crecimiento: La Experiencia de Chile, 1973–89." *Pensamiento Iberoamericano* 21: 33–55.

Filmer, Deon, and Lant Pritchett. 1999a. "Educational Enrollment and Attainment in India: Household Wealth, Gender, Village, and State Effects." *Journal of Educational Planning and Administration* 13(2): 135–63.

_____. 1999b. "The Effect of Household Wealth on Educational Attainment: Evidence from 35 Countries." *Population and Development Review* 25(1): 85–120.

_____. 1999c. "The Impact of Public Spending on Health: Does Money Matter?" *Social Science and Medicine* 49(10): 1309–23.

Filmer, Deon, Jeffrey Hammer, and Lant Pritchett. Forthcoming. "Health Policy in Poor Countries: Weak Links in the Chain." *World Bank Economic Observer.*

Fine, B., and K. Fine. 1974a. "Social Choice and Individual Rankings I." *Review of Economic Studies* 41(3): 303–322

_____. 1974b. "Social Choice and Individual Rankings II." *Review of Economic Studies* 41(4): 459–75.

Fischer, Stanley. 1993. "The Role of Macroeconomic Factors in Growth." *Journal of Monetary Economics* 32(3): 485–512.

_____. 1998. "Capital Account Liberalization and the Role of the IMF." In *Essays in International Finance Series,* 207. Princeton, New Jersey: Princeton University, Department of Economics, International Finance Section.

Fischer, Stanley, Richard N. Cooper, Rudiger Dornbusch, Peter M. Garber, Carlos Massad, Jaques J. Polak, Dani Rodrik, and Savak S. Tarapore. 1998. *Should the IMF Pursue Capital-Account Convertibility?*

Fishlow, Albert. 1995. "Inequality, Poverty, and Growth; Where Do We Stand?" In Michael Bruno and Boris Pleskovic, eds., *Annual World Bank Conference on Development Economics 1995.* Washington, D.C.: World Bank.

Fisman, Raymond, and Roberta Gatti. 2000. "Decentralization and Corruption: Evidence across Countries." Policy Research Working Paper no. 2290. World Bank, Development Research Group, Washington, D.C. Available at www.wbln0018.worldbank.org/research/workpapers.nsf/.

Fisman, Raymond, and Jakob Svensson. 1999. "The Effects of Corruption and Taxation on Growth: Firm-Level Evidence." Processed.

Foster, Andrew, and Mark R. Rosenzweig. 1995. "Learning by Doing and Learning from Others: Human Capital and Technical Change in Agriculture." *Journal of Political Economy* 103: 1176–1209.

Fournier, Gary, and David Rasmussen. 1986. "Targeted Capital Subsidies and Economic Welfare." *Cato Journal* 6(1): 295–312.

Fox, Jonathan. 1997. "The World Bank and Social Capital: Contesting the Concept in Practice." *Journal of International Development* 9(7): 963–71.

Frank, Robert. 1998. *Luxury Fever: Why Money Fails to Satisfy in an Era of Excess*. New York: Free Press.

Freedom House. 1998. *Freedom in the World: Political Rights and Civil Liberties*. New York.

Furman, Jason, and Joseph Stiglitz. 1998. "Economic Crises: Evidence and Insights from East Asia." *Brookings Papers on Economic Activity* (2nd issue for 1998): 1–114.

Furtado, Jose, Nalin Kishor, G. V. Rao, and Catherine Wood. 1999. *Global Climate Change and Biodiversity: Challenges for the Future and the Way Ahead*. Washington D.C.: World Bank Institute.

Galeotti, Marzio, and Alessandro Lanza. 1999. "Desperately Seeking (Environmental) Kuznets." Paper presented at the 1998 World Congress of Environment and Resource Economists, June 25-27, Venice, Italy.

Gallego, Francisco, Leonardo Hernandez, and Klaus Schmidt-Hebbel. 1999. "Capital Controls in Chile: Effective? Efficient?" Working Paper. Central Bank of Chile, Santiago.

Galor, Oded, and J. Zeira. 1993. "Income Distribution and Macroeconomics." *Review of Economic Studies* 60: 35–52.

Gandhi, V., D. Gray, and R. McMorran. 1997. "A Comprehensive Approach to Domestic Resource Mobilization for Sustainable Development." Paper presented to the Fourth Expert Group Meeting on Financial Issues of Agenda 21, January 6-8, Santiago, Chile, United Nations, Department for Policy Coordination and Sustainable Development, New York.

Garrett, Geoffrey. 1998. "Global Markets and National Politics: Collision Course or Virtuous Circle?" *International Organization* 52(4): 787–824.

Gazetta Mercantil. 1999. An international weekly. New York, May 21.

GEF (Global Environmental Facility). 1998. *Valuing the Global Environment: Actions and Investments for a 21st Century*, vol. 1. Washington, D.C.

Gilson, Stuart. 1995. "UAL Corporation." Case Study 9-295-130. Harvard University Business School, Cambridge, Massachusetts.

Gold, Joseph. 1977. *International Capital Movements under the Law of the International Monetary Fund*. Washington D.C.: International Monetary Fund.

Gonzalez de Asis, Maria. 2000. "Reducing Corruption: Lessons from Venezuela." PREM Note no. 39. World Bank, Washington, D.C.

Goodman, L. A., and H. Markowitz. 1952. "Social Welfare Functions Based on Individual Rankings." *American Journal of Sociology* 58.

Gray, Cheryl W., and Daniel Kaufmann. 1998. "Corruption and Development." *Finance and Development* 35(1): 7–10.

Greaney, Vincent, and Thomas Kellaghan. 1996. "Monitoring the Learning Outcomes of Education Systems." Direction in Development Papers. World Bank, Washington, D.C.

Griliches, Zvi. 1971. *Price Indexes and Quality Changes: Studies in New Methods of Measurement*. Cambridge, Massachusetts: Harvard University Press.

_____. 1997. "Education, Human Capital, and Growth: A Personal Perspective." *Journal of Labor Economics* 15(1, part 2): s330–42.

Grossman, Gene M., and Elhanan Helpman. 1989. "Growth and Welfare in a Small Open Economy." Working Paper no. 2970. National Bureau of Economic Research.

_____. 1990. "Comparative Advantage and Long Run Growth." *American Economic Review*, 80: 796–815.

Grossman, Gene M., and A. B. Krueger. 1995. "Economic Growth and the Environment." *Quarterly Journal of Economics* 112: 353–78.

Gulati, Ashok, and Sudha Narayanan. 2000. "Demystifying Fertilizer and Power Subsidies in India." *Economic and Political Weekly*, March 4, pp. 784–94.

Gupta, Sanjeev, Hamid Davoodi, and Rosa Alonso-Terme. 1998. "Does Corruption Affect Income Inequality and Poverty?" Working Paper no. WP/98/76. International Monetary Fund, Fiscal Affairs Department, Washington, D.C.

Haldane, Andrew. 1999. "Private Sector Involvement in Financial Crisis." *Financial Stability Review* (November) Bank of England.

Hall, Robert E., and Charles I. Jones. 1999. "Why Do Some Countries Produce So Much More Output Per Worker Than Others?" *Quarterly Journal of Economics* 114(1): 83–116.

Hamilton, Kirk, and Ernst Lutz. 1996. "Green National Accounts: Policy Uses and Empirical Experience." Environment Department Paper no. 39. World Bank, Environment Department, Washington, D.C.

Hammer, Jeffrey S., and Sudhir Shetty. 1995. "East Asia's Environment: Principles and Priorities for Action." World Bank Discussion Paper no. 287. World Bank, Washington D.C.

Hanrahan, David, David Wheeler, Michelle Keene, and David Shaman. 1998. "Developing Partnerships for Effective Pollution Management." *Environment Matters* Annual Review(Fall): 62–65.

Hanushek, Eric. 1995. "Interpreting the Recent Research on Schooling in Developing Countries." *World Bank Research Observer* 10(2):227–46.

Hanushek, Eric A., and Dongwook Kim. 1995. "Schooling, Labor Force Quality, and Economic Growth." Research Working Paper no. 5399. National Bureau of Economic Research, Cambridge, Massachusetts.

Harr, Jonathan. 1995. *A Civil Action*. New York: Vintage Books.

Harris, Richard I. D. 1991. "The Employment Creation Effects of Factor Subsidies: Some Estimates for Northern Ireland Manufacturing Industry, 1955–1983." *Journal of Regional Science* 31(1): 49–64.

Harriss, John, ed. 1997. "Policy Arena: 'Missing Link' or Analytically Missing? The Concept of Social Capital." *Journal of International Development* 9(7, special section): 919–71.

Harsanyi, J.C. 1953. "Cardinal Utility in Welfare Economics and in the Theory of Risk-Taking." *Journal of Political Economy* 61: 434–35.

Helleiner, Eric. 1994. *States and the Reemergence of Global Reform: From Brettan Woods to the 1990s.* Ithaca, New York: Cornell University Press.

Hellman, Joel, Geraint Jones, and Daniel Kaufmann. 2000a. "Seize the State, Seize the Day: An Empirical Analysis of State Capture and Corruption in Transition Economies." Paper presented at the Annual Bank Conference on Development Economics, April 18–20, Washington, D.C. Available at http://www.worldbank.org/wbi/governance/.

_____. 2000b. "Far from Home: Do Transnationals Import Better Governance in the Capture Economy." World Bank, Washington, D.C. Processed. Available at http://www.worldbank.org/wbi/governance/.

Hellman, Joel S., Geraint Jones, Daniel Kaufmann, and Mark Schankerman. 2000. "Measuring

Governance, Corruption, and State Capture: How Firms and Bureaucrats Shape the Business Environment in Transition." Policy Research Working Paper no. 2313. World Bank, Washington, D.C.

Hernandez, Leonardo, and Klaus Schmidt-Hebbel. 1999. "Capital Controls in Chile: Effective? Efficient? Endurable?" Paper presented at the World Bank Conference on Capital Flows, Financial Crisis and Policies, April 15–16, Washington, D.C.

Herrera, Alejandra. 1992. "The Privatization of the Argentine Telephone System." *CEPAL Review* 47: 149–61.

Hettige, Hemamala, Muthukumara Mani, and David Wheeler. 1998. "Industrial Pollution in Economic Development (Kuznets Revisited)." Policy Research Working Paper no. 1876. World Bank, Development Research Group, Washington, D.C.

Hicks, Norman, and Paul Streeten. 1979. "Indicators of Development: The Search for a Basic Needs Yardstick." *World Development* 7(6): 567–80.

Hill, Kenneth, Rohini Pande, Mary Mahy, and Gareth Jones. 1999. *Trends in Child Mortality in the Developing World: 1960–96.* New York: United Nations Children's Fund.

Hindriks, Jean, Michael Keen, and Abhinay Muthoo. 1999. "Corruption, Extortion, and Evasion." *Journal of Public Economics* 74(3): 395–430.

Hirschman, Albert O. 1958. *The Strategy of Economic Development.* New Haven, Connecticut: Yale University Press.

_____. 1970. *Exit, Voice, and Loyalty: Responses to Decline in Firms, Organizations, and States.* Cambridge, Massachusetts: Harvard University Press.

_____. 1981. *Essays in Trespassing: Economics to Politics and Beyond*, Cambridge, U.K.; and New York: Cambridge University Press.

Hoeffler, Anke. 1997. "The Augmented Solow Model and the African Growth Debate." University of Oxford, U.K. Processed.

Holtz-Eakin, Douglas, and Thomas M. Selden. 1995. "Stoking the Fires? CO_2 Emissions and Economic Growth." *Journal of Public Economics* 57: 85–101.

Hoy, Michael, and Emmanuel Jimenez. 1997. "The Impact of the Urban Environment of Incomplete Property Rights." Working Paper no. 14. Research Project on Social and Environmental Consequences of Growth-Oriented Policies. World Bank, Policy Research Department, Washington, D.C.

Hughes-Hallet, A. J. 1989. "Econometrics and the Theory of Economic Policy: The Tinbergen-Theil Contributions 40 Years on." *Oxford Economic Papers* 41(January): 189–214.

Huntington, Samuel P. 1964. "Modernization and Corruption." In Arnold J. Heidenheimer, ed., *Political Corruption: Readings in Comparative Analysis.* New York: Holt Reinehart.

_____. 1968. *Political Order in Changing Societies.* New Haven: Yale University Press.

IDB (Inter-American Development Bank). 1998. *Facing Up to Inequality in Latin America. Economic and Social Progress in Latin America. 1998–1999 Report.* Baltimore, Maryland: The Johns Hopkins University Press.

IMF (International Monetary Fund). 1998. "Fiscal Reforms in Low-Income Countries: Experiences under IMF-Supported Programs." Occasional Paper no. 160. Washington, D.C.

_____. 1999. *Government Financial Statistics.* Washington, D.C.

_____. Various issues. *Exchange Arrangements and Exchange Restrictions: Annual Report.* Washington, D.C.

India Today. 1999. "The Poisoning of India." Special collectors issue, January (Living Media India, New Delhi).

International Country Risk Guide. 1982–95. Computer file. Syracruse, New York: PRS Group. Available to World Bank and International Monetary Fund staff at http://jolis. worldbankimflib.org/nldbs.htm

International Finance Corporation. Various years. *Emerging Stock Markets Factbook.* Washington, D.C.

Isham, Jonathan, and Daniel Kaufmann. 1999. "The Forgotten Rationale for Policy Reform: The Productivity of Investment Projects." *Quarterly Journal of Economics* 114(February): 149–84.

Isham, Jonathan, Daniel Kaufmann, and Lant H. Pritchett. 1997. "Civil Liberties, Democracy, and the Performance of Government Projects." *World Bank Economic Review* 11(2): 219–42.

Islam, Nazrul. 1995. "Growth Empires: A Panel Data Approach." *The Quarterly Journal of Economics* 110: 1127–70.

James, Estelle, Elizabeth King, and Ace Suryadi. 1996. "Finance, Management, and Cost of Public and Private Schools in Indonesia." *Economics of Education Review* 15(4): 387–98.

Jimenez, Emmanuel, and Vicente Paqueo. 1996. "Do Local Contributions Affect the Efficiency of Public Primary Schools?" *Economics of Education Review* 15(4): 377–86.

Jimenez, Emmanuel, and Yasuyuki Sawada. 1999. "Do Community-Managed Schools Work? An Evaluation of El Salvador's EDUCO Program." *The World Bank Economic Review* 13(3): 415–41.

Jimenez, Emmanuel, Bernard Kugler, and Robin Horn. 1986. "An Economic Evaluation of a National Job Training System: Columbia's Servicio Nacional de Aprendizaje (SENA)." EDT24. World Bank, Education and Training Department, Washington, D.C.

Johnson, Simon, Daniel Kaufmann, and Andrei Shleifer. 1997. "The Unofficial Economy in Transition." *Brookings Papers on Economic Activity* (2). Washington, D.C.

Johnson, Simon, Daniel Kaufmann, and Pablo Zoido-Lobatón. 1998. "Regulatory Discretion and the Unofficial Economy." *American Economic Review* 88(2): 387–92.

Jones, Charles I. 1995. "Time Series Tests of Endogenous Growth Models." *Quarterly Journal of Economics* 110(2): 495–525.

Kakwani, Nanak. 1993. "Performance in Living Standards: An International Comparison." *Journal of Development Economics* (Netherlands) 41(August): 307–336.

Kaminsky, Graciela, and Carmen Reinhart. 1999. "Twin Crises: The Causes of Banking and Balance of Payments Problems." *American Economic Review* 89(3): 473–500.

Kanbur, Ravi. 1999. "Why Is Inequality Back on the Agenda?" Paper presented at the Annual Bank Conference on Development Economics, April 28–30, World Bank, Washington D.C.

_____. 2000. "Income Distribution and Development." In A. Atkinson and F. Bourguignon, eds., *Handbook of Income Distribution.* Amsterdam: North-Holland.

Kapstein, Ethan B. 1989. "Resolving the Regulator's Dilemma: International Coordination of Banking Regulations." *International Organization* 43(2): 323–47.

Kates, Robert W., and Viola Haarmann. 1992. "Where the Poor Live: Are the Assumptions Correct?" *Environment* (U.S.) 34(May): 4–11, 25–28.

Kato, Kazu. 1996. "Grow Now, Clean Up Later? The Case of Japan." In *Effective Financing of Environmentally Sustainable Development*. Environmentally Sustainable Development Proceedings Series no. 10. Proceedings of the Third Annual Conference on Environmentally Sustainable Development. Washington D.C.: World Bank.

Kaufmann, Daniel. 1998. "Challenges in the Next Stage of Anticorruption." *In New Perspectives on Combating Corruption*. Washington, D.C. Transparency International and the World Bank Institute.

Kaufmann, Daniel, and Yan Wang. 1995. "Macroeconomic Policies and Project Performance in the Social Sectors: A Model of Human Capital Production and Evidence from LDCs." *World Development* 23(5): 751–65.

Kaufmann, Daniel, and Shan-Jin Wei. 1999. "Does 'Grease Money' Speed up the Wheels of Commerce?" World Bank Policy Research Working Paper no. 2254. World Bank, Washington, D.C.

Kaufmann, Daniel, Aart Kraay, and Pablo Zoido-Lobatón. 1999a. "Aggregating Governance Indicators." Policy Research Working Paper no. 2195. World Bank, Policy Research Department, Washington, D.C. Available at http://www.worldbank.org/wbi/governance/.

———. 1999b. "Governance Matters." Policy Research Working Paper no. 2196. World Bank, Policy Research Department, Washington, D.C.

———. 2000. "Governance Matters: From Measurement to Action." *Finance and Development*. Available at http://www.imf.org/faudd/2000/06/kauf.htm. International Monetary Fund, Washington, D.C.

Kaufmann, Daniel, Sanjay Pradhan, and Randi Ryterman. 1998. "New Frontiers in Anti-corruption Empirical Diagnostics: From In-Depth Survey Analysis to Action Programs in Transition Economies." Poverty Reduction and Economic Management Note no. 7. World Bank, Washington, D.C.

Keefer, Philip, and Stephen Knack. 1997. "Why Don't Poor Countries Catch Up? A Cross-National Test of Institutional Explanation." *Economic Inquiry* 35(3): 590–602.

Keller, Wolfgang. 1995. "International R&D Spillovers and Intersectoral Trade Flows: Do They Match?" Yale University, New Haven, Connecticut. Processed.

———. 1998. "Are International R&D Spillovers Trade-Related? Analyzing Spillovers among Randomly Matched Trade Partners." *European Economic Review* 42(8): 1469–81.

Kelley, Allen C. 1988. "Economic Consequences of Population Change in the Third World." *Journal of Economic Literature* 26(4): 1685–1728.

———. 1998. "The Impacts of Rapid Population Growth on Poverty, Food Provision, and the Environment." Working Paper. Duke University, Chapel Hill, North Carolina.

Kelley, Allen C., and Robert M. Schmidt. 1999. "Economic and Demographic Change: A Synthesis of Models, Findings, and Perspectives." Working Paper no. 99-01. Duke University, Chapel Hill, North Carolina. Forthcoming in Nancy Birdsall, ed., *Population Change and Economic Development*.

Khan, Mohsin S. 1996. "The Implications of International Capital Flows for Macroeconomic and Financial Policies." *International Journal of Finance and Economics* (U.K.) 1(July): 155–60.

Kim, Jong-Il, and Lawrence J. Lau. 1994. "The Sources of Economic Growth of the East Asian Newly

Industrialized Countries." *Journal of the Japanese and International Economies* 8(3): 235–71.

Kim, Jooseop, Harold Alderman, and Peter F. Orazem. 1999. "Can Private School Subsidies Increase Schooling for the Poor? The Quetta Urban Fellowship Program." *World Bank Economic Review* 13(3): 443–65.

King, Elizabeth M., and M. Anne Hill, eds. 1993. *Women's Education in Developing Countries: Barriers, Benefits, and Policy.* Baltimore, Maryland: The Johns Hopkins University Press.

King, Elizabeth M., Peter F. Orazem, and Darin Wohlgemuth. 1999. "Central Mandates and Local Incentives: The Colombia Education Voucher Program." *World Bank Economic Review* 13(3): 467–91.

King, Robert G., and Ross Levine. 1993. "Financial Intermediation and Economic Development." In Colin Mayer and Xavier Viver, eds., *Capital Markets and Financial Intermediation.* Cambridge, U.K.: Cambridge University Press.

King, Robert G., and Sergio Rebelo. 1990. "Public Policy and Economic Growth: Developing Neoclassical Implications." *Journal of Political Economy* 98(5) part 2: s126–50.

_____. 1993. "Transitional Dynamics and Economic Growth in the Neoclassical Model." *American Economic Review* 83(4): 908–931.

Kishor, Nalin M., and Luis Constantino. 1994. "Sustainable Forestry: Can it Compete?" *Finance and Development* 31(4): 36–39.

_____. 1996. "Voting for Economic Policy Reform." Dissemination Note no 15. World Bank, Latin America Technical Environment Department, Washington, D.C.

Klenow, Peter and Andrés Rodríguez-Clare. 1997a. "Economic Growth: A Review Essay." *Journal of Monetary Economics* (40): 597–618.

_____. 1997b. "The Neoclassical Revival in Growth Economics: Has It Gone Too Far?" In *NBER Macroeconomic Annual 1997.* Cambridge, Massachusetts: National Bureau of Economic Research.

Klitgaard, Robert. 1988. *Controlling Corruption.* Berkeley, California, and London: University of California Press.

Klitgaard, Robert, Ronald Maclean-Abaroa, and H. Lindsey Parris. 2000. *Corrupt Cities: A Practical Guide to Cure and Prevention.* Oakland, California and Washington, D.C.: ICS Press and World Bank Institute.

Knack, Stephen, and Philip Keefer. 1995. "Institutions and Economic Performance: Cross-Country Tests Using Alternative Institutional Measures." *Economics and Politics* 7: 207–27.

_____. 1997. "Does Social Capital Have an Economic Payoff? A Cross-Country Investigation." *Quarterly Journal of Economics* 112: 1251–88.

Knight, J. B., and R. H. Sabot. 1983. "Educational Expansion and the Kuznets Effect." *American Economic Review* 73(5): 1132–36.

Knight, John B., and Li Shi. 1991. "The Determinants of Educational Attainment in China." Oxford Applied Economics Discussion Paper no. 127. Oxford University, Oxford, U.K

Kornai, Janos. 2000. "Ten Years After 'The Road to a Free Economy.' The Author's Self-Evaluation." Paper presented at the Annual Bank Conference on Development Economics, April 20, World Bank, Washington, D.C.

Krongkaew, Medhi. 1999. "A Tale of an Economic Crisis: How the Economic Crisis Started, Developed, and Ended in Thailand." Paper presented at the International Conference on Economic Crisis and Impacts on Social Welfare, June 14–15, Taipei, China.

Krueger, Anne O. 1974. "The Political Economy of the Rent-Seeking Society." *American Economic Review* 64(3): 291–301.

Krueger, Anne O., Maurice W. Schiff, and Alberto Valdés, eds. 1991. *The Political Economy of Agricultural Pricing Policy*, vols. 1–5. Baltimore, Maryland: The Johns Hopkins University Press.

Krugman, Paul. 1996. "The Myth of Asia's Miracle." *Pop Internationalism*, Cambridge, Massachusetts: MIT Press (reprint). *Foreign Affairs* 73(6): 62–78, 1994 (original).

_____. 1998. "Fire-Sale FDI." Paper prepared for the National Bureau of Economic Research Conference on Capital Flows to Emerging Markets. Cambridge, Massachusetts. Processed. Also available at http://web.mit.edu/krugman/www/FIRESALE.htm.

Kuznets, S. 1955. "Economic Growth and Income and Income Inequality." *American Economic Review* 45:1–28.

_____. 1968. *Toward a Theory of Economic Growth: With Reflections on the Economic Growth of Modern Nations.* New York: Norton.

La Porta, Rafael, and Florencio Lopez-De-Silanes. 1999. "The Benefits of Privatization: Evidence from Mexico." *Quarterly Journal of Economics* 114(4):1193–1242.

La Porta, Rafael, Florencio Lopes-de-Silanes, Andrei Shleifer, and Robert Vishny. 1999. "The Quality of Government." *Journal of Law, Economics, and Organization* 15(1): 222-79.

Lam, David, and Deborah Levison. 1991. "Declining Inequality in Schooling in Brazil and its Effects on Inequality in Earnings." *Journal of Developmental Economics* 37(1–2): 199–225.

Lanjouw, Peter, and Nicholas Stern. 1989. "Agricultural Change and Inequality in Palanpur 1957–84." Discussion Paper no. 24. London: London School of Economics and Political Science, Development Economics Research Programme.

_____. 1998. *Economic Development in Palanpur over Five Decades.* New York: Oxford University Press.

Lee, Jong Wha. 1996. "Government Interventions and Productivity Growth." *Journal of Economic Growth* 1(3): 392–415.

Lee, Jong-Wha, and Robert J. Barro. 1997. "Schooling Quality in a Cross-Section of Countries." Working Paper no. 6198. National Bureau of Economic Research, Cambridge, Massachusetts.

Leff, Nathaniel H. 1964. "Economic Development through Bureaucratic Corruption." *The American Behavior Scientist* 2: 8–14.

Leipziger, Danny M., ed. 1997. *Lessons from East Asia.* Ann Arbor, Michigan: University of Michigan Press.

Leipziger, D. M., David Dollar, A. F. Shorrocks, and S. Y. Song. 1992. *The Distribution of Income and Wealth in Korea.* Washington, D.C.: World Bank Institute.

Lerner, A. P. 1944. *Economics of Control.* New York: Macmillan.

Levine, Ross. 1997a. "Financial Development and Economic Growth: Views and Agenda." *Journal of Economic Literature* 35(2): 688–726.

_____. 1997b. "Napoleon, Bourse, and Growth in Latin America." Conference on the Development of Securities Markets in Emerging Economics: Obstacles and Preconditions for Success, October 28–29, Washington, D.C.

_____. 1999. "Law, Finance, and Economic Growth." *Journal of Financial Intermediation* 8(1–2): 8–35.

Levine, Ross, and Sara Zevos. 1998a. "Capital Control Liberalization and Stock Market Development." *World Development* 26(7): 1169–83.

_____. 1998b. "Stock Markets, Banks, and Economic Growth." *American Economic Review* 88(3): 537–58.

Levinsohn, James, Steven Berry, and Jed Friedman. 1999. "Impacts of the Indonesian Economic Crisis: Price Changes and the Poor." Working Paper no. 7194. National Bureau of Economic Research, Cambridge, Massachusetts.

Lewis, W. Arthur. 1955. *The Theory of Economic Growth.* New York: Harper Torchbooks.

Li, Hongyi, Lyn Squire, and Heng-Fu Zou. 1998. "Explaining International and Intertemporal Variations in Income Inequality." *Economic Journal* 108: 26–43.

Lim, David. 1992. "Capturing the Effects of Capital Subsidies." *Journal of Development Studies* 28(4): 705–16.

Lin, Justin Yifu. 1992. "Rural Reforms and Agricultural Growth in China." *American Economic Review* 82(1): 34–51.

Liu, Francis. 1985. "An Equilibrium Queuing Model of Bribery." *Journal of Political Economy* 93(4): 760-81.

Lockheed, E. Marlaine, and Adriaan M. Verspoor. 1991. *Improving Primary Education in Developing Countries.* New York: Oxford University Press.

Loh, Jonathan, Jorgen Randers, Alex MacGillivray, Val Kapos, Martin Jenkins, Brian Groombridge, and Neil Cox. 1998. "Living Planet Report 1998." World Wildlife Fund International, New Economics Foundation, and World Conservation Monitoring Center, Gland, Switzerland.

Londoño, Juan Luis. 1990. "Kuznetsian Tales with Attention to Human Capital." Paper presented at the Third Inter-American Seminar in Economics, Rio de Janeiro, Brazil.

López, Ramon 1997. "Protecting the 'Green' Environment in a Context of Fast Economic Growth: The Case for Demand-Based Incentives." University of Maryland, College Park, Maryland. Processed.

_____. 1998a. "Growth and Stagnation in Natural Resource-Rich Economies." University of Maryland, College Park, Maryland. Processed.

_____. 1998b. "Where Development Can or Cannot Go: The Role of Poverty-Environment Linkages." Paper presented at the Annual Bank Conference on Development Economics, April 30–May 1, World Bank, Washington, D.C.

López, Ramon, and A. Valdes. 2000. *Rural Poverty in Latin America: Analytics, New Empirical Evidence, and Policy.* London and New York: MacMillan Press and St. Martin's Press.

López, Ramón, T. Thomas, and Vinod Thomas. 1998. "Economic Growth and the Sustainability of Natural Resources." University of Maryland, Department of Agricultural and Resource Economics, College Park, Maryland.

López, Ramón, Vinod Thomas, and Yan Wang. 1998. "Addressing the Education Puzzle: The Distribution of Education and Economic Reform." Policy Research Working Paper no. 2031. World Bank, Washington, D.C.

Lopez-Mejia, Alejandro. 1999. "Large Capital Flows—A Survey of the Causes, Consequences, and Policy Responses." Working Paper no. WP/99/17. International Monetary Fund, Washington, D.C.

Loury, Glenn C. 1999. "Social Exclusion and Ethnic Groups: The Challenge to Economics." Paper presented at the Annual Bank Conference on Development Economics, April 28–30, World Bank, Washington D.C.

Lucas, R. 1988. "On the Mechanics of Economic Growth." *Journal of Monetary Economics* 22(1): 3–42.

Lucas, Robert E. 1993. "Making a Miracle." *Econometrica* 61(2): 251–72.

Lundberg, Mattias, and Lyn Squire. 1999. "Growth and Inequality: Extracting the Lessons for Policymakers." World Bank, Washington, D.C.

Lustig, Nora. 1999. "Crises and the Poor: Socially Responsible Macroeconomics." Inter-American Development Bank, Sustainable Development Department, Poverty and Inequality Advisory Unit, Washington, D.C.

Lvovsky, Kseniya, Maureen Cropper, James Listorti, A. Edward Elmendorf, Candace Chandra, Julian Lampiette, Ronald Subida, and Meghan Dunleavy. 1999. "Environmental Health." Background Paper for the Environment Strategy. Draft. World Bank, Environment Department, Washington, D.C.

Lynch, Owen J., and Kirk Talbott. 1995. "Balancing Acts: Community-Based Forest Management and National Law in Asia and the Pacific." World Resources Institute, Washington D.C.

Maas, Jacob van Lutsenburg, and Geert Criel. 1982. "Distribution of Primary School Enrollments in Eastern Africa." Working Paper no. 511. World Bank, Washington, D.C.

Mamingi, Nlandu, Kenneth Chomitz, David Gray, and Eric Lambin. 1996. "Spatial Patterns of Deforestation in Cameroon and Zaire." Working Paper no 8. Research Project on Social Environmental Consequences of Growth-Oriented Policies. World Bank, Policy Research Department, Washington, D.C.

Mankiw, Gregory N., David Romer, and David N. Weil. 1992. "A Contribution to the Empirics of Economic Growth." *Quarterly Journal of Economics* 105(2): 407–37.

Mauro, Paolo. 1995. "Corruption and Growth." *Quarterly Journal of Economics* 110(3): 681–712.

_____. 1997. "The Effects of Corruption on Growth, Investment, and Government Expenditure: A Cross–Country Analysis." In Kimberly Ann Elliot, ed., *Corruption and the Global Economy.* Washington D.C.: Institute for International Economics.

_____. 1998. "Corruption and the Composition of Government Expenditure." *Journal of Public Economics* 69(2): 263–79.

McGranahan, Donald. 1972. *Contents and Measurement of Socioeconomic Development.* New York: Praeger.

McKinley, Terry. 1996. *The Distribution of Wealth in Rural China.* New York: M. E. Sharpe.

McKinnon, Ronald I., and Huw Pill. 1997. "Credible Liberalizations and International Capital Flows: The Over-Borrowing Syndrome." *American Economic Review, Papers and Proceedings* 87(2): 189–93.

Megginson, William J., and Jeffrey M. Netter. 2000. "From State to Market: A Survey of Empirical Studies on Privatization." Working Paper. Norman, Oklahoma: The University of Oklahoma Press.

Mehrez, Gil, and Daniel Kaufmann. 2000. "Transparency, Liberalization, and Banking Crises." World Bank Policy Research Working Paper no. 2286. World Bank Institute, Washington, D.C.

Middleton, John, Adrian Ziderman, and Arvil Van Adams. 1993. *Skills for Productivity*. New York: Oxford University Press.

Milanovic, Branko. 1997. *Income Inequality and Poverty during the Transition from Planned to Market Economy*. Washington, D.C.: World Bank.

Mincer, Jacob. 1962. "On the Job Training Costs: Returns and Some Implications." *Journal of Political Economy* 70(October) supplement, part 2:50–79.

_____. 1974. *Schooling, Experience, and Earnings*. New York: Columbia University Press.

Mingat, Alain, and Jee-Peng Tan. 1998. "The Mechanics of Progress in Education, Evidence from Cross-Country Data." Policy Research Working Paper no. 2015. World Bank, Washington, D.C.

Mink, Stephen D. 1993. "Poverty, Population, and the Environment." World Bank Discussion Paper no. 189. World Bank, Washington, D.C.

Mishkin, Frederic S. 1997. "Understanding Financial Crises: A Developing Country Perspective." In *Proceedings of World Bank Annual Conference on Development Economics*. Washington, D.C.: World Bank.

Montiel, Peter. 1998. "The Capital Inflow Problem." Working Paper. World Bank Institute, Washington, D.C.

Moore, Stephen. 1999. "Corporate Subsidies in the Federal Budget." Testimony before the Budget Committee, the U.S. House of Representatives, June 30, 1999. Available at http://www.cato.org/testimony/ct-sm063099.html.

Morris, M. D. 1979. *Measuring the Condition of the World's Poor: The Physical Quality of Life Index*. New York: Pergamon Press

Mueller, Dennis C. 1998. "Constitutional Constraints on Governments in a Global Economy." *Constitutional Political Economy* 9(3): 171–86.

Munasinghe, Mohan. 2000. "Towards Sustainomics: A Trans-Disciplinary Metaframework for Making Development more Sustainable." In M. Munasinghe, O. Sunkel, and C. de Miguel, eds., *The Sustainability of Long-Term Growth: Socioeconomic and Ecological Perspectives*. London: Edward Elgar.

Murphy, Kevin, Gary S. Becker, and Edward Glaeser. 1999. "Population and Economic Growth." *American Economic Review* 89(May): 145–49.

Murphy, Kevin M., Andrei Shleifer, and Robert W. Vishny. 1989. "Industrialization and the Big Push." *Journal of Political Economy* 97(5): 1003–1026.

_____. 1991. "The Allocation of Talent: Implications for Growth." *Quarterly Journal of Economics* 106(2): 503–530.

Murray, Christopher J. L., and Alan D. López, eds. 1996. *The Global Burden of Disease and Injury Series*, vol. 1. Cambridge, Massachusetts: Harvard School of Public Health for the World Health Organization and World Bank.

Narayan, Deepa, with Raj Patel, Kai Schafft, Anne Rademacher, and Sarah Koch-Schulte. 2000. *Voices of the Poor: Can Anyone Hear Us?* New York: Oxford University Press.

Narayan, Deepa, and Lant Pritchett. 1999. "Cents and Sociability: Household Income and Social Capital in Rural Tanzania." *Economic Development and Cultural Change* 47(4): 871–97.

Nehru, Vikram, and Ashok Dhareshwar. 1993. "A New Database on Physical Capital Stock: Sources, Methodology, and Results." *Revista de Analisis Economico* 8(1): 37–59.

Nehru, Vikram, Eric Swanson, and Ashutosh Dubey. 1995. "A New Database on Human Capital Stock in Developing and Industrial Countries: Sources, Methodology, and Results." *Journal of Development Economics* 46(2): 379–401.

Nelson, Richard R., and Howard Pack. 1998. "The Asian Miracle and Modern Growth Theory." Policy Research Working Paper no. 1881. World Bank, Development Research Group, Washington, D.C.

New Steel. 1998. Editorial comment 14(8).

Nordhaus, William D., and James Tobin. 1972. *Is Economic Growth Obsolete?* Fiftieth Anniversary Colloquium V. National Bureau of Economic Research. New York: Columbia University Press.

North, Douglass C. 1989. "Institutions and Economic Growth: An Historical Introduction." *World Development* 17(9):1319–32.

_____. 1993. "The Ultimate Sources of Economic Growth." In Adam Szirmai, Bart Vanark, and Dirk Pilat, eds., *Explaining Economic Growth: Essays in Honor of Angus Maddison.* Amsterdam: North-Holland.

Nurkse, Ragnar. 1953. *Problems of Capital Formation in Underdeveloped Countries.* New York: Oxford University Press.

Obstfeld, Maurice. 1996. "Models of Currency Crises with Self-Fulfilling Features." *European Economic Review* 40(3–5): 1037–47.

OECD (Organisation for Economic Co-operation and Development). 1990. *Liberalization of Capital Movements and Financial Services in the OECD Area.* Paris.

Oman, Charles P. 2000. "Policy Competition for Foreign Direct Investment." OECD Development Centre, Paris. Processed.

O'Neill, Donal. 1995. "Education and Income Growth: Implications for Cross-Country Inequality." *Journal of Political Economy* 103(6): 1289–1301.

Ostrom, Elinor. 1990. *Governing the Commons: The Evolution of Institutions for Collective Action.* Cambridge, U.K.: Cambridge University Press.

Owen, Ann L. 1995. "International Trade and the Accumulation of Human Capital." Board of Governors of the Federal Reserve System, Finance and Economics Discussion Series 95/49 November, Washington, D.C.

Panayotou, Theodore. 1997. "Demystifying the Environmental Kuznets Curve: Turning a Black Box into a Policy Tool." *Environment and Development Economics* 2(4): 465–84.

Park, Jae Ha. 2000. "Korea's Crisis Resolution and Future Policy Directions." Paper presented at the World Bank Institute senior policy seminar on Managing Capital Flows in a Volatile Financial Environment, February 21–24, Bangkok, Thailand.

Pauly, Louis W. 1995. "Capital Mobility, State Autonomy, and Political Legitimacy." *Journal of International Affairs* 48(2): 369–88.

_____. 1997. *Who Elected the Bankers?* Ithaca, New York, and London: Cornell University Press.

Pearce, David, and Jeremy J. Warford. 1993. *World without End: Economics, Environment, and Sustainable Development.* New York: Oxford University Press.

Persson, Torsten, and Guido Tabellini, eds. 1994. "Growth, Distribution, and Politics." In *Monetary and Fiscal Policy*, vol. 2, *Politics*. Cambridge, Massachusetts: MIT Press.

Pritchett, Lant. 1996. "Where Has all the Education Gone?" Policy Research Working Paper no. 1581. World Bank, Policy Research Department, Poverty and Human Resources Division, Washington, D.C.

———. 1998. "Patterns of Economic Growth: Hills, Plateaus, Mountains, and Plains." Policy Research Working Paper WPS 1947. World Bank, Washington, D.C.

Psacharopoulos, George, and Ana-Maria Arriagada. 1986. "The Educational Attainment of the Labor Force: An International Comparison." Report no. EDT38. World Bank, Washington, D.C.

Putnam, Robert D. (with Robert Leonardi and Raffaella Nanetti). 1993. *Making Democracy Work: Civic Traditions in Modern Italy*. Princeton, New Jersey: Princeton University Press.

Qian, Yingyi. 1999. "The Institutional Foundation of China's Market Transition." Paper presented at the Annual Bank Conference on Development Economics, April 28–30, World Bank, Washington D.C.

Quinn, Dennis. 1997. "The Correlates of Change in International Financial Regulation." *American Political Science Review* 91(3): 531–51.

Quinn, Dennis, and Carla Inclan, 1997. "The Origins of Financial Openness: A Study of Current and Capital Account Liberalization." *American Journal of Political Science* 41(July): 771–813.

Quinn, Dennis, and A. Maria Toyoda. 1997. "Measuring International Financial Regulation." Georgetown University, Washington, D.C. Processed.

Radelet, Steven, and Jeffrey Sachs. 1998. "The East Asian Financial Crisis: Diagnosis, Remedies, Prospects." In William C. Brainard and George L. Perry, eds., *Brookings Papers on Economic Activity*, No. 1. Washington, D.C.: The Brookings Institution.

Ram, Rati. 1982a. "Composite Indices of Physical Quality of Life, Basic Needs Fulfillment, and Income: A 'Principal Component' Representation." *Journal of Development Economics* 11(October): 227–47.

———. 1982b. "International Inequality in the Basic Needs Indicators." *Journal of Development Economics* 10(1): 113-17.

———. 1990. "Educational Expansion and Schooling Inequality: International Evidence and Some Implications." *Review of Economics and Statistics* 72(2): 266–74.

Ramey, Garey, and Valerie A. Ramey. 1995. "Cross-Country Evidence on the Link between Volatility and Growth." *American Economic Review* 85(5): 1138–51.

Ranis, Gustav, Frances Stewart, and Alejandro Ramirez. 2000. "Economic Growth and Human Development." *World Development* 28(2): 197–219.

Ravallion, Martin. 1997. "Can High-Inequality Developing Countries Escape Absolute Poverty?" *Economics Letters* 56: 51–57.

Ravallion, Martin, and Shaohua Chen. 1997. "What Can New Survey Data Tell Us about Recent Changes in Distribution and Poverty?" *World Bank Economic Review* 11(2): 357–82.

Ravallion, Martin, and Gaurav Datt. 1998. "Why Have Some Indian States Done Better Than Others at Reducing Rural Poverty?" *Economica* 65: 17–38.

_____. 1999. "When Is Growth Pro-Poor? Evidence from the Diverse Experiences of India's States." Policy Research Working Paper no. 2263. World Bank, Development Research Group, Washington, D.C.

Ravallion, Martin, and Binayak Sen. 1994. "Impacts on Rural Poverty of Land-Based Targeting: Further Results for Bangladesh." *World Development* 22(6): 823–38.

Ravallion, Martin, Mark Heil, and Jyotsna Jalan. 1997. "A Less Poor World, but a Hotter One?" Working Paper no. 13. Research Project on Social and Environmental Consequences of Growth-Oriented Policies.World Bank, Policy Research Department, Washington, D.C.

Rawls, John. 1971. *A Theory of Justice.* Cambridge, Massachusetts: Harvard University and Belknap Press.

Razin, Assaf, and Andrew K. Rose. 1994. "Business-Cycle Volatility and Openness: An Exploratory Cross-Sectional Analysis." In Leonardo Leiderman and Assaf Razin, eds., *Capital Mobility: The Impact on Consumption, Investment, and Growth.* Cambridge, U.K.: Cambridge University Press.

Rebelo, Sergio. 1991. "Long-Run Policy Analysis and Long-Run Growth." *Journal of Political Economy* 99(3): 500–21.

Reinhart, Carmen, and Graciela Kaminsky. 1999. "On Crises, Contagion, and Confusion." Processed.

Robboy, Rebeca. 1999. *Today,* Sept. 8. World Bank, Washington, D.C.

Roberts, J. Timmons, and Peter E. Grimes. 1997. "Carbon Intensity and Economic Development 1962–91: A Brief Exploration of the Environmental Kuznets Curve." *World Development* 25(2): 191–98.

Rodriguez, Andres Gerardo. 1993. "The Division of Labor, Agglomeration Economics, and Economic Development." Ph. diss., Stanford University, Palo Alto, California.

Rodrik, Dani. 1994. "Getting Interventions Right: How South Korea and Taiwan Grew Rich." National Bureau of Economic Research Working Paper no. 4964. National Bureau of Economic Research, Cambridge, Massachusetts.

_____. 1997a. "TFPG Controversies, Institutions, and Economic Performance in East Asia." Working Paper 5914. National Bureau of Economic Research, Cambridge, Massachusetts.

_____. 1997b. *Has Globalization Gone too Far?* Washington, D.C.: Institute for International Economics.

_____. 1998. "Where Did All the Growth Go? External Shocks, Social Conflict, and Growth Collapses." Discussion Paper Series 1789. Center for Economic Policy Research, London. Available at www.cepr.demon.co.uk/pubs/papers.htm.

_____. 1999. *The New Global Economy and Developing Countries: Making Openness Work.* Policy Essay no. 24. Washington, D.C.: Overseas Development Council (distributed by The Johns Hopkins University Press).

Roemer, John E. 1993. "A Pragmatic Theory of Responsibility for the Egalitarian Planner." *Philosophy and Public Affairs* 22: 146–66.

Rogers, Everett. 1983. *Diffusion of Innovations.* New York: Free Press.

Romer, Paul. 1986. "Increasing Returns and Long Run Growth." *Journal of Political Economy* 90(6): 1002–37.

_____. 1990. "Endogenous Technological Change." *Journal of Political Economy* 98(5): s71–102.

_____. 1993. "Two Strategies for Economic Development: Using Ideas and Producing Ideas." In *Proceedings of the Annual World Bank Conference on Development Economics 1992 Supplement.* Washington, D.C.: World Bank.

Rose-Ackerman, Susan. 1989. "Corruption and the Private Sector." In Arnold J. Heidenheimer, Michael Johnston, and Victor T. Levine, eds., *Political Corruption: A Handbook.* New Brunswick, New Jersey; and Oxford, U.K.: Transaction Books.

_____. 1997a. *Corruption and Government: Causes, Consequences, and Reform.* Cambridge, U.K.; New York; and Melbourne: Cambridge University Press.

_____. 1997b. "The Political Economy of Corruption." In Kimberly Ann Elliot, ed., *Corruption and the Global Economy.* Washington D.C.: Institute for International Economics.

Ruggie, John G. 1983. "International Regimes, Transactions, and Change: Embedded Liberalism in the Postwar Economic Order." In Stephen D. Krasner, ed., *International Regimes.* Ithaca, New York: Cornell University Press.

Ruitenbeek, H. Jack. 1989. "Social Cost-Benefit Analysis of the Korup Project, Cameroon." World Wildlife Fund for *Nature* (London). Processed.

Ruzindana, Augustine. 1997. "The Importance of Leadership in Fighting Corruption in Uganda." In Kimberly Ann Elliot, ed., *Corruption and the Global Economy.* Washington D.C.: Institute for International Economics.

Sachs, Jeffrey, Aaron Tornell, and Andrés Velasco. 1996. "Financial Crises in Emerging Markets: The Lessons from 1995." Discussion Paper no. 1759. Harvard University, Harvard Institute of Economic Research, Cambridge, Massachusetts.

Sally, Razeen. 1998. "Classical Liberalism and International Economic Order: An Advance Sketch." *Constitutional Political Economy* 9(1): 19–44.

Sandel, Michael J. 1996. *Democracy's Discontent: America in Search of a Public Philosophy.* Cambridge, Massachusetts: The Belknap Press of Harvard University.

Schaffer, Mark E. 1995. "Government Subsidies to Enterprises in Central and Eastern Europe: Budgetary Subsidies and Tax Arrears." In David M. B. Newberry, ed., *Tax and Benefit Reform in Central and Eastern Europe.* London: Centre for Economic Policy Research.

Schmidheiny, Stephan, and Federico Zorraquin. 1996. *Financing Change.* Cambridge, Massachusetts: MIT Press.

Schultz, T. Paul. 1998. "Inequality in the Distribution of Personal Income in the World: How It Is Changing and Why." *Journal of Population Economics* 11(3): 307–344.

Schultz, T. W. 1961. "Investment in Human Capital." *American Economic Review* 51(1):1–17.

Selden, Thomas M., and Daqing Song. 1994. "Environmental Quality and Development: Is There a Kuznets Curve for Air Pollution?" *Journal of Environmental Economics and Management* 27(2): 147–62.

Sen, Amartya K. 1980. "Equality of What?" In S. McMurrin, ed., *Tanner Lectures on Human Values,* vol I. Cambridge, U.K.: Cambridge University Press.

_____. 1988. "The Concept of Development." In H. Chenery and T. N. Srinivasan, eds., *Handbook of Development Economics,* vol. I. New York: Elsevier Science Publishers.

_____. 1994. "Economic Regress: Concepts and Features." In *Proceedings of the World Bank Annual*

Conference on Development Economics. Washington, D.C.: World Bank.

_____. 1997a. "Development Thinking at the Beginning of the 21st Century." *Development Economics Research Programme* No. 2 (March), London School of Economics.

_____. 1997b. "What Is the Point of a Development Strategy?" Development Economics Research Programme No.3 (April), London School of Economics.

Sengupta, Jati K., and Karl A. Fox. 1969. *Economic Analysis and Operations Research: Optimization Techniques in Quantitative Economic Models*. Amsterdam: North-Holland.

Shafik, Nemat. 1994. "Economic Development and Environmental Quality: An Econometric Analysis." *Oxford Economic Papers* 46(5):757–73.

Shafik, Nemat, and Sushenjit Bandyopadhyay. 1992. "Economic Growth and Environmental Quality: Time Series and Cross-Country Evidence." Policy Research Working Paper WPS 904. World Bank, Washington, D.C.

Shleifer, Andrei, and Robert W. Vishny. 1994. "The Politics of Market Socialism." *Journal of Economic Perspectives* 8(2): 165–76.

_____. eds. 1998. *The Grabbing Hand: Government Pathologies and Their Cures*. Cambridge, Massachusetts: Harvard University Press.

Sieh Lee, M. L. 1998. "Competing for Foreign Direct Investment: The Case of Malaysia." Processed.

Simon, Julian. 1976. "Population Growth May Be Good for LDCs in the Long Run: A Richer Simulation Model." *Economic Development and Cultural Change* 24(2): 309–337.

Slottje, Daniel J. 1991. "Measuring the Quality of Life across Countries." *Review of Economics and Statistics* 73(4): 684–93.

Smith, John H. 1973. "Aggregation of Preferences with Variable Electorate." *Econometrica* 41(6): 1027–41.

Solow, Robert M. 1997. "Georgescu-Roegen Versus Solow/Stiglitz." *Ecological Economics* 22(3): 267–68.

Srinivasan, T. N. 1995. "Long-Run Growth Theories and Empirics: Anything New?" In Takatoshi Ito and Anne Krueger, eds., *Growth Theories in Light of the East Asian Experience*. Chicago: University of Chicago Press.

_____. 1997. "As the Century Turns: Analytics, Empirics, and Politics of Development." Discussion Paper no. 783. Yale University, New Haven, Connecticut.

_____. 2000. "Growth, Poverty, and Inequality." Yale University, New Haven Connecticut. Processed.

Steinherr, Alfred. 1998. *Derivatives: The Wild Beast of Finance*. New York: John Wiley.

Stern, David I., Michael Common, and Edward Barbier. 1996. "Economic Growth and Environmental Degradation: The Environmental Kuznets Curve and Sustainable Development." *World Development* 24(7): 1151–60.

Stern, Nicholas. 1998. "The Future of the Economic Transition." Working Paper (International) no. 30. European Bank for Reconstruction and Development, London.

Stiglitz, Joseph E. 1975. "The Theory of 'Screening,' Education, and the Distribution of Income." *American Economic Review* 65(3): 283–300.

_____. 1993. "The Role of the State in Financial Markets." In *Proceedings of the World Bank Conference on Development Economics, 1993*. Washington. D.C.: World Bank.

_____. 1997. "Georgescu-Roegen Versus Solow/Stiglitz." *Ecological Economics* 22(3): 269–70.

_____. 1998. "More Instruments and Broader Goals: Moving toward the Post-Washington Consensus." Paper presented at the 1998 World Institute for Development Economics Research Annual Lecture, January, Helsinki, Finland.

_____. 1999. "Whither Reform? Ten Years of the Transition." Paper presented at the Annual Bank Conference on Development Economics, April 28–30, World Bank, Washington D.C.

Stiglitz, Joseph E., and Amar Bhattacharya. 1999. "Underpinnings for a Stable and Equitable Global Financial System: From Old Debates to a New Paradigm." Paper presented at the Annual Bank Conference on Development Economics, April 28–30, World Bank, Washington D.C.

Summers, Lawrence H. 2000. "A New Framework for Multilateral Development Policy." Remarks to the Council on Foreign Relations, March 20, New York.

Summers, Robert, and Alan Heston. 1991. " The Penn World Table (Mark 5): An Expanded Set of International Comparisons. 1950–88." *Quarterly Journal of Economics* 106(2): 327–68.

Tan Jee-Peng, Julia Lane, and Gerard Lassibille. 1999. "Student Outcomes in Philippine Elementary Schools: An Evaluation of Four Experiments." *World Bank Economic Review* 13(3): 493–508.

Tanzi, Vito. 1998. "Corruption around the World: Causes, Consequences, Scope, and Cures." *International Monetary Fund Staff Papers* 45(4): 559–94.

Tanzi, Vito, and Hamid Davoodi. 1997. "Corruption, Public Investment, and Growth." Working Paper no. WP/97/139. International Monetary Fund, Washington, D.C.

Temple, Jonathan, and Paul A. Johnson. 1998. "Social Capability and Economic Growth." *Quarterly Journal of Economics* 63(3): 965–90.

Thomas, Vinod. 1998. "Economic Globalization and Sustainable Development in Costa Rica." Paper presented at the conference on Stability and Economic Development in Costa Rica: The Pending Reforms, April 23–25, Acadamy of Central America, Costa Rica.

Thomas, Vinod, and Tamara Belt. 1997. "Growth and Environment: Allies or Foes." *Finance and Development* 34(June): 22–24.

Thomas, Vinod, and Yan Wang. 1996. "Distortions, Interventions, and Productivity Growth: Is East Asia Different?" *Economic Development and Cultural Change* 44(2): 265–88.

_____. 1997. "Education, Trade, and Investment Returns." Working Paper. World Bank Institute, Washington, D.C.

Thomas, Vinod, Nalin Kishor, and Tamara Belt. 1998. "Embracing the Power of Knowledge and Partnerships for a Sustainable Environment." Background paper prepared for the *World Development Report 1998/99*. Processed.

Thomas, Vinod, Yan Wang, and Xibo Fan. 2000. "Measuring Education Inequality: Gini Coefficients of Education." Working Paper. World Bank Institute, Washington, D.C.

Townsend, Robert. 1999. "Agricultural Incentives in Sub-Saharan Africa: Policy Challenges." Technical Paper no. 444. World Bank, Washington, D.C.

UNCTAD (United Nations Conference on Trade and Development). 1994. *Directory of Import Regimes, Part I: Monitoring Import Regimes.* Geneva: United Nations.

_____. 1997. "Income Inequality and Development." In *Trade and Development Report 1997*. New York and Geneva: United Nations.

UNDP (United Nations Development Program). 1998. *Human Development Report 1998*. New York: Oxford University Press.

_____. 2000. *Human Development Report 2000*. New York: Oxford University Press.

UNESCO (United Nations Educational, Scientific, and Cultural Organization). 1998. *World Education Report*. Paris.

UNRISD (United Nations Research Institute for Social Development). 1970. "Studies in the Methodology of Social Planning." Geneva.

Van Rijckeghem, Caroline, and Beatrice Weder. 1999. "Sources of Contagion: Finance or Trade?" Working Paper no. WP/99/146. International Monetary Fund, Washington, D.C.

Verdier, Daniel. 1998. "Domestic Responses to Capital Market Internationalization under the Gold Standard, 1870–1914." *International Organization* 52(1): 1–34.

Vishwanath, Tara, and Daniel Kaufmann. 1999. "Towards Transparency in Finance and Government." World Bank, Washington, D.C. Processed. Available at http://www.worldbank.org/wbi/governance.

Wang, Hua, and Ming Chen. 1999. "Industrial Firms' Pollution Control Efforts under a Charge-Subsidy System: An Empirical Analysis of Chinese Top Polluters." World Bank, Policy Research Department, Washington, D.C.

Wang, Hua, and David Wheeler. 1996. "Pricing Industrial Pollution in China: An Econometric Analysis of the Levy System." Policy Research Working Paper no. 1644. World Bank, Policy Research Department, Washington, D.C.

Warford, Jeremy J., Mohan Munasinghe, and Wilfrido Cruz. 1997. "The Greening of Economic Policy Reform," vols.1 and 2. World Bank, Environment Department and World Bank Institute, Washington, D.C.

Warford, Jeremy J., A. Schwab, W. Cruz, and S. Hansen. 1994. "The Evolution of Environmental Concerns in Adjustment Lending: A Review." Working Paper no. 65. World Bank, Environment Department, Washington, D.C.

Watson Robert, John Dixon, Steven Hamburg, Anthony Janetos, and Richard Moss. 1998. *Protecting Our Planet, Securing Our Future: Linkages among Global Environmental Issues and Human Needs*. Nairobi and Washington, D.C.: United Nations Environment Programme, United States National Aeronautics and Space Administration, and World Bank.

Webb, Michael C. 1994. *The Political Economy of Policy Coordination: International Adjustment since 1945*. Ithaca, New York; and London: Cornell University Press.

Wei, Shang-Jin. 1997. "How Taxing Is Corruption on International Investors." Working Paper no. 6030. National Bureau of Economic Research, Cambridge, Massachusetts.

_____. 1999. "Corruption in Economic Development: Beneficial Grease, Minor Annoyance, or Major Obstacle?" Policy Research Working Paper 2048. World Bank, Development Research Group, Public Economics, Washington, D.C.

Wessels, J. H. 1993. "Redistribution from a Constitutional Perspective." *Constitutional Political Economy* 4(3): 425–48.

Wheeler, David, and Shakeb Afsah. 1996. "Going Public on Polluters in Indonesia: BAPEDAL's PROPER-PROKASIH Program International Executive Reports." World Bank, Washington, D.C.

WHO (World Health Organization). 2000. *The World Health Report 2000*. Geneva.

Williamson, John, and Molly Mahar. 1998. "A Survey of Financial Liberalisation." In *Essays in International Finance Series*, 211. Princeton, New Jersey: Princeton University, Department of Economics, International Finance Section.

Wolfensohn, James D. 1998, October. "Address to the Board of Governors." World Bank, Washington, D.C. Processed.

_____. 1999. "A Proposal for a Comprehensive Development Framework." World Bank, Washington, D.C. Processed.

Woolcock, Michael. 1998. "Social Capital and Economic Development: Toward a Theoretical Synthesis and Policy Framework." *Theory and Society* 27: 151–208.

World Bank. 1990. *World Development Report 1990*. New York: Oxford University Press.

_____. 1991. *World Development Report 1991: The Challenge of Development*. New York: Oxford University Press.

_____. 1992. *World Development Report 1992: Development and the Environment*. New York: Oxford University Press.

_____. 1994. *Averting the Old Age Crisis: Politics to Protect the Old and Promote Growth*. Washington, D.C.: World Bank and Oxford University Press.

_____. 1996a. *Global Economic Prospects 1996*. Washington, D.C.

_____. 1996b. *World Development Report 1996: From Plan to Market*. New York: Oxford University Press.

_____. 1997a. *Can the Environment Wait in East Asia? Priorities for East Asia*. Washington, D.C.

_____. 1997b. "Chile: Poverty Reduction and Income Distribution in a High-Growth Economy: 1987–95." Report no. 16377-CH. World Bank, Latin America and the Caribbean Region, Washington, D.C.

_____. 1997c. *Clear Water Blue Skies. China's Environment in the New Century*. China 2020 series. Washington D.C.

_____. 1997d. *Expanding the Measures of Wealth: Indicators of Environmentally Sustainable Development*. In Environmentally Sustainable Development Studies and Monograph Series no. 17. Washington, D.C.

_____. 1997e. *Five Years after Rio: Innovations in Environmental Policy*. In Environmentally Sustainable Development Studies and Monograph Series no. 18. Washington, D.C.

_____. 1997f. *Private Capital Flows to Developing Countries: The Road to Financial Integration*. World Bank Policy Research Report Series. Oxford, U.K.; and New York: Oxford University Press.

_____. 1997g. *Sharing Rising Incomes: Disparities in China*. China 2020 Series. Washington, D.C.

_____. 1997h. *Trends in Developing Economies*. Washington, D.C.

_____. 1997i. *World Development Indicators*. Washington, D.C.

_____. 1997j. *World Development Report 1997*. Oxford University Press: New York.

_____. 1998a. *Assessing Aid: What Works, What Doesn't, and Why? A World Bank Policy Research Report*. Oxford University Press: New York.

_____. 1998b. *East Asia: The Road to Recovery.* Washington D.C.

_____. 1998c. "The Business Environment and Corporate Governance." Discussion Draft. Private Sector Development Department, Business Environment Group.

_____. 1999a. *Education Sector Strategy.* Washington, D.C.

_____. 1999b. "Environmental Implications of the Economic Crisis and Adjustment in East Asia." East Asia Environment and Social Development Unit Discussion Paper Series no.1. Washington, D.C.

_____. 1999c. *Global Development Finance.* Washington, D.C.

_____. 1999d. "Poverty Trends and Voices of the Poor." Poverty Reduction and Economic Management, Human Development, and Development Economics, Washington, D.C. Processed. Also available at http://www.worldbank.org/poverty/data.

_____. 1999e. *World Development Indicators.* Washington, D.C.

_____. 1999f. *Transition toward a Healthier Environment: Environmental Issues and Challenges in the Newly Independent States.* Washington, D.C.

_____. 1999g. "Towards Collective Action to Improve Governance and Control Corruption in Seven African Countries." Action programs prepared by African countries for the ninth Annual International Conference Against Corruption, October 10-15, Durban, South Africa. Available at http://www.worldbank.org/wbi/governance.

_____. 1999h. "New Empirical Tools for Anticorruption and Institutional Reform: A Step-by-Step Guide to their Implementation." Washington, D.C.: Europe and Central Asia Public Sector.

_____. 2000a. *Global Economic Prospects and the Developing Countries.* Washington, D.C.

_____. 2000b. *World Development Report 1999/2000: Entering the 21st Century.* Washington, D.C.

_____. 2000c. *World Development Indicators.* Washington, D.C.

_____. 2000d. *Greening Industry: New Rules for Communities, Markets, and Governments.* New York: Oxford University Press.

_____. 2000e. *Bolivia, Ecuador, and Paraguay Governance and Anticorruption Empirical Diagnostic Studies.* Washington, D.C.: World Bank Institute. Available at http://www.worldbank.org/wbi/governance.

_____. 2000f. *East Asia: Recovery and Beyond.* Washington, D.C.

_____. 2000g. *Engendering Development.* New York: Oxford University Press.

_____. 2000h. *Anticorruption in Transition: Confronting the Challenge of State Capture.* Washington, D.C. Forthcoming.

_____. 2000i. *World Development Report 2000/2001: Attacking Poverty.* Washington, D.C.

_____. 2000j. "Reforming Public Institutions and Strengthening Governance: A World Bank Strategy." A Sectoral Strategy Paper. Public Sector, Poverty Reduction, and Economic Management Network, Washington, D.C.

_____. Various issues. *Commodities Quarterly.* Washington, D.C.

_____. Various issues. *Global Development Finance.* Washington, D.C.

World Commission on Forestry and Sustainable Development. 1999. "Our Forests, Our Future." In *Summary Report of the World Commission on*

Forestry and Sustainable Development. Winnipeg, Manitoba, Canada.

Wyplosz, Charles. 1999. "Ten Years of Transformation: Macroeconomic Lessons." Paper presented at the Annual Bank Conference on Development Economics, April 28–30, Washington, D.C.

Young, Alwyn. 1991. "Learning by Doing and the Dynamic Effects of International Trade." *Quarterly Journal of Economics* 106(2): 369–405.

_____. 1992. "Tale of Two Cities: Factor Accumulation and Technical Change in Hong Kong and Singapore." *NBER Macroeconomics Annual 1992.* Cambridge, Massachusetts; and London: MIT Press.

_____. 1994. "Lessons from East Asian NICS: A Contrarian View." *European Economic Review* 38(3–4): 964–73.

_____. 1995. "The Tyranny of Numbers: Confronting the Statistical Realities of the East Asian Growth Experience." *Quarterly Journal of Economics* 110(3): 641–80.

Zanowitz, Victor. 1999. "Theory and History behind Business Cycles: Are the 1990s the Onset of a Golden Age?" *Journal of Economic Perspectives* 13(2): 69–90.